The Media in Contemporary France

NATIONAL MEDIA

Series editor: Brian McNair
Queensland University of Technology

National Media is a series of books designed to give readers an insight into some of the most important media systems throughout the world. Each book in the series provides a comprehensive overview of the media of a particular country or a geographical group of countries or nation states.

Titles in the series

The Media in Russia
Anna Arutunyan

The Media in Italy: Press, Cinema and Broadcasting from Unification to Digital
Matthew Hibberd

The Media in Contemporary France
Raymond Kuhn

The Media in Latin America
Ed. Jairo Lugo

THE MEDIA IN CONTEMPORARY FRANCE

Raymond Kuhn

Open University Press

Open University Press
McGraw-Hill Education
McGraw-Hill House
Shoppenhangers Road
Maidenhead
Berkshire
England
SL6 2QL

email: enquiries@openup.co.uk
world wide web: www.openup.co.uk

and Two Penn Plaza, New York, NY 10121—2289, USA

First published 2011

A catalogue record of this book is available from the British Library

ISBN-13: 9780335236220(pb) 9780335236213(hb)
ISBN-10: 0335236227(pb) 0335236219(hb)

Typeset by Kerrypress, Luton, Bedfordshire
Printed in the UK by CPI Antony Rowe, Chippenham, Wiltshire

The *McGraw·Hill* Companies

To the Lisbon Lions

CONTENTS

LIST OF TABLES

ABBREVIATIONS

ADSL	asymmetric digital subscriber line
AEF	Audiovisuel Extérieur de la France
AFP	Agence France-Presse
AOL	America OnLine
ARD	Arbeitsgemeinschaft der öffentlich-rechtlichen Rundfunkanstalten der Bundesrepublik Deutschland
BBC	British Broadcasting Corporation
CNCL	Commission nationale de la communication et des libertés
CNN	Cable News Network
CNNI	Cable News Network International
CSA	Conseil Supérieur de l'Audiovisuel
DDM	Direction du Développement des Médias
DSL	digital subscriber line
EU	European Union
FM	frequency modulation
FR3	France Régions 3
GATT	General Agreement on Tariffs and Trade
HADOPI	Haute autorité pour la diffusion des œuvres et la protection des droits sur Internet
INA	Institut national de l'audiovisuel
LCI	La Chaîne Info
LVMH	Louis Vuitton, Moët Hennessy
MAC	Multiplexed analogue components
MTV	Music Television
NRJ	Nouvelle Radio des Jeunes
ORTF	Office de Radiodiffusion-Télévision Française
PS	Parti socialiste
RAI	Radiotelevisione Italiana
RFI	Radio France Internationale
RSS	really simple syndication
RTF	Radiodiffusion-Télévision Française
RTL	Radiodiffusion-Télévision Luxembourg
TDF1	Télédiffusion Française 1
TF1	Télévision Française 1
TPS	Télévison par satellite
UK	United Kingdom
UMP	Union pour un mouvement populaire
UN	United Nations
USA	United States of America
WTO	World Trade Organization

ACKNOWLEDGEMENTS

I should like to thank Brian McNair, the series editor, for inviting me to write this book and all those at Open University Press who were involved in its commissioning, production and marketing, notably Sarah Cassie, Christopher Cudmore, Stephanie Frosch, Melanie Havelock, Katherine Morton and Claire Munce. I am also indebted to Jon Ingoldby for his detailed copy-editing work.

I am grateful to all my colleagues in the Department of Politics at Queen Mary University of London, for providing an atmosphere support-ive of research and writing and to the institution itself for granting me leave to complete this book. Huge thanks are due to Ian Campbell, my doctoral research supervisor at the University of Warwick, who much longer ago than I care to remember first ignited my interest in the politics of the French media. I should also like to acknowledge the help and friendship of the following colleagues with whom I have shared an interest in the study of media policy and political communication over many years: Christopher Flood, Peter Humphreys, Ralph Negrine, Erik Neveu, Sheila Perry, Paul Smith, James Stanyer, Jeanette Steemers, Thierry Vedel and Mark Wheeler. I am especially grateful to the Reuters Institute for the Study of Journalism at the University of Oxford and in particular to the Institute's director, David Levy, for appointing me to what proved to be an intellectually stimulating Visiting Research Fellowship in 2010. Above all, I should like to thank my wife and companion, Shirley Jordan, for her love, support and unfailing encouragement.

This book is dedicated to the 'Lisbon Lions'. This was the name given to the Celtic football team that won the European Cup (the forerunner of the European Champions League) in Lisbon on 25 May 1967 when they defeated Internazionale Milan by two goals to one: Ronnie Simpson, Jim Craig, Tommy Gemmell, Bobby Murdoch, Billy McNeill, John Clark, Jimmy Johnstone, Willie Wallace, Steve Chalmers, Bertie Auld and Bobby Lennox (manager: Jock Stein). At the time of my writing this dedication (spring 2010) three of this team, plus the manager, are no longer alive – Simpson, Johnstone and my own personal favourite, Bobby Murdoch, who played in midfield and was the driving force for the whole side. Not only were Celtic the first club from a non-Mediterranean country to win this coveted European trophy, but all of the players were reputedly born within 30 miles of the stadium in Glasgow. In an era where the game has become a global commodity and top footballers are fêted, often undeserv-edly, as media celebrities, the Celtic team of 1967 stands as a poignant reminder of a different football age. In the words of the Celtic song, it truly was 'a grand old team to see'.

INTRODUCTION

This national case study of the media in contemporary France is designed for readers with little or no previous knowledge of the subject matter. It is necessarily selective in its coverage and does not pretend to provide a fully comprehensive survey of a complex and wide-ranging field. This selectivity operates at four levels: conceptualization (which media?), territorial boundaries (where?), field of inquiry (what aspects of the media?) and disciplinary approach (from what academic perspective?). First, while the concept of 'the media' embraces a broad spectrum of means of communication, sources of entertainment and technologies of distribution – including the film industry, comics, book publishing and recorded music among others (Albertazzi and Cobley, 2010: 75–275) – this book focuses only on what are now conventionally regarded as the principal media in terms of information provision and significant audience reach: namely, the news media of the press, radio, television and the internet.

The lack of attention paid to cinema may at first sight seem surprising, given the strength of the film industry and of film culture in France, as well as the international popularity of many French film directors (Jäckel, 2010). In the current era, however, the film industry is not commonly regarded as a news medium and it certainly does not fulfil this function for audiences in contemporary France. In any case, there are many excellent books on French cinema that have no difficulty in treating film on its own merits as a largely distinct medium of art house culture or mass entertainment (Hayward, 2005; Powrie, 2006).

Second, the book is concerned solely with the news media based in metropolitan France – officially called 'the European territory of France' – and so excludes consideration of those public, private and community media that cater for audiences in the French overseas departments, regions and territorial authorities, such as Guadeloupe, Martinique and La Réunion. Third, the book deals only with selected aspects of the structures and functioning of the media, including the issues of pluralism and regulation, major public policy questions and some key features of political communication. Other topics such as entertainment content, media genres and audience effects are covered only marginally or not at all. Finally, and linked to the previous point, the book is written from a politics perspective, in the academic rather than partisan sense. The focus is very much on the interdependence between politics and the media in contemporary France. A publication with the same title written by an economist, a sociologist or a specialist in cultural studies would in all likelihood highlight other features of the French media and would certainly adopt a different disciplinary approach in its treatment of the subject matter.

The rationale for this book is twofold: one general – regarding the pertinence of national case studies – and the other specific – about the particular relevance of France. First, in an age where increasing emphasis in academic literature on the media is given over to comparative inquiry, this book reflects the author's belief that national case studies remain important both in their own terms for what they tell us about the media in a particular society and as an essential building block for informed comparative research. For instance, whatever the common features of media systems across contemporary Europe and however strong are processes of cross-national homogenization and convergence, it remains the case that 'in most European states the media are still predominantly national' (Kleinsteuber, 2010: 61). Moreover, as a significant proportion of the comparative media literature tends to be based on findings drawn mainly from the experience of English-speaking countries, notably the UK and the USA, there is a clear and ever-present danger of ethnocentric bias that can be countered only through the systematic provision of detailed case studies of non-Anglophone national media systems.

Second, France is a country whose media are eminently worthy of such study. Although it can have no claim nowadays to be a global super-power, contemporary France is nonetheless a major player within the European Union (EU) and a significant 'second tier' economic, cultural and political power on the world stage. In contrast to some smaller European states – such as Austria and Ireland, whose media structures and content are to a significant extent shaped by their proximity to larger and more powerful neighbouring countries with which they share a common language (Germany and the UK respectively) – France is a sufficiently well-populated country with its own national language to support a highly developed indigenous media system that well serves the needs of its over 60 million citizen-consumers. Even in an era of the apparent weakening of the nation state and the increasing transnational-ization of media technology, capital and product (Chalaby, 2004, 2009), France benefits from a media system with historically well-implanted national roots (Kuhn, 1995). It also ranks as one of the major countries among EU member states in terms of the economic turnover and audience usage of the media. Finally, although claims to exceptionalist status should be treated with due caution (Kuhn, 2005a), the French media system does possess certain distinctive traits in comparison with the structures and functioning of the media in other developed democracies, including its closest European neighbours. In their seminal comparative study of media systems in the developed capitalist democracies of Western Europe and North America, for instance, Hallin and Mancini experienced considerable difficulty in slotting the French case into its allotted typological category of 'the Mediterranean or Polarized Pluralist Model' (along-side Greece, Italy, Spain and Portugal) with anywhere near total conviction, as the authors themselves explicitly acknowledged at several points of their analysis (2004: 89–142).

This book is structured as follows. Chapter 1 analyses, explains and evaluates some of the key events and issues in the history of the French media from the latter part of the nineteenth century until the final years of the twentieth, with a particular focus on developments since the Liberation in 1944. It thus covers the period from the emergence of a mass newspaper press to the dawn of the digital, multimedia age. Such a historical overview is important in helping to situate elements of continuity and change in the French media over time. While history does not determine either the structures or operations of the media landscape in contemporary France, it does act as an important formative influence. Some knowledge of the history of the French media is therefore necessary to understand the ways in which they are presently organized and function and to appreciate the issues at stake in current policy debates on topics such as the future of the press, the status of public service broadcasting and the relationship between the media and the state.

Chapter 2 provides an analysis of key structural and operational features of the contemporary media landscape. The first section looks at some of the influential factors – technological, economic, sociocultural and transnational – that have helped form the French media environment of today. Succeeding sections examine a particular media sector – the press, radio, television and the internet respectively – situating each within the context of a media system whose constituent components have to a significant extent become more interdependent than in the past, largely as a result of the technological convergence that is a central feature of the digital age.

Chapter 3 examines media pluralism, both external (range of outlets) and internal (diversity of political content within a specific outlet). The expansion of the French media in recent years, notably in the broadcasting and online sectors, has opened up the possibility for greater pluralism in supply and increased diversity of content. At the same time it has also given established media companies the opportunity to consolidate and extend their existing stakes both within and across different market sectors. This chapter examines the extent of ownership concentration in the contemporary media and considers the issue of whether ownership matters. It looks at the structural rules on media ownership that have been in place for many years in an attempt to secure an acceptable level of external pluralism. With regard to internal pluralism, newspapers, news magazines and internet websites are free to disseminate politically partisan opinions and to be as one-sided as they like in their editorial content. In contrast, radio and television are supposed to ensure internal pluralism in the expression of political viewpoints and not to favour one political tendency or opinion above another. This means that broadcast media outlets are the object of significant regulatory supervision in the sensitive area of political content provision, whereas the press and the internet are subject to minimal oversight in this regard.

Chapter 4 focuses on media policy and regulation. Because of their political, cultural and economic significance, the media continue to be the object of various public policy provisions. This chapter emphasizes the continued importance of the political dimension in policy-making and in particular the key role played by the political executive and powerful media groups in shaping media policy. It looks at two key policy initiatives undertaken by President Nicolas Sarkozy, affecting the press and television respectively. The chapter also considers the tradition of state regulation in the media, particularly in the broadcasting sector, and the role of the relevant regulatory authority, the Conseil Supérieur de l'Audiovisuel.

Chapter 5 examines the news management activities of the political executive in contemporary France. Using examples largely taken from the Chirac and Sarkozy presidencies, the chapter argues that the executive's capacity to act as a 'primary definer' for the news media is considerable, particularly given the significant attention paid to this area of activity by President Sarkozy. While fragmentation of the core executive has posed problems for effective news management, the nature of the journalistic culture in France, especially among broadcasting journalists, means that the French executive is normally subject to less adversarial contestation from the news media than is often the case in Anglo-American democracies.

Chapter 6 examines the mediatization of elite politicians in contemporary France – including the two main contenders in the 2007 presidential election, Sarkozy and Ségolène Royal. The chapter focuses on selected features of image projection and the changing public/private interface. It outlines the traditional French approach to the management of the public/private boundary in the mediatization of elite political figures, considers the way in which politicians have increasingly accepted the desirability of marketing aspects of their private lives via the media for electoral purposes, and examines the factors that underpin a more personalized and even intimate form of media coverage of politicians in the contemporary era.

Chapter 7 covers selected activities of the French media in the global arena, including the export of media content and formats, the work of the French news agency, Agence France-Presse, ownership shares of French companies in foreign media markets and the role of external broadcasting via transnational radio and television provision. In particular, the chapter provides an in-depth analysis and evaluation of a specific recent initiative – the launch of the international rolling news channel, France 24 – as a case study of the strengths and weaknesses of France's media activities on the world stage in the first decade of the twenty-first century.

1 HISTORICAL DEVELOPMENT OF THE MEDIA IN FRANCE

> - Origins of a mass press
> - The advent of radio
> - The media in the Second World War
> - Postwar reconstruction of the media system
> - The growth of television
> - The liberalization of broadcasting
> - Conclusion

This chapter analyses, explains and evaluates some of the key events and issues in the history of the French media from the latter part of the nineteenth century until the final years of the twentieth, with a particular focus on developments since the Liberation in 1944. It thus covers the period from the emergence of a mass newspaper press to the dawn of the digital, multimedia age. Such a historical overview is important in helping to situate elements of continuity and change in the French media over time. While history does not determine either the structures or operations of the media landscape in contemporary France, it does act as an important formative influence. Some knowledge of the history of the French media is therefore necessary to understand the ways in which they are presently organized and function. It is also essential if one is fully to appreciate the issues at stake in current policy debates on topics such as the future of the press, the status of public service broadcasting and the relationship between the media and the state. Adopting an overarching chronological framework, this chapter devotes a section to each of the following topics: origins of a mass press; the advent of radio; the media in the Second World War; the postwar reconstruction of the media system; the growth of television; and the liberalization of broadcasting.

Origins of a mass press

Newspapers have by far the longest history among the media still functioning in contemporary France. The first weekly periodical, *La Gazette*, was published in 1631, while the first national daily newspaper, *Le Journal de Paris*, appeared in 1777. As was the case right across Europe, readership of French newspapers in the eighteenth and for much of the nineteenth centuries was restricted to elite sections of society (Sassoon, 2006: 194–9). Despite some short-lived explosions in the number of newspaper titles after the 1789 and 1848 Revolutions, it was not until the last quarter of the nineteenth century that the press experienced a period of unprecedented expansion during which it achieved the status of a mass medium in terms of news provision to an audience of significant size.

More particularly, in the years between the collapse of the Second Empire in 1870 and the outbreak of the First World War in 1914 – the so-called 'golden age' of the French press – newspapers underwent a massive expansion in both the number of different titles published and the size of their total readership (Martin, 2005a: 13–52). As a result, in 1914 with a total print run of over nine million copies, France occupied pole position in Europe for the circulation of daily newspapers per head of population: 244 copies for every 1,000 inhabitants, compared with only 73 in 1881 (Chupin et al., 2009: 44). The opening up of newspaper sales to a mass public was underpinned on the demand side by the spread of literacy and the extension of the electoral franchise, and on the supply side by innovations in printing technology, such as the rotary press, and improvements in distribution through new means of transportation, notably the railways. Through the use of mass production techniques, the industrialization of the publication process led to a lowering in the cover price of newspapers, which in turn helped boost sales.

At the same time the period saw the emergence of leading industrialists and financiers, who were prepared to invest in the press as a business enterprise. Recognizing that progress in technology could be harnessed to create a new popular market for newspapers, they regarded the press as an economic sector ripe for commercial development and exploitation. In 1863 the sale of Le Petit Journal at five centimes a copy led to the introduction into the market of what were to become mass circulation newspapers, 'specifically designed for the masses and not for those interested in politics' (Zeldin, 1977: 526). Four newspapers – Le Petit Journal, Le Petit Parisien, Le Journal and Le Matin – each had a daily print run of over one million copies prior to the outbreak of the First World War (Charon, 2005: 14).

Meanwhile, the relationship between the state and the press underwent radical change. After a long history of interference in editorial content, whereby for much of the nineteenth century the state employed a range of mechanisms to seek to ensure a compliant press, the 1881 press statute – the Law on the Liberty of the Press – began with the words 'Printing and publishing are free'. Guaranteeing freedom of opinion and the right to publish, this reform brought a formal end to a variety of practices, including state censorship, legal restraints on content and restrictive financial measures, all of which had curtailed the functioning of a free press in the past. The new legislation was thus indicative of a major change of attitude on the part of the authorities towards the print media, with the dominant political forces in the new parliamentary regime of the Third Republic seeking to encourage the growth of a democratic political culture in support of republican values and institutions in the struggle against conservative and reactionary forces and ideas.

Yet the 1881 statute did not put a definitive end to state interference in newspaper content. This was particularly evident at times of national crisis. During the First World War, for example, the government severely censored the press in the interest of keeping popular morale high. Moreover, from a sense of patriotic duty, much of the press for most of the time was more than happy to comply with government directives and presented to their readers a highly misleading and optimistic picture of events at the front (D'Almeida and Delporte, 2010: 17–54). There also emerged in peacetime a negative side to the newly discovered press freedom. Loosed from the shackles of state repression, the press did not always exercise social responsibility, with newspapers sometimes engaging in reporting of a scurrilous nature. This aspect of press behaviour was to become especially marked in the final years of the regime and was to contribute to the destabilization of the political system when economic crisis and political scandal rocked France in the 1930s. Nonetheless, in general the 1881 statute marked a major advance in the status of the press and in an explicit symbolic acknowledgement of its contribution to the cause of media freedom, the first line of the Socialist government's 1982 reform of broadcasting stated that 'Audiovisual communication is free' (Fillioud, 2008: 103–7).

The First World War brought the 'golden age' of the French press to an inglorious end. The factual inaccuracy and unbounded patriotic zeal of newspaper stories during the conflict led to the alienation of many readers, while adverse economic circumstances after the end of the war – including an acute shortage of labour, severe restrictions on the supply of paper, troublesome transportation problems, a marked reduction in advertising revenue and a general increase in production costs – seriously affected newspaper production and distribution. During the inter-war years there was a decline in the number of daily titles published, although print run figures for national and provincial newspapers combined had edged up from 9.5 million in 1914 to 11 million in 1939. Provincial papers in particular were becoming more important players in the newspaper market: indeed, by the start of the Second World War they had caught up with the sales of those papers produced in Paris. Yet although the total circulation of daily papers increased gradually between the wars, the per capita growth was small. Moreover, international comparison showed the extent to which the French press was falling behind in relative terms: while 261 newspapers per 1,000 inhabitants were sold in France in 1939, in Britain the corresponding figure had already reached 360.

The inter-war period saw powerful press barons coming to the fore, notably the textile magnate, Jean Prouvost, a future owner of *Le Figaro*. Magazines emerged as major media outlets during the years running up to the outbreak of the Second World War. In 1937 Prouvost established the title *Marie-Claire*, one of a range of magazines specifically aimed at women readers that emerged at this time. The following year he took over the small sports magazine *Match* and turned it into a weekly photonews magazine, with sales of over a million by the summer of 1939. A few years after the war the magazine was relaunched with the slightly new title of *Paris Match*. As an illustrated weekly news magazine, *Paris Match* was to constitute 'one of the most glaring successes of the postwar French press' (Hewitt, 1991: 111), with nearly two million copies sold in 1957.

The advent of radio

The first radio station to broadcast regularly was Radio-Tour Eiffel, which was established in 1921 as a state service linked to the Ministry of Posts. The first private radio station to transmit officially was Radio-Paris (originally called Radiola), which had the backing of the national syndicate of radio-electric industries and began broadcasting at the end of 1922. During the inter-war period there was strong competition in Paris between different public and private stations, such as Radio-Tour Eiffel, Paris-PTT and Radio-Paris. Rivalry between stations was also fierce in the provinces. The private stations broadcast mainly entertainment programmes and were funded principally from advertising revenue. The public service stations were also funded in part from advertising until 1933 when the radio-receiving licence was introduced. The licence fee was designed to give a solid funding base to the state sector at a time when radio was just beginning to establish itself as a mass medium: by 1938 there were over four million radio sets in France, compared with just under two million at the start of 1935. Public and private stations continued to coexist up until the start of the Second World War.

French newspaper owners were particularly concerned by the uptake of the new medium, as they faced up to the challenge radio posed to the political influence and economic viability of the press. One response, prefiguring that adopted by press groups in adjusting to the legalization of private local stations in the 1980s, was to acquire their own stake in radio. In 1924, for instance, *Le Petit Parisien* was the first newspaper to establish a radio station, Le Poste Parisien. As competition between public and private stations intensified, news bulletins became part of the programme output of radio, raising issues of political balance and impartiality. Worried about losing readership, the press in general was opposed to coverage of politics on the radio. However, as newspaper owners were unable to prevent this development, they adapted to the new circumstances by encouraging listeners to purchase their company's newspapers so as to complement their audio news diet. Radio also began to make an impact on French political debate, with the medium first being formally used in an election campaign in 1936. Before the outbreak of the Second World War, however, French politicians were only just beginning to appreciate the potential of radio as a means of mass persuasion.

The media in the Second World War

On the eve of the Second World War, in response to the signing of the non-aggression pact between Nazi Germany and the Soviet Union, the French government moved to ban the publication of the Communist press, including the daily *L'Humanité*, and as a result the party's publishing ventures were forced underground. Inevitably the defeat of 1940 entailed massive dislocating consequences for the French press, as the population came to terms with the psychological shock of the military collapse, the reality of Nazi occupation in the north and the authoritarian Vichy regime of Marshal Pétain in the south. In terms of press organization, the fall of France led to many Paris newspapers fleeing to the southern zone. Others simply stopped publishing altogether. Strict censorship was established by the Nazis and the Vichy state in their respective zones (Kedward, 1978: 187–8). After the German invasion of the southern zone in November 1942, most of the Paris dailies that had earlier moved south abandoned publishing. In the northern zone the officially sanctioned press was naturally dominated by collaborationist papers for the whole period of the German occupation.

During the war the influence of the pro-Vichy and pro-Nazi press was to some extent offset by the publication of clandestine newspapers sympathetic to the views of de Gaulle and the Resistance (Jackson, 2001: 402–26). This clandestine press was a vital means of spreading the ideals of the Resistance, mobilizing support for its activities and maintaining a sense of solidarity. The launch of a clandestine newspaper was a major gesture of defiance against the authorities and those who took this initiative of political engagement ran a considerable risk of discovery and punishment (Kedward, 1985: 52). The number of different clandestine titles was impressive, as was the political spectrum covered: Catholic, Socialist, Communist and Gaullist among others. Moreover, the longer the war continued, the more the clandestine press became well organized and highly professional in its operations. As the defeat of the Nazis came to seem the likeliest outcome of the war, the clandestine press formed a national federation at the end of 1943. In agreement with the Resistance organizations and the Provisional Government, this federation was to help shape the content of legislation on the press after the Liberation.

It was the outbreak of the Second World War that thrust radio into an incontrovertible position of political prominence. From 1940 to 1944 France was the scene of a verbal battle over the air involving radio stations articulating views sympathetic to the Nazis (Radio-Paris), Pétain (Radio-Vichy) and the Resistance (Radio-Londres) (Amaury, 1969: 409–22; Eck, 1985). Pétain frequently used radio to try to rally support for the Vichy regime, while de Gaulle broadcast over the BBC as the symbol of French resistance (Smith, 1973: 157). Although some politicians were already becoming fascinated with the power of the medium of radio, de Gaulle was virtually unique among the military in appreciating its significance. His first and most famous broadcast, the appeal of 18 June

1940 from the London studios of the BBC, was a call to his compatriots to continue the struggle against the Nazis. As the Second World War progressed, the BBC became one of the authentic voices of French resistance. The military and political conflict of the war thus found a reflection in a propaganda battle of the airwaves as each side strove to impose its views through the medium of radio.

Postwar reconstruction of the media system

It is impossible to overestimate the impact of the Second World War on the media landscape that emerged in France after the Liberation. The wartime period marked an almost wholly clean break with the prewar media system, with both press and broadcasting sectors effectively rebuilt from scratch once the conflict was over. This reconstruction was heavily influenced by the statist and anti-capitalist ideals of the National Council of the Resistance. Moreover, although values associated with the market, first in the press and much later in broadcasting, effectively challenged the initial hegemonic dominance of the postwar media settlement, nonetheless the ethos of the Liberation continued to influence both the attitudes of various media policy stakeholders and the framing of different elements of media policy throughout the second half of the twentieth century and even into the first decade of the twenty-first.

The press

In the press sector the sum of the changes introduced in the immediate postwar period amounted to nothing short of a revolution. Newspapers accused of collaboration with the Nazi occupiers were closed down and their assets redistributed to owners untainted by collaboration. As a result, of the 206 daily newspaper titles that had been published in France in 1939, only 28 were able to resume operations after the war (Guil-lauma, 1988: 19). At the same time, the old prewar press groups were eliminated and a new press system was reconstituted from independent companies. Small press groups, including those of Catholic and Communist sensibilities, established themselves in the new system.

Many new titles were established in both Paris and the provinces in the months following the Liberation. Party political titles were particularly in evidence in the initial postwar period (Martin, 2002: 307–27). So too were politically committed 'opinion' newspapers, of which the most famous example was *Combat*, in which the philosopher Albert Camus played a leading role. The quality daily *Le Monde* was also set up in 1944 to provide France with a newspaper of reference in the style of the prewar *Le Temps*. There was some shrinkage in the number of different daily newspaper titles, with the number of Paris dailies (i.e. national titles) dropping slightly from 31 in 1939 to 28 in 1946, while the total of provincial dailies remained constant at 175.

The immediate post-Liberation period saw a sharp increase in the total print run of daily newspapers in comparison to prewar figures: over 15 million in 1946, an increase of more than four million compared with 1939. This meant that 370 newspapers were sold in 1946 for every 1,000 inhabitants, a statistic that has never been surpassed since. The explosion in circulation figures can be explained by an enormous hunger for information after the famine of the war years, the pace of institutional and political change, and the flourishing of new social and economic ideas. Most of this increase benefited the provincial press, whose print run went up from 5.5 million in 1939 to over nine million in 1946. The legacy of the Second World War helped the provincial press in its battle against the Paris papers. The wartime division of the country into an occupied and an unoccupied zone, with the capital firmly under Nazi control, increased the importance of the provincial press over its Paris counterpart (Pedley, 1993: 150). Another factor working in favour of the provincial press was that in the immediate postwar period, when rationing was still in force, local and regional newspapers were the major source of information regarding the availability of food supplies in the locality.

Organizational change in the press sector was underpinned by legislative reform. Many in the Resistance were critical of the prewar newspaper industry and wanted to vent their wrath on those owners who had controlled the press before the war. The dominance of the inter-war press by capitalist financiers was anathema to those forces that dominated French politics immediately after the Liberation. Their attention, however, was not confined to a mere settling of personal accounts, though that certainly formed part of their revanchist agenda. More importantly, proponents of reform wanted to address what they regarded as the structural weaknesses of the prewar press system that had allowed it to fall into the hands of capitalist entrepreneurs. In their eyes the market had failed both to provide real choice and to reflect the diversity of opinion in French society, while it had concentrated power and influence in the hands of a few unscrupulous proprietors. An increased role for the state was designed to counter what were regarded as the undesirable consequences of the operation of a free market in the press. Reformers therefore concentrated their attention on the organizational framework of the press and on the liberal values that had underpinned its operation since 1881. In short, rather than just the ritual scapegoating of those proprietors who had abused their freedom to publish under the Nazis and Vichy, a full scale reorganization of the press was considered essential by the parties in power after the Liberation.

This concern of the postwar government to reform the legislative framework of the press system found embodiment in the ordinance of 26 August 1944, the main provisions of which were intended to guarantee pluralism, prevent concentration of ownership and introduce transparency into the financial dealings of newspapers. The measures aimed to establish a more positive framework to protect the press from economic pressures that might limit the independence of newspapers. The reform sought to make patterns of ownership and control more visible through a combination of initiatives that compelled newspapers to declare their economic interests and make public their financial situation. In particular, the ordinance made it illegal for the same person to be the publishing boss of more than one daily newspaper.

The 1944 ordinance was thus a very different piece of legislation from the press statute of 1881. The laissez-faire provisions of the nineteenth-century legislation were now perceived as an inadequate means of ensuring pluralism in ownership and diversity in content. In its emphasis on the need for new legislation to secure these objectives, the postwar government was trying to make a clean break with the liberal paradigm instituted over 60 years previously. The 1881 legislation had been introduced at a time of expansion and as a counter to the previous practice of excessive state control. In the eyes of the postwar government the inadequacies of this free market approach had been exposed during the inter-war period. Whereas in 1881 the concern of the legislators had been to promote the liberty of the press by protecting it from *political* control by the state, in 1944 the emphasis was placed on removing *economic* threats to press freedom from capitalist owners.

In 1944, therefore, state intervention was not viewed as a means of impeding editorial freedom. It was not intended to mark a return to nineteenth-century censorship and governmental interference in content. Rather it was advocated as a prerequisite for countering the ineffective functioning of the market. The state, it was argued, could help deliver a more pluralistic and responsible press. At the same time the government hoped that the result would be a press system more sympathetic to the viewpoint of the dominant centre-left parties in politics and of progressive forces in society. Thus, a mixture of altruism and self-interest lay behind the introduction of the new legislation.

Overall, the role of the state in the organization of the press was massively increased after the Liberation. The radical provisions of the 1944 ordinance, the establishment of a national press agency, Agence France-Presse, and the institution of a system of financial aid were all indicative of the state's desire to play a more proactive role in the affairs of the press than had been the case prior to the outbreak of the Second World War. So too was the creation in 1947 of a new cooperative system of distribution to replace Hachette's prewar private monopoly.

The daily newspaper market was in an apparently healthy condition in 1946. Circulation figures for daily newspapers had never been higher, while the large inter-war drop in the number of newspaper titles had been virtually halted. Yet this postwar boom was short-lived. Sales began to decline, the number of titles shrank and the ethos of the Resistance quickly evaporated. By 1952 the number of Paris and provincial newspaper titles had fallen to 14 and 117 respectively, while total print run figures dropped below the ten million mark. Meanwhile, the number of papers sold per 1,000 inhabitants had declined to 218.

As interest in news subsided and the economy stagnated, the new papers were forced gradually either out of business or into the hands of people willing to apply new capital to their development. In 1947 a month-long printers' strike led to the loss of scores of papers, and the sudden miracle of a 'decapitalized' press was over, together with much of the spirit of the Resistance. Many of the pre-war press-owners, including Prouvost, who had been banned from owning papers at the Liberation, returned to their businesses, and France ceased to be among the major newspaper-consuming countries of the world.

(Smith, 1979: 176)

Not surprisingly, the postwar emphasis on a strong role for the state in press matters has not been without its critics. For example, in comparing what he terms 'the French model' unfavourably with the more laissez-faire regimes in Germany and Great Britain, Charon puts forward a critique of the excesses of statism. He argues that the powers taken by the French state in press matters have facilitated political control, prevented the implementation of decisions that were desirable on economic grounds and made essential rationalization in the newspaper industry more difficult than would otherwise have been the case (Charon, 1991).

It has also been argued that the ideals of the Resistance were utopian and their fulfilment soon undermined by the re-emergence of hard-nosed economic realities. According to this interpretation of events, the 'political phase' of the postwar press was very short lived. State regulation and financial aid may have tempered some of the less desirable aspects of market competition, but the parties of the Resistance were unable to impose their anti-capitalist values on the functioning of the press. Within a few years of the end of the war, many newspapers had gone out of business. The inexperience of some of the new press owners played a part in this retrenchment. Economic factors also came into play. As the price of newspapers increased, the circulation figures of some fell, while those of others went up. Advertising tended to go to those papers whose circulation was already healthy, thereby giving a further downward push to the weaker papers. Meanwhile, readers preferred to read newspapers of a general information character rather than party political papers with their ideologically partisan content (Guillauma, 1988: 21). Another reason why the objectives of the 1944 legislation were not fully realized was that several politicians themselves became press owners and had no interest in seeing its provisions tested in court amid a blaze of critical publicity. The further the experience of the Resistance receded into the background, the more economic factors and commercial concerns asserted their importance.

Yet this does not mean that the innovations of the Liberation were a total failure. Whatever its limitations in practice, the 1944 legislation did have some impact in checking a tendency towards concentration of ownership and the emergence of large press groups in the postwar period. What evolved was a market system in which the state played an important but by no means all-embracing role in aiding pluralism and diversity.

If this revolution was not as durable as its promoters in the Resistance or in exile had hoped, at least it did for a time make a *tabula rasa* of the past, put in place new titles, men and organizations and defined a different regime from that of 1881. Developments since the Liberation have profoundly transformed this new press; economic factors have favoured concentration. The constraints of commercial journalism have rendered inoperative many of the prescriptions of 1944 and 1945. The Resistance was able to give an opportunity to a very wide spectrum of newspapers and journalists: it could not guarantee to each the same success.

(Albert, 2008: 206)

Overall, the strongest legacy of the postwar reform of the press was to legitimize the role of the state as a positive enabling force in this sector of the media, a legitimacy which the state enjoys among many policy stakeholders to this day (see Chapter 4).

Broadcasting

French radio emerged from the war ripe for reorganization. Not surprisingly the medium had expanded only very gradually during the conflict, with 5.5 million sets in use by 1946. In comparison, the UK had almost twice as many radio sets as France in the same year. The main concern for French politicians, however, was not so much to encourage consumer demand for radio as to ensure that the medium would serve the objectives of the postwar state. The role played by radio during the conflict was to have a spillover effect on French broadcasting policy once peace had been restored and in particular to have a crucial impact on the postwar organization and development of the medium. Politicians emerged from the steep learning curve of the war not just conscious of radio's power, but also determined to harness that power for their own political purposes. This meant creating structures for broadcasting that would facilitate the achievement of those goals that were at the heart of the economic and political programmes of the centre-left governing coalition of Christian Democrats, Socialists and Communists.

The role played by radio during the war was, therefore, a decisive factor in the formulation of broadcasting policy by the political forces active in the Resistance, since it was decided during the wartime period that the provision of broadcasting services would be nationalized following the Liberation. With all private radio licences cancelled, the private stations that had been allowed to broadcast up until the outbreak of hostilities were compelled either to cease broadcasting altogether or to transmit from outside French territory. Installations and equipment belonging to the private radio companies were requisitioned by the state, though some staff from the prewar private stations obtained posts in the new state service. The Vichy laws on broadcasting were reinstated after temporary repeal.

The main provision of the immediate postwar legislation was the affirmation of broadcasting as a state monopoly with public service goals, placed under the responsibility of a Minister of Information. Among the parties of the governing coalition the state monopoly represented without any doubt the optimal organizational framework for broadcasting. The Liberation government thus legitimized the framework within which broadcasting in France was to develop and attain maturity: a state monopoly with a formal public service role, but in practice closely subordinated to the political interests of the government of the day (Thomas, 1976: 2–5). The propaganda role played by radio during the Second World War thus had the unfortunate consequence of linking two separate ideas – state monopoly and political control – in the minds of French politicians (Eck, 1991). Evident under the wartime Vichy regime, this fusion of state monopoly and government control was to continue during the Fourth Republic (1946–58), when representatives of various political forces – Socialists, Radicals, Christian Democrats and assorted conservatives and independents – all sought to exploit radio for their own partisan political ends.

Right up until the early 1980s the state monopoly in the provision of radio services was enshrined in all major pieces of postwar legislation on French broadcasting. In theory this meant that only state radio could transmit from within French territory. No privately owned or commercially managed competition was allowed under the provisions of the various pieces of legislation which applied to broadcasting in the period before François Mitterrand's presidential election victory in 1981. In practice, however, the situation was significantly more complicated. The monopoly status of state radio in the postwar period did not go unchallenged, with strong competition coming from the so-called 'peripheral stations' (*postes périphériques*) such as Europe 1, Radio Luxembourg and Radio-Monte-Carlo. These advertising-funded stations transmitted to French audiences from just outside the national territory and their existence was tolerated by the French state, which even had a stake in managing their operations. The 'peripheral stations' were considered by French audiences to be less stuffy and politically tainted than their state counterpart and they were to play a particularly important role in news dissemination during the 1968 'events', when state radio was heavily controlled by the Gaullist government.

The growth of television

Compared with some other industrialized countries, such as the USA and Great Britain, France was slow to enter the television era. Though French television was officially established in 1935 and regular transmissions began after the Second World War, it was not until the late 1950s that a significant mass audience began to emerge: in 1961 fewer than 20 per cent of French households had a television set, whereas over

80 per cent possessed a radio. Financial constraints within the state broadcasting services, which were still geared up primarily for radio broadcasts, meant that the transmission network and programme output of television were slow to expand and attract a large nationwide audience. In contrast, during the 1960s the take-off of the sale of television sets was impressive. The number of households owning a set steadily increased – from below two million in 1960 to just over ten million in 1969. The amount of time spent watching television by the average French adult also increased from 57 minutes per day in 1964 to 107 minutes in 1969, almost wholly because of the expanding market penetration of the medium rather than through any radical changes in individual viewing habits.

A second national channel was established in 1964, while colour television arrived in 1967. Daily programme schedules were lengthened with the result that the total supply of television programming doubled during the decade. These measures were designed not just to raise viewing figures and widen choice, but also to boost sales of domestically manufactured television sets. By the end of the 1960s television had displaced the press and radio as the principal mass medium of national and international information for the French public – a status it has maintained ever since. Television also became the primary source of domestic entertainment and the single most important disseminator of culture. It was held responsible for various social phenomena, such as the decline in cinema attendance and newspaper reading. While the specific nature of the impact of television in any particular sphere of political or cultural activity may be open to debate, there is no doubt that by the time General de Gaulle resigned from the presidential office in 1969, television had become the most pervasive mass medium in French history.

From the very beginning of its public transmissions after the Liberation, French television was organized within the framework of the state broadcasting monopoly. France was by no means unique in adopting such an organizational principle for its new television service. A state monopoly was common practice in several Western European countries in the immediate postwar period. Yet there were also specific domestic factors that Smith argues worked in favour of the application of the state monopoly model to French television.

> Firstly, there was the tradition of government control of the telegraph initiated in the middle of the nineteenth century because of fear of its use by enemies of the regime.
>
> Secondly, there was no real debate within France over who was to control broadcasting ... State control was a convenience rather than the result of a firm policy.
>
> Thirdly, the newspapers seeing that radio elsewhere, and later of course television, was potentially a usurper of advertising revenue became staunch supporters of a system by which the state would guarantee the financial viability of a French system of broadcasting.

Fourthly, broadcasting was seen as a primary instrument of the traditional French policy of cultural diffusion. In private hands, as in the United States, broadcasting automatically became an instrument of low culture; the French ... saw that centralised control of broadcasting was the only guarantee that the instrument would be employed to ensure that high culture would prevail.

Finally, there had been throughout the century an anxiety in many sections of French society that their state lacked coherence and a centre of gravity; there were fears constantly that French society might crack up altogether and the knowledge that broadcasting was centralised and in public hands made society as a whole that much more secure.

(Smith, 1973: 158–9)

Of these five explanatory factors, two are uncontroversial: the opposition of the press to commercial television and the prime role of the state in cultural diffusion. As it had done in the case of radio in the 1920s, the newspaper industry was deeply concerned about the potential threat from television as a competitor for advertising revenue. In these circumstances, a state-owned television service funded from licence revenue was the least worst result for the French press. That this service should aim not to pander to the lowest common denominator of taste but instead to act as a vehicle for the best of French culture was an important part of the public service ethos, especially in the 1950s and 1960s. In part this cultural emphasis was due to the approach taken by key individuals involved in broadcasting management, such as Jean d'Arcy; in part to government policy that emphasized the role of the state in cultural provision, notably evident under President de Gaulle's Minister of Culture, André Malraux, in the 1960s; and in part to the influential role of various leading television directors, many of whom had sympathies for the French Communist Party, who were opposed to the Americanization of French television content.

Conversely, the tradition of government control of the telegraph, though an important historical antecedent, had not prevented the flourishing of private radio stations in the inter-war period. Moreover, Smith's arguments that the broadcasting monopoly came about because 'state control was a convenience rather than the result of a firm policy' and that 'the state lacked coherence and a centre of gravity' are less convincing. The monopoly may well have been a convenient policy response, but it was also a deliberate policy output that could mobilize a wide cross-section of political and social groups in its support. There was a large degree of consensus among the political elites in the immediate postwar period in favour of the monopoly solution to the organization of broadcasting. In the postwar climate of antipathy to capitalist forces and enthusiasm for collectivist solutions to problems of economic management in the form of public ownership of key utilities, it was not difficult to defend the state's appropriation of the main means of mass communication. Adherence to the principle of the state monopoly found favour among Gaullists, Christian Democrats, Socialists, Communists and trade union confederations among others. The incorporation of television into the enlarged sector of state activities testified more to the growing power of the state after the Liberation than to its incoherence and rootlessness. In any event, the Liberation government established a state monopoly that was defended by politicians of different political persuasions for virtually the next 40 years, during which time no private commercial competition was allowed to enter the market for the supply of television programming to viewers.

Until 1975 this state monopoly was organized in a single, public corporation – its last institutional embodiment being the Office de Radiodiffusion-Télévision Française (ORTF), established by the Gaullist government in 1964. The ORTF was a large organization of over 16,000 staff with a stake in all aspects of broadcasting – production, programming and transmission – in both radio and television sectors. Commercial advertising was introduced as an additional means of funding to the licence fee in 1968, while a third channel with a regional vocation was established in 1973. By the early 1970s the ORTF was one of the European broadcasting giants, embodying a specific French variant of public service values and ranking alongside other public service broadcasting organizations such as the BBC in Britain, the RAI in Italy and the ARD in West Germany in terms of organizational size and range of broadcast output.

In the eyes of its critics, however, the ORTF had grown to dysfunctional proportions, become difficult to manage and was prone to service disruptions by powerful trade unions. Politically it was a strong symbol of Gaullist control of the state. Under these circumstances it is not surprising that reform of the broadcasting sector was a priority for the first non-Gaullist President of the Fifth Republic, Valéry Giscard d'Estaing. The 1974 Giscardian reform dismantled the ORTF and created separate organizational entities that included three public television companies – TF1, Antenne 2 and FR3 (Bachmann, 1997). This reform encouraged a significant degree of competition between the three channels for audiences and advertising revenue, but maintained the legal status of the monopoly for public broadcasting and eschewed any private intervention in the market. Vedel describes the organization of French television prior to the Giscardian reform as one of 'state television', while he calls the period between 1974 and the Socialist reform of 1982 'commercialized state television'. Following the 1974 reform the essential features of the Giscardian 'commercialized state' model compared to its Gaullist predecessor were: greater organizational fragmentation; a larger role for commercial advertising as a funding mechanism; more competition between television channels for viewers and advertisers; and more attention given to audience ratings (Vedel, 2009: 261–3).

By the end of Giscard d'Estaing's presidency in 1981, French television was characterized by the following key features: limited supply consisting of a maximum of three channels with restricted daytime schedules; highly regulated output with all three channels subject to French-style public service obligations; terrestrial distribution, which meant that the over-whelming majority of the French audience was restricted to the output of the three state channels; and no minority, niche or thematic channels, with the result that programme schedules were for the most part designed for mass audience consumption. French television was thus an overwhelm-ingly national medium, protected by a combination of technologically imposed limitations and public policy decisions. The strong national television culture (Steemers, 2004: 1–19) evident in the French case, especially during the period of 'state television', is hardly surprising since in the medium's formative years television was consciously and explicitly used by politicians and state officials, most notably President de Gaulle, as a cultural, educational and informational tool to help construct a popular national consensus around the new political institutions of the Fifth Republic (Chalaby, 2002).

The liberalization of broadcasting

On 10 May 1981, François Mitterrand became the first President of the Fifth Republic to be elected from the ranks of the Socialist-Communist left. His government's 1982 reform of broadcasting heralded two impor-tant innovations in public policy: the abolition of the state monopoly and the establishment of a new regulatory authority for the broadcasting sector. In the wake of this reform French radio and television underwent an uneven process of economic and political liberalization over the next few years.

The monopoly was abandoned for a variety of reasons. One was the realization among policy-makers that the technological straitjacket in which radio and television transmissions had been constrained for so long was now outmoded. Advances in new communication technologies, such as the frequency modulation (FM) waveband for radio and cable and satellite for television distribution, opened up the way for a more diverse broadcasting system and called into question the technical rationale for monopoly in a field that was no longer a scarce public resource. There were also powerful economic arguments in favour of an expansion of the broadcasting system and the entry of new non-state actors as financial contributors and programme providers. Domestic manufacturers of hard-ware, advertisers and programme production companies all hoped to gain from the expansion in television provision. Politically, President Mitter-rand and the Socialist government hoped to benefit from the electoral popularity that was expected to result from the expansion of broadcast supply.

In the radio sector the abolition of the monopoly was quickly felt. The pirate stations (*radios libres*) that had started broadcasting in the late 1970s and been repressed by the Giscardian government were now free to transmit their programmes, although the state retained the power to grant licences and organize the allocation of frequencies. The radio sector became more competitive after 1982 as many new stations competed for audiences and funding. While the original intention of the Socialist government had been to promote small-scale community stations financed from donations and public subsidies, in practice it was not long before advertising-funded national private networks such as NRJ came to dominate. Advertising for private local radio was authorized in 1984. Since Radio France had been long accustomed to competition with the commercial networks of the 'peripheral stations', the culture shock of the new broadcasting landscape was much less strong for public radio than was to be the case for public television.

Change was slower to come in television. It was not until late 1984 that Europe's first terrestrial pay-TV channel, Canal+, began transmissions. Initially received with considerable public scepticism, Canal+ quickly became a major force for innovation within French television and by the 1990s was a key media player at both the national and supranational levels. At the start of 1986 two free-to-air commercial television networks (La Cinq and TV6) were established, financed from advertising revenue. For those French viewers who had not subscribed to Canal+, these two channels marked the end of the total domination of television supply by public sector monopoly providers. Finally, niche channels were also made available via cable and satellite systems, although audience take-up of these alternative means of programme distribution was comparatively low by the standards of some other Western European countries. Thus, while the 1974 Giscardian reform had confined itself to institutionalizing competition within the framework of the state monopoly, the 1982 Socialist statute introduced competition between public and private providers. Moreover, whereas in the past the television system had grown very slowly, with one channel being added every ten years or so, the Socialists effectively doubled the number of channels in less than five years. It is important to note that this expansion in television supply was closely managed by state officials from the top down. This state-controlled economic liberalization in France contrasted sharply with the so-called 'savage deregulation' of the television system in Greece, Portugal and Italy at the same time (Hallin and Mancini, 2004: 124–7).

The second major plank of the 1982 reform was the creation of a new regulatory agency – the High Authority for Audiovisual Communication (*la Haute Autorité de la Communication Audiovisuelle*) – to act as a buffer between the government and broadcasting, especially public radio and television. The avowed intention of the Socialist government was that this would help cut the umbilical cord that had tied broadcasting to the state during the Gaullist and Giscardian eras (Bourdon, 1999; Bédeï, 2008). The decision to set up the High Authority represented an attempt by the Socialists to address what was widely perceived as a defect of the postwar statist model: excessive governmental interference in key broadcasting appointments and in news content. The stated objective was that while the government would continue to determine the regulatory framework for broadcasting, it would not intervene in day-to-day management.

In particular, the new authority took over from the government responsibility for appointing the chief executives of the public radio and television companies. This change in the method of appointment was a crucial symbolic break with the former practice of government patronage. The chairperson of the new body, Michèle Cotta, was an experienced journalist whose professional reputation had been enhanced by her role as one of the two interviewers in the Giscard d'Estaing-Mitterrand television debate during the 1981 presidential election campaign. Her political sympathies were left-of-centre, but she was not seen as politically tainted.

Between 1982 and 1986 the High Authority managed with some success to establish itself as an independent agency in the broadcasting system (Chauvau, 1997). However, it is also the case that with one exception the political executive always succeeded in ensuring that nobody was appointed to a top position in public broadcasting without the approval of the President. In practice, it proved very difficult for the Socialists to make a clean break with the tradition of political interference in broadcasting. Yet ultimately the main drawback of the High Authority was not so much that it was politically manipulated, but rather that many of the most important developments in French broadcasting fell outside its jurisdiction. For example, the High Authority was not even consulted before the decision was taken in 1985 to set up two new commercial television channels (Cotta, 1986: 238). The result was that the High Authority was never a major player in the key policy decisions that determined the configuration of the television system in the mid-1980s. Its abolition by the incoming right-wing government in 1986 was more a symbolic measure of partisan revenge than an acknowledgement of the High Authority's power and influence.

The creation of the High Authority represented an important, if limited, step in the direction of the political liberalization of broadcasting. Of course, such a structural innovation could not change habits overnight. Long-established elite attitudes and patterns of behaviour remained, as traditional concerns regarding access, patronage and control of content continued to be raised. While the establishment of a regulatory authority represented an important symbolic break with previous practices of direct political control, it took some time for the notion of an independent regulatory authority to be accepted across the political class. Appointments to key posts in broadcasting were still scrutinized by politicians and commentators for their political significance, while television's political output remained a contested arena, closely monitored by politicians of all parties for indications of bias. In short, the 1982 reform did not remove broadcasting from the realm of political controversy.

In 1986 the parties of the mainstream right won a majority at the parliamentary elections, thus introducing the first period of executive cohabitation (1986–8) whereby the President and Prime Minister came from opposing party coalitions. One of the early reforms of the new conservative government under Jacques Chirac's premiership was yet another reorganization of broadcasting. While the economic liberalization of television by the Socialists was welcomed, the Gaullist-Giscardian government wanted to extend this through the privatization of the main free-to-air public channel, TF1 (Frèches, 1989: 155–88). The privatization of TF1 was the centrepiece of the 1986 statute – the jewel in the crown of the mainstream right's audiovisual reform package. In addition, the new government replaced the High Authority with a new regulatory body, the National Committee for Communication and Freedoms (*Commission Nationale de la Communication et des Libertés* – CNCL), and reallocated the franchises for the commercial channels La Cinq and TV6 (now renamed M6). In carrying out these reform measures, the government ensured that persons and interests sympathetic to the political right dominated both the new regulatory body and the management of the commercial television companies.

In 1988, Mitterrand won a second seven-year presidential term and after new parliamentary elections a centre-left government was elected. Condemned by Mitterrand for its political partisanship, the CNCL was replaced in 1989 by yet another regulatory authority, the Higher Audio-visual Council (*Conseil Supérieur de l'Audiovisuel* – CSA) (Franceschini, 1995). During Mitterrand's second term, public television provision grew with the creation of the Franco-German cultural channel, Arte, and the educational channel, La Cinquième, both of which came to public prominence when they jointly took over the terrestrial transmission network vacated by the bankrupt La Cinq in 1992. Despite this expansion of the public sector, however, the main beneficiary of the new competitive environment in television was undoubtedly TF1, which after privatization was able to pursue the mass audience, especially in prime time, subject to fewer regulatory constraints than previously.

TF1 was able to take advantage of its nationwide transmission network, its programming know-how and its sheer experience in the business to establish itself as the market leader. Conversely, the public service channels were thrown on to the defensive, competing against TF1 not just for audiences but also for advertising revenue in a new broadcasting environment that tended to favour the commercial sector and a market ethos dominated by audience ratings. A revealing insight into the thinking of programme schedulers working for private channels was later provided by the chairman of TF1, Patrick Le Lay, when he stated: 'There are many ways to talk about television, but from a business perspective, let's be realistic: basically, the job of TF1 is to help Coca Cola, for example, to sell its product' ('*Il y a beaucoup de façons de parler de la télévision, mais dans une perspective business, soyons réaliste: à la base, le métier de TF1, c'est d'aider Coca-Cola, par exemple, à vendre son produit*') (Le Lay, 2004). Yet it is also the case during this period that 'while commercial concerns became increasingly dominant, the French broadcasting system did not turn into a full marketplace and remained highly regulated' (Vedel, 2009: 262).

Conclusion

Five main conclusions can be drawn from this brief overview of the historical development of the French media from the latter part of the nineteenth century up to the final years of the twentieth. First, the period saw the successive emergence of different media sectors as means of mass information, communication and entertainment: beginning with newspapers, followed by radio and finally television. This was an era of truly mass media, with usage not confined to a highly restricted audience of social elites as had previously been the case with newspapers. Instead, the intended target of much media content (with the notable exception of magazines) was a largely undifferentiated mass audience that covered all classes and sections of society.

Second, the successive arrival and popularization of print, audio and visual media did not result in the disappearance of pre-existing media sectors. Newspapers adjusted to the establishment of radio in the 1920s, while both radio and the press adapted to the advent and routinization of television from the 1950s onwards. The content and formats of the already established media were undoubtedly altered in response to competition from new sources of supply and changes in patterns of audience usage. Television viewing, for instance, had a huge impact on radio listening habits. Yet in no case did a new medium simply replace an existing one. Instead audiences regarded the press, radio and television as largely complementary in terms of their functions and usage.

Third, the increased supply of media outlets and channels created new audience demands and modes of behaviour. Media consumption became a large part of everyday social life. By the latter part of the twentieth century French citizens spent a significant amount of time per day interacting with media: reading a newspaper and/or magazine, listening to the radio and watching television. Official government statistics (Ministry of Culture, 2009) revealed that in 1997 over 70 per cent of the population aged 15 and above read a daily newspaper, with about half of these reading a paper practically every day; over 80 per cent regularly read a magazine; 90 per cent watched television, with over 75 per cent doing so every day; and over 85 per cent listened to the radio, with nearly 70 per cent doing so every day. The average amount of time spent watching television in 1997 was 21 hours per week, while the corresponding figure for radio listening was 15 hours. As the time available for leisure expanded, so the media implanted themselves as an integral part of social activity. Well before the end of the twentieth century, France had become a highly mediatized society.

Fourth, there were some signs towards the end of this period that the era of mass media had peaked. Some media aimed at a mass audience either had been in slow decline for many years (e.g. sales of daily newspapers) or had witnessed audience dispersal as a result of increased competition (for instance, the established generalist networks after the growth in radio supply from the 1980s onwards). While many examples of mass media audience usage were still evident, especially in television where generalist channels still dominated, a clear parallel trend toward niche outlets (e.g. magazines and specialist radio stations) had also emerged. This should not be equated with a return to an elite-oriented media system; rather it constituted a segmentation on the supply side as a range of media providers targeted different audience groups. The result was the beginning of a shift, more marked in some media sectors than others, towards the fragmentation of the mass audience by the end of the twentieth century.

Finally, the nature of the linkages between the state and the media altered dramatically over the period. In the press sector the 1881 reform seemed to put an end to repressive practices of state censorship. Such censorship was to reappear during the two World Wars and, more controversially, during the bloody Algerian conflict of the late 1950s and early 60s (see Chapter 5). Nonetheless, during the twentieth century the press enjoyed greater editorial freedom in its relationship with the state than had been the case during most of the nineteenth century.

In the broadcasting sector the state enjoyed a (near) monopoly in the provision of radio and television services for almost four decades after the Liberation. The abolition of the monopoly in 1982, followed by the privatization of TF1 and other media companies later in the decade, shifted the balance of ownership from public to private in the space of a few years. Economic liberalization of broadcasting was a marked feature of the French media landscape in the final couple of decades of the twentieth century. Political liberalization of broadcasting after years of governmental interference that reached its height during the de Gaulle presidency of the 1960s was harder to achieve. The creation of successive regulatory authorities revealed an apparent willingness on the part of the political executive to establish a buffer between the government and the broadcasting companies. Yet broadcasting remained an area in which the state remained strongly implicated. Some of this political involvement, for instance in the appointment to key posts in public radio and television, showed how difficult it was for French politicians of both left and right to put aside long-established practices of partisan interference.

In short, it is clearly not possible to talk about a simple all-encompassing retreat of the state in its interrelationship with the media over the time period covered in this chapter. In terms of ownership, there was a huge expansion of state involvement in broadcasting at the end of the Second World War. In contrast, by the 1990s, ownership of newspapers and a large slice of the radio and television market was firmly in the hands of private sector actors, while commercial companies had also taken a major stake in cable and satellite broadcasting. Yet the state was still more directly involved in media ownership in 1995 than it had been a hundred years earlier. Moreover, it was still very much involved in controlling entry into the broadcasting market. In terms of financial patronage, the state also played an important role both directly and indirectly in supporting the media: subsidies to newspapers, licence fee funding for public radio and television, and government advertising across all media. Finally, the state's policy-making and regulatory role remained substantial at the end of the twentieth century, as public policy sought among other things to protect national ownership of media companies and domestic production of media content (see Chapter 4).

Key dates in the history of the French media

1631   Publication of the first weekly periodical *La Gazette*

1777   Publication of the first national daily newspaper *Le Journal de Paris*

1837   Legislation establishes a state monopoly in telegraph communication

1866   *Le Figaro* becomes a daily newspaper

1881   Major legislative reform of the press: 'Printing and publishing are free'

1904   Launch of *L'Humanité*, which becomes the Communist Party daily newspaper after the split between the Socialist and Communist Parties in 1920

1918   Adoption of a code of ethics by the newly formed Syndicat des journalistes

1920   Creation of the French version of the magazine *Vogue*

1921   First radio station to broadcast, Radio-Tour Eiffel

1927   The Socialist Party newspaper *Le Populaire* becomes a daily paper

1933   Introduction of the licence fee as a means of financing public radio

1933   Launch of the Luxembourg radio company, the future RTL

1935   First experimental television broadcasts

1935   Statutory recognition of the profession of journalist

1938   A year after its launch, *Marie-Claire* becomes the top-selling weekly magazine

1939   Ban on Communist press introduced prior to the outbreak of the Second World War

1940   Establishment by the Vichy regime of the first Ministry of Information

1941–3   Creation of Radio-Paris and then Télévision-Paris by the occupying German authorities

1944   Ordinance on the press

1944+   Wholesale restructuring of the press system

1944   Establishment of the national daily newspaper *Le Monde*

1944   First copy of the regional newspaper *Ouest-France*

1944   Establishment of the Agence France-Presse news agency

1945   State monopoly in broadcasting established

1946   First copy of the sports daily *L'Équipe*

1949   Establishment of the Radiodiffusion-Télévision Française (RTF) as the state broadcasting organization

1949   The radio licence fee is extended to cover television sets ➡

1949   First television news programme
1949   Launch of the photo news magazine *Paris Match*
1953   Launch of the news magazine *L'Express*
1955   Creation of peripheral radio station Europe 1
1964   Introduction of second state television channel
1964   Establishment of the Office de Radiodiffusion-Télévision
        Française (ORTF) as the state broadcasting corporation
1964   *L'Express*, originally established in 1953, becomes the first
        French weekly news magazine
1967   Introduction of colour television
1968   Introduction of commercial advertising on state television
1968   Major strike of staff at the ORTF in protest against Gaullist
        control of broadcasting
1969   Creation of competition between the newsrooms of the first
        and second channels of the ORTF and abolition of the
        Ministry of Information as part of the New Society project
        of Prime Minister Jacques Chaban-Delmas
1970   President Georges Pompidou talks of ORTF journalists as
        being the voice of France
1972   Broadcasting   statute   limits   advertising   revenue   to
        25 per cent of the total revenue of the ORTF
1973   Introduction of third state television channel to serve the
        needs of the regions
1973   Establishment of the daily newspaper *Libération*
1974   First presidential television debate, between Valéry Giscard
        d'Estaing and François Mitterrand
1974   Break-up of the ORTF into separate public radio and
        television companies
1977   First broadcast of the pirate radio station Radio Verte
1978   Legislation by the Giscardian presidency to strengthen the
        state monopoly in the face of the challenge from pirate
        radio stations
1979   Launch of the first local radio stations of Radio France
1981   Legalization of private local radio by President Mitterrand's
        Socialist government
1981   Creation of NRJ radio station
1982   Abolition of the state monopoly in broadcasting
1982   Establishment of the first independent regulatory authority
        for broadcasting, the High Authority for Audiovisual Com-
        munication (*Haute Autorité de la Communication Audiovis-
        uelle*)
1982   The state-managed cable plan is approved by the Socialist
        government with the aim of installing cable television and
        communication networks across France
1984   Creation of the terrestrial pay-TV channel Canal+
1984   Introduction of advertising on private local radio
1984   Establishment of the international francophone television
        channel TV5   ➡

1984	Creation of a public fund to support non-advertising funded local private radio stations
1986	First broadcasts of free-to-air commercial television channels five (La Cinq) and six (TV6, later renamed M6)
1986	Communications statute privatizes the public television channel TF1
1986	Establishment of a new regulatory authority for broadcasting, the National Committee for Communication and Freedoms (*Commission Nationale de la Communication et des Libertés*)
1986	Launch of Skyrock radio network
1986	Launch of Paris Première, the first cable thematic channel
1987	The franchise for La Cinq is awarded to the French press mogul Robert Hersant and the Italian media magnate Silvio Berlusconi
1987	The franchise for the privatized TF1 is awarded to the Bouygues company
1987	Creation of France Info radio station
1989	Establishment of a new regulatory authority for broadcasting, the Higher Audiovisual Council (*Conseil Supérieur de l'Audiovisuel*)
1989	Establishment of a single top management for the two public television channels, Antenne 2 and FR3
1989	Adoption of the Television Without Frontiers directive
1991	Loi Évin bans television sponsorship and advertising for alcohol and tobacco
1992	Financial collapse of the commercial television channel La Cinq
1992	Launch of the Franco-German public service cultural channel ARTE
1992	Launch of the satellite distribution system CanalSatellite
1993	France obtains recognition of the idea of a 'cultural exception' for broadcasting and audiovisual services at the General Agreement on Tariffs and Trade (GATT) talks
1994	Liberalization of rules on ownership share of a television channel by single individual or company
1994	Launch of the rolling news channel LCI
1994	*Paris Match* publishes photos of Mitterrand's daughter, Mazarine Pingeot
1995	First broadcast of new public television channel, La Cinquième, renamed France 5 in 2002
1996	Launch of the digital satellite service Télévison par satellite (TPS)
1997	Launch of the news magazine *Marianne*
1999	Legislation creates the parliamentary channels, La Chaîne parlementaire de l'Assemblée nationale and Public Sénat
2000	Vivendi group buys Universal Studios to create the global multimedia conglomerate Vivendi Universal ➡

2000	France Télévisions is established as a holding company consisting of three channels: France 2, France 3 and La Cinquième
2000	Legislation reduces the amount of advertising on public television
2001	Reality programme *Loft Story*, a French version of *Big Brother*, shown on M6
2002	Launch of free newspapers *Métro* and *20minutes*
2004	Law on electronic communications: radio and television services on the internet to comply with similar obligations governing those on cable and satellite
2005	Launch of digital terrestrial television
2006	Launch of the international news channel France 24
2007	Creation of independent news website Rue 89
2007	Merger between CanalSatellite and TPS to create a single digital satellite television distributor, CanalSat
2008	President Sarkozy announces the withdrawal of commercial advertising from public television
2009	Major reform of public television, including the creation of a single public television company and the direct appointment of its chief executive by the President
2009	Publication of the findings of the official forum on the state of the French press (*Les états généraux de la presse écrite*)
2009	Introduction of the Hadopi law (*Haute Autorité pour la diffusion des œuvres et la protection des droits sur Internet*), designed to prevent peer-to-peer internet file sharing and to protect intellectual property rights on the web

2 THE CONTEMPORARY MEDIA LANDSCAPE

- Formative influences
- The press
- Radio
- Television
- The internet
- Conclusion

Ranging from local newspapers with small circulations to the global reach of new information and communication technologies, the media landscape of contemporary France is diverse and multilayered, as befits a country with a rich history, highly developed economy and complex, heterogeneous society. There has been a notable expansion of supply over the past 30 years through the proliferation of local radio stations, digital broadcasting services and internet websites. Mapping the terrain of this landscape, this chapter provides an analysis of key structural and operational features of the French media in the early years of the twenty-first century. The first section – entitled 'Formative influences' – considers the different factors that have helped form the French media landscape of today. Succeeding sections examine a particular media sector – the press, radio, television and the internet respectively – situating each within the context of a media system whose constituent components have to a significant extent become more interdependent than in the past, largely as a result of the technological convergence that is a central feature of the digital, multimedia age.

Formative influences

In the previous chapter we examined some of the key events and issues in the historical development of the French media from the latter part of the nineteenth century until the final years of the twentieth, noting for example the major impact of the Second World War on the restructuring of the press and broadcasting after the Liberation. The configuration of the contemporary media landscape can be seen as a product of this long historical sequence – of past choices that have either opened up possibilities for change or closed off potential decision-making options. For instance, the policy choices made after the Liberation in strengthening the role of the state exerted a powerful influence on the structures and functioning of the media that in path-dependent fashion are still evident over 65 years later in practices ranging from financial subsidies for newspapers to regulation of broadcast content.

In addition to the impact of history, other variables have influenced essential features of the French media landscape of today. Four are covered in this section: technological, economic, sociocultural and transnational factors. While in practice these formative influences are often mutually interdependent – for instance, the introduction of new communications technology with a global reach may have significant consequences for the economic viability of certain media outlets and may also radically alter how some social groups access media content – here we deal with each of them separately for the purposes of analysis. It is also important to note at this stage the impact of one more formative influence – that of political intervention through the process of media policy-making – that will be covered separately in Chapter 4.

The first major formative influence on the contemporary media landscape is technological change. Since the media are technologically dependent industries, advances in technology will necessarily have an impact on the production and distribution of content, as well as its mode of reception by audiences. This has always been the case; it is certainly not an innovation of the digital era. For example, the development of new printing methods in the 1970s and 80s radically altered the process of newspaper production; the introduction of FM in the 1970s permitted a significant expansion in the supply of radio services, notably at the local level, even if many new stations were not legalized until the early 1980s; and the exploitation of new distribution technologies, such as cable and direct-to-home satellite broadcasting, opened up the potential of multichannel, analogue television in the final two decades of the twentieth century. The introduction of new communications technology has tended to speed up production processes, improve distribution and increase diversity of supply. At its most radical, technological innovation may even lead to the introduction of wholly new types of media, as was the case with the invention of radio towards the end of the nineteenth century and of television in the early part of the twentieth.

The most recent development in the technological field, described by many as revolutionary, is the shift from analogue to digital (Murdock, 2000). Through its capacity for signal compression, digital technology allows for significantly more efficient use of transmission platforms (terrestrial, cable, satellite, ADSL, mobile communication) than was previously the case with analogue. The digitization of networks makes it possible to deliver far more content over the same spectrum, with digital television, for example, usually delivering up to six channels in the spectrum previously required for one analogue channel. Digitization therefore has massively increased the potential number of television channels available to audiences, giving a new impetus to the distribution of multi-channel television to French households. As a result, for many media users the impact of digital change has come to be associated primarily with a huge expansion in the provision of television programming and therefore in viewer choice.

Certainly the switch to digital is the most important technological change in television supply since the medium was first rolled out to a mass audience in France in the 1960s. Digital allows for even greater segmentation of programme supply in the form of thematic and niche channels. It also facilitates access to video-on-demand services and a host of interactive possibilities. The impact of digitization, therefore, cannot simply be evaluated in terms of an increase in the quantity of content transmitted to viewers – more television output in a traditional linear model of distribution, whereby programmes are selected and packaged for audiences within the framework of a constructed schedule. Instead, the advent of the digital age opens up a different type of television than its analogue predecessor, with content capable of being accessed via the internet, mobile phone and personal mobile television as well as the traditional television screen, and with greater empowerment for the service user (no longer just a 'viewer') to construct their own patterns of content access and media usage through personal video recorders, catch-up television (*télévision de rattrapage*) via the internet and video-on-demand services. With the spread of digital the viewing experience is moving towards a more fragmented and customized model. As a result, in the eyes of some, digitization alters the power balance between producer and consumer, as a previously highly restricted, producer-dominated market is replaced by a more competitive set of arrangements in which consumers can now exercise greater freedom of choice.

The impact of digitization on the traditional television sector is, however, only a small part of a much larger change. In the analogue era, clear distinctions could generally be made between media, based on their use of different technologies, their operation in discrete markets and the relative lack of substitutability in their social modes of consumption. In the digital era, France's media and communication industries are more technologically and economically integrated than in the past. The most significant consequence of the arrival of digital has been the growing technological convergence among communications media, with the result that the same media product can now be delivered through a range of different platforms. Online newspapers, electronic publishing, radio and television broadcasts on the internet, video images via the telephone and e-mail accounts on television monitors are just a few examples of the crossover of traditional sectoral boundaries in the contemporary communications media. On the distribution side, the boundaries of industries are blurring, with telecommunication companies becoming involved in the broadcasting sector. In terms of audience reception, the growing convergence embracing press, telephony, radio, television and the internet has meant that consumers may now access various types of media content via an array of household and portable devices, such as smartphones, while the possibilities for interactive media usage are also greatly enhanced. In the opinion of one of the most influential commentators on the changes brought about by digital media, we have witnessed a shift from mass and personal media to media of 'mass self-communication' – self-generated, self-directed and self-selected communication that can potentially reach a global audience (Castells, 2009).

Economic factors comprise a second set of formative influences on the contemporary media landscape. The French media form an economic sector with a turnover of over €30 billion and on which more than 400,000 persons rely for employment, including 60,000 directly (Giazzi, 2008: 3). Since most media outlets (apart from public radio and television) are private businesses run for a profit, their commercial health is to a significant extent linked to the performance of the wider economy. In a period of economic downturn, reduced advertising budgets and declining consumer expenditure, media companies may have to retrench and downgrade certain activities, while the capacity for new investment, for instance in online services, may well be threatened. For example, the cyclical economic crisis that began in 2008, and the accompanying fall in media advertising, greatly exacerbated the long-standing structural problems of the newspaper industry.

Ultimately the financial bottom-line may even have an adverse effect on the very survival of media outlets. Various daily newspapers have gone into liquidation in the past, including *J'informe* (1977), *Le Matin de Paris* (1988), *La Truffe* (1991) and *Info-Matin* (1996). A national commercial television channel, La Cinq, went bankrupt in 1992 because of its inability to secure an audience of sufficient size or the desired socioeconomic composition to attract advertisers. In 2009 the independent news website bakchich.info, founded three years previously, declared its incapacity to pay its bills in the face of a shortfall in income. Even among public sector media the size of budgets has a significant impact on operational capacity. For example, the international rolling news channel, France 24, funded by the state, is significantly less well resourced than its BBC equivalent, BBC World News, and as a result has fewer journalists employed around the globe (see Chapter 7).

Changes in French society and in cultural practices form a third set of formative influences on contemporary media structures and operations. Particular sections of society – including women, ethnic minorities, the gay community and the young – have emerged as target markets for different media outlets. Their tastes and interests are catered for by a range of niche media in the print, broadcasting and online sectors, including different genre magazines, minority interest radio stations, themed television channels and a host of dedicated websites. The range of media practices now evident across a society differentiated by age, sex, income, social class, ethnic origin and educational qualifications means that the era of the undifferentiated mass audience is now largely a historical memory. Media usage has become more individualized than in the past and media consumers are more demanding that content should meet their particular personal needs. Moreover, in a society that places a high premium on leisure activities, a lot of media product is designed for entertainment purposes as consumers seek to distract themselves from the more mundane aspects of their existence. The impact of the entertainment imperative has not just been reflected in the expansion of those media sectors specifically geared for this purpose, such as film channels and music stations. It can also be seen in programme genres such as news, where the need to attract and hold audiences has become an important constraint on the behaviour of media practitioners.

The most important sociological variable governing practices of media usage is generational. An official report on the cultural practices of the French in the digital age divides French society into four generational groups (Donnat, 2009: 11). The first is the prewar generation, which retains a strong attachment to the print media and is the least involved in digital media usage; the second is the postwar babyboom generation, marked by the music culture of the 1960s and the arrival of television; and the third group consists of persons in their thirties, who grew up with the expansion of radio and television supply and the commercialization of broadcasting, and who have adapted with relative ease to the changes brought about by digitization. The final group, the generation below the age of 30, has matured in a screen-dominated environment (television, computers, games consoles), the virtual world of cyberspace and the rolling-out of broadband internet services. This last generation of 'digital natives' and 'netizens' (internet citizens) is fully at ease with all aspects of the digitized multimedia universe.

A fourth formative influence is transnationalization, whereby the structures, operations and regulation of the contemporary media land-scape in France are affected by European/global trends and practices that show little or no respect for national borders (Chalaby, 2004, 2009). Transnationalization embraces such diverse phenomena as the expanding role of global multimedia companies, trade in television programmes between countries and supranational regulatory intervention by the EU. An important part of transnationalization is technologically driven. In the latter part of the twentieth century the proliferation of communication satellites in geostationary orbit above the earth not only radically transformed the scope and speed of media content distribution, but also opened up previously well protected national broadcasting systems to non-domestic content providers in a range of genres including news (for example, CNNI) and music (MTV). The quintessential transnational communications infrastructure is the internet, whose operations are not nationally bounded.

Another aspect of transnationalization can be found in the field of media content and formats. The huge worldwide growth in media outlets has created a demand for a large amount of product. In television, for example, there is a global market in programming whereby series of programmes are traded between broadcasters in different countries (Steemers, 2004). In addition, programme formats move across national frontiers, sometimes accompanied by fine-tuning to suit the tastes of local audiences. The French media are significant importers of broadcast content, particularly from the USA, including popular series such as *CSI* (*Les Experts*) and children's cartoons. Programme formats are also imported into France and adapted for domestic consumption. One of the best known examples of this was the hugely popular *Loft Story* programme, a French version of the Dutch *Big Brother*, first screened on M6 in 2001. The impact of transnationalization is also evident in the press sector where the phenomenon of free newspapers has been imported into France from abroad with papers such as *Métro*, which originated in Sweden, and *20minutes*, which is partly owned by the Norwegian press group Schibsted.

Transnationalization is clearly an important feature of the French media landscape in the digital era. Yet it is also important to place this phenomenon in perspective. It is certainly not new, since the media in France have been exposed to transnational developments for many years, notably in the field of television programme imports. More importantly, the influence of transnationalization should not be overstated. The impact of transnational trends needs to be offset against the continued strength of national and sub-national specificities across the contemporary French media: national issues are high on the media policy agenda and national actors dominate the process of media policy-making (see Chapter 4). In addition, market pressures ensure that much press, broadcast and web content covers French events and issues (crime, sport, politics and showbusiness), while regulation and convention have ensured that French broadcasting in particular has catered for its national audiences with predominantly domestically produced output that is often highly appreciated by listeners and viewers.

The press

The press in contemporary France faces a series of interlocking and overlapping challenges to its ongoing prosperity. Newspapers in both the national and regional markets are in trouble; indeed, in the eyes of some industry analysts, their long-term survival – at least in their traditional hard copy form – is seriously at risk. Until recently the magazine sector was generally healthy, although some genres have experienced difficulties in attracting readers and advertising over the past few years. While the problems in the newspaper industry are structural, those in the magazine sector are mainly cyclical. The French newspaper industry is in need of radical reform, while the magazine sector may just need to ride out what it hopes will be a temporary downturn in advertising revenue.

Newspapers

Newspapers produced in hard copy (newsprint newspapers) and financed mainly through a combination of advertising and direct payment by the consumer are more then ever before engaged in a battle for audiences and revenue in highly competitive media markets. Both the huge expansion of broadcasting provision in recent years, including the introduction of rolling news services, and the growing availability of free newspapers in urban areas, have provided unwelcome competition. However, by far the principal challenge to the economic sustainability and social relevance of paid-for newsprint newspapers (*la presse payante*) undoubtedly comes from the internet. The two main objective symptoms of the difficulties facing the French newspaper industry are falling circulations among paid-for titles and declining share of advertising revenue relative to other media sectors. In addition to these quantitative indices, one can also find qualitative evidence of public disaffection with newspaper content and widespread concern among journalists about their professional role in the age of digitized information production and distribution.

The newspaper industry in contemporary France is made up of two distinct markets: national titles (i.e. those produced in Paris) and local/regional papers. At first sight the daily national market is broad-ranging in the choice offered to readers. This consists of three upmarket quality titles (*Le Figaro*, *Libération* and *Le Monde*); two popular titles (*France-Soir* and *Le Parisien-Aujourd'hui en France*); three so-called 'opinion' papers (*La Croix* – reformist Catholic, *L'Humanité* – Communist and *Présent* – nationalist/traditionalist Catholic/extreme-right); two financial titles (*Les Echos* and *La Tribune*); and one sports daily (*L'Équipe*). The most obvious gap on the supply side among national dailies and the main reason for their low total circulation nationwide is the absence of a popular title with tabloid journalistic values: France notably lacks the equivalent of *The Sun* in Britain or *Bild* in Germany. The national titles sell mainly in the greater Paris area (see Table 2.1 for circulation figures of national daily titles). In 2000 three out of four French citizens never read a daily national newspaper (DDM, 2002: 97) and there is no reason to believe that this statistic has changed for the better in the intervening years.

In 2007 the daily regional market consisted of 57 separate titles. It is these regional dailies, often centred on a provincial conurbation, that dominate sales nationwide. Of the eight million total print run of daily newspapers, just over six million are regional titles and fewer than two million are national. The biggest selling daily is *Ouest-France* (Rennes) with a circulation of 762,000 in 2009. In 2006 the Ouest-France group published no fewer than 42 local editions of its main daily newspaper, employed around 1,200 journalists and had a network of about 5,000 correspondents who provided local information to the newsdesk (Tessier and Baffert, 2007: 38). Other high circulation regional dailies (2009 figures) include *Sud-Ouest* (Bordeaux: 298,000), *La Voix du Nord* (Lille: 274,000), *Le Dauphiné Libéré* (Grenoble: 235,000) and *Le Progrès* (Lyons: 209,000). Just like the national titles, none of the regional newspapers seeks to attract readers on the basis of tabloid-style journalism.

Table 2.1   Circulation of national daily newspapers (1981–2009) (in 000s)

	1981	1994	2000	2006	2007	2008	2009
La Croix	118	97	90	97	97	95	95
Les Echos	67	124	154	119	119	121	121
L'Équipe	223	337	401	361	323	311	303
Le Figaro	336	383	368	333	327	320	315
France-Soir	429	197	60*	34	21	24	23
L'Humanité	141	67	55	52	51	49	48
Libération	70*	174	171	133	132	123	112
Le Monde	439	354	402	350	317	300	288
Le Parisien-Aujourd'hui en France	343	431	492	510	524	513	489
La Tribune	n/a	78	104	77	78	77	67

*Estimated circulation

Note: The figures across the years may not be methodologically wholly comparable, as different criteria for the calculation of circulation figures may have been used.

Sources: Albert (1998: 121, 2008: 140); Organisme de Justification de la Diffusion (2010).

The great importance attached to local identity in France has no doubt contributed to the powerful position of these regional papers in their particular geographic catchment areas. Strong identification with hetero-geneous sub-national cultural traditions and local communities has helped underpin the strength of local and regional newspapers in their competi-tion with the national dailies. Despite the creation of ever-faster and more efficient communication and transportation networks, many French peo-ple cling strongly to their local roots, taking a great interest in informa-tion relevant to events and personalities in their particular locality or region. The provincial papers have been well placed to satisfy this demand, with their extensive coverage of local and regional information. They also tend to be cheaper to buy than the national dailies as well as being more successful in securing regular readers through subscription and home delivery.

The structures of the French political system have also helped the provincial press. Top national politicians generally seek to legitimize their position through control of a local/regional power base: for instance, Martine Aubry, leader of the main opposition party (the Parti Socialiste – PS) is mayor of Lille, Alain Juppé, a leading member of the governing centre-right party, the Union pour un mouvement populaire (UMP), is mayor of Bordeaux and Ségolène Royal, the defeated Socialist candidate in the 2007 presidential election, is head of the regional council of Poitou-Charentes. Well-known national politicians are thus locally embed-ded in a way that directs at least some media attention away from a purely metropolitan focus. As a result, politicians of national standing are obliged to take a keen interest in their mediation by the relevant local/regional news media. Local and regional titles may also influence the content and tone of national political debate. Not surprisingly, French politicians are always keen to harness the support of a regional daily in their election campaigns, with Jacques Chirac even declaring his candidacy for the 1995 presidential election via a regional newspaper, *La Voix du Nord*.

The contemporary newspaper business shows a significant fall in the number of daily paid-for newspaper titles since the high point of the immediate postwar years (see Table 2.2). The combined total of 67 national and regional daily newspaper titles in 2007 was a marked drop from the 203 on sale in 1946. In circumstances of a declining readership for daily newspapers and a very competitive advertising market, there has been limited scope for new entrants. This is particularly the case as the entry costs of a new title into the market are very high. Since the immediate postwar boom only two new national daily newspapers – *Libération* and *La Tribune* – have been established and still survive. Several other titles have fallen by the wayside. On a more positive note, there has been little change in the combined total of paid-for national and regional daily titles since the mid-1990s, while between 2001 and 2007 ten free newspaper titles also entered the daily market.

Table 2.2   Number of daily newspaper titles (1946–2007)

Year	National	Regional	Total paid-for	Free
1946	28	175	203	
1950	16	126	142	
1955	13	116	129	
1960	13	98	111	
1965	13	92	105	
1970	13	81	94	
1975	12	71	83	
1980	12	73	85	
1985	12	70	82	
1990	11	62	73	
1995	12	58	70	
2000	10	56	66	0
2005	10	58	68	6
2007	10	57	67	10

Source: DDM (2009: 106).

One of the most obvious causes for concern for the French newspaper industry is falling circulations. In the 1950s the national daily *France-Soir* regularly sold over one million copies; however, there is currently no paid-for newspaper in France with a circulation anywhere near this figure. The best selling national daily, *Le Parisien-Aujourd'hui en France*, had an average circulation of just over half a million copies in 2008 (in formal terms *Le Parisien* is a regional newspaper for the greater Paris area, but the sales figures for the two papers are usually reported as one since they both have very similar content). Total print runs for paid-for newspapers have declined from the high point of over 15 million daily papers in 1946 to just over eight million in 2007. The slight increase in print run figures in 2007 compared to the previous year can probably be explained by the public's interest in the presidential election (see Table 2.3).

Table 2.3   Daily newspaper print run figures (1946–2007) (in 000s)

Year	National	Regional	Total paid-for	Free
1946	5,959	9,165	15,124	
1950	3,678	7,256	10,934	
1955	3,779	6,823	10,602	
1960	4,185	7,170	11,355	
1965	4,211	7,857	12,068	
1970	4,278	7,587	11,865	
1975	3,195	7,411	10,606	
1980	2,913	7,535	10,448	
1985	2,777	7,109	9,886	
1990	2,741	7,010	9,751	
1995	2,844	6,881	9,725	
2000	2,186	6,719	8,905	0
2005	1,995	6,277	8,272	1,517
2006	1,901	6,159	8,060	1,655
2007	1,995	6,247	8,242	2,740

Source: DDM (2009: 106).

Cross-national statistical data regarding per capita newspaper circulations across selected advanced democratic societies is provided in Table 2.4. If one just compares France with its major EU neighbours (Great Britain, Germany and Italy), two points are particularly worthy of note. First, mainly because of their large tabloid readerships, Britain and Germany hugely outperform France and Italy. Second, despite population growth and increased levels of formal educational qualifications, per capita newspaper sales declined in all four countries between 1960 and 2005 – dramatically so in France and Great Britain, marginally in Germany and Italy.

Table 2.4   Number of copies of daily newspapers per 1,000 inhabitants (1960–2005)

	1960	1970	1979	1990	1995	2000	2005
France	252	238	196	155	156	180	156
Germany (West)	307	326	323	343	314	371	298
Great Britain	514	463	426	393	317	383	335
Italy	122	144	93	118	108	128	116
Australia	358	321	336	221	185	202	179
Belgium	285	260	228	187	167	175	163
Canada	222	218	241	230	191	189	170
Denmark	353	363	367	355	310	371	287
Finland	359	392	480	562	464	543	515
Japan	396	511	569	591	576	664	631
Netherlands	283	315	325	313	310	363	287
Norway	377	383	456	615	600	705	601
Spain	70	–	–	82	–	106	110
Sweden	490	537	526	529	464	543	466
USA	326	302	282	253	226	274	241

Source: Albert (2008: 39).

For many French citizens reading a newspaper remains a daily ritual. Observance of this ritual is, however, less widely maintained than previously. According to official government statistics, in 2008 69 per cent of French citizens above the age of 15 sometimes read a daily newspaper (compared with 73 per cent in 1997), but only 29 per cent did so (almost) every day (36 per cent in 1997) (Donnat, 2009: 6). Only 11 per cent read a *national* daily more than once a week (13 per cent in 1997), while 32 per cent read a *regional* daily with the same frequency (38 per cent in 1997). Of all the sociological variables – educational qualifications, gender, ethnic origin, employment status – potentially linked to the decline in newspaper reading, age is the most important. In 2008, 58 per cent of 15–24 year-olds sometimes read a daily newspaper (70 per cent in 1997), but only 10 per cent did so (almost) every day (20 per cent in 1997) (Donnat, 2009: 6). Young people are particularly resistant to paying for a newspaper and there is a fear among newspaper owners and journalists that the current generation of young people may never properly acquire the habit of regular reading of a newsprint newspaper even as they grow older. If so, we are witnessing a generational change in media consumption patterns to which newspapers will be obliged to respond if they are, quite simply, not to go out of business.

For instance, a recent study of readership of the regional press in France revealed not just the extent to which young people were less interested than their elders in reading newspapers, but also that this represented a generational rather than simply an age effect (Rouger, 2008). One of the main reasons given was that this particular younger generation was less attached to the locality than its predecessors, with the result that what had previously been a strong aspect of the journalism of regional newspapers – a focus on local news – was much less valued by this new generational cohort. In similar vein, the attractiveness for young urban professionals of free newspapers has been attributed in part to the way in which the journalistic content and format of these titles are more suited to a postmodern lifestyle where media usage is characterized by mobility, free access to information and 'soft' news (Rieffel, 2010: 41–68). In short, one of the key drivers of change in the relationship between the public and newspapers in contemporary France is to be found in the modifications undergone by French society in recent years and in particular the different lifestyles and media consumption habits of the young.

One factor in suppressing demand for newspapers in France is their high cover price. Newsprint newspapers remain expensive to produce and distribute. The introduction of new printing technology in the last quarter of the twentieth century did not lower production costs as much as had been hoped and did nothing to reduce distribution costs. Newspapers are more expensive to produce in France than in many other comparable countries. In part this is because of overstaffing and restrictive practices in the print industry, which has been dominated since the Liberation by the powerful trade union, the Syndicat du Livre. Reducing the price of newspapers as a way to boost sales is not, however, within the capacity of most newspaper groups in France, since they lack the scale of media interests to sustain significant price cuts over time. In any case, while high cover prices may deter potential readers, they may still be necessary for the newspaper's economic balance-sheet since a large element of production costs are fixed irrespective of the length of print runs. In short, lowering the unit price of newspapers to gain more readers may not make financial sense, while raising the price increases consumer disaffection and depresses sales even further. Another factor adversely affecting both supply and demand lies in the distribution network. The number of newsagents and sales points has been on the decline in France, while subscription and home delivery are much less well established than in other major EU countries such as Germany. Distribution of newspapers in their newsprint form is currently a major headache for the industry.

There is also the relatively recent challenge posed by the arrival of free newspapers such as *DirectMatin*, *Métro* and *20minutes*. Distributed at the entrance to underground and railway stations, these titles are available in different local editions in major French towns and cities. They have proved particularly popular with women and the young. In 2007 *20minutes* was the most popular daily newspaper in France (2.5 million readers per day), while its competitor *Métro* was not far behind (2.3 million readers per day). At the end of 2009 *20minutes* had a circulation of 757,000 copies, *Métro* 622,000, *DirectMatin* 413,000 and *DirectSoir* 340,000 (Rieffel, 2010: 25).

The attitude of traditional newspaper companies to the arrival of free newspapers has evolved over time. While originally opposed to this new and unexpected challenge, some established press groups have become involved in the ownership of free newspapers, most notably the Ouest-France group in *20minutes*. From one perspective free newspapers can be seen as a valuable addition in the battle facing the newspaper industry as a whole against other media sectors. They are popular with consumers and until the advertising downturn were one of the few growth areas in newsprint newspapers. Supporters argue that they provide a useful way of attracting new readers, especially among the young, who it is hoped will then migrate to paid-for newspapers as the habit of reading a daily paper takes hold. Free newspapers do not pose a significant direct challenge to the circulations of their paid-for counterparts, since most readers of the free titles are new consumers of daily newspapers, accustomed to receiving their news via the broadcasting media (Rieffel, 2010: 31). In contrast, opponents have argued that free newspapers are the cuckoo in the nest of the newspaper industry, as they undermine the economics of traditional production and distribution. Their content has been criticized for its superficiality, while the reliance on advertising places a premium on what some condemn as 'journalism lite' largely based on a cut-and-paste of press releases. In any event, the cyclical drop in advertising expenditure as a result of the economic crisis of 2008–9 severely undermined the financial viability of this sector of the daily newspaper market.

In addition to falling circulations, the other major issue of concern for the newspaper industry relates to finance, particularly advertising revenue. The majority of newspapers rely on advertising for a significant slice of their income, even if the extent of this dependence varies from title to title. In respect of advertising funding, the health of the newspaper sector within the wider national media market depends on the interaction of two factors: the total amount of resources devoted to advertising across all media sectors (television, radio, the press, cinema, internet, etc.) and the percentage share of the media's advertising budget that newspapers manage to secure. The worst-case scenario for newspapers is a 'double whammy': a reduction in the total amount of money spent by firms on media advertising combined with a reduced percentage share for newspapers – in other words, a smaller slice of a shrinking cake. The share of media advertising taken by the press has been on the decline for many years (see Table 2.5) and this trend is set to continue as television and, even more so, the internet, increase their market share. Regional newspapers, for example, have been badly affected in recent years by the loss of classified advertising to the internet, while for the national titles Google has become an unwanted competitor for brand advertising. These structural changes in the media advertising market were compounded in 2008–9 by the cyclical downturn in the performance of the French economy. The combined impact was catastrophic for the financial well-being of the daily newspaper sector across both national and regional markets.

Table 2.5   Sectoral market share of media advertising (as % of total media advertising budget)

	1982	1990	1995	2003	2007
Press	58.0	56.2	42.8	42.6	36.7
Television	16.0	24.9	32.8	34.5	36.0
Radio	9.0	6.6	8.8	8.5	8.0
Internet	n/a	n/a	n/a	1.5	6.2
Posters	15.0	11.5	14.8	12.1	11.9
Cinema	2.0	0.8	0.8	0.8	1.2

Source: Giazzi (2008: 36).

What about the power of French newspapers? The days are long gone when newspapers enjoyed a virtual monopoly as suppliers of information in the mediated public sphere. They now face stiff competition from other media for access to sources, content, advertising revenue and audiences. In addition, surveys of public opinion show that audiences consider newspapers on the whole to be less accurate and trustworthy in their news coverage than the broadcasting media, particularly radio. On the face of it, therefore, the power of newspapers to influence audiences appears weak.

Yet it would be a mistake simply to write newspapers off as irrelevant commentators on events. They continue to perform key functions, notably agenda-setting and acting as watchdogs, even if it is frequently difficult precisely to evaluate the extent of their influence. The sales superiority of regional titles does not mean that national newspapers have a lower status or exert little influence. Whereas in some other European countries, such as Italy and Germany, large non-metropolitan urban centres publish high quality, prestige newspapers, this is not the case in France. As far as the publication of elite opinion-forming newspapers is concerned, there is no French equivalent of Milan or Frankfurt. On the contrary, despite their comparatively low nationwide circulations, in key respects the national dailies are the dominant agenda-setters in the French press system. Whereas the provincial dailies may be important sources of information for the mass of society, it is the national dailies that reflect the concerns of elites. In particular, the quality national dailies such as *Le Monde*, *Le Figaro* and *Les Echos* exercise a strong influence among key political and economic decision-makers, help set the agenda for the other news media and act as a major forum for the discussion of new ideas in social and cultural matters.

This privileged position of the national press among elites is scarcely surprising, given that the capital is the centre of French political, economic and cultural life. As a result, even provincial titles based far from the capital complement their local and regional content with stories that have a national resonance. In contrast, the national titles largely ignore local and regional news, except when this has a strong human interest dimension, such as a natural disaster. Newspapers are also often in the vanguard in the performance of the media's role as watchdog on behalf of the public, whether as citizens or consumers. Very occasionally newspapers take the initiative through investigative journalism in exposing political scandal or corruption. More frequently, they act as an echo chamber for other political actors, such as pressure groups and the judiciary, by giving publicity to particular campaigns such as the exposure of financial corruption by political parties in the 1990s.

Are French newspapers in structural crisis or simply undergoing a somewhat painful transition? Times are certainly difficult for many newspaper titles. The financial model of traditional newspaper publishing has been hit by a combination of technological, economic and social factors – most notably, the internet, shrinking advertising budgets, competition from free newspapers and disaffection among the younger generation to the product in its paid-for newsprint form. Some individual newsprint titles may well go out of business in the next few years, unable to adjust to new market conditions. Of course, there is nothing new in the closure of individual newspaper titles. What is new is that such titles are now unlikely to be replaced in the offline market as tended to be the case in the past. These new challenges have been superimposed on particular long-standing structural problems: for instance, French press groups have for many years been small and under-capitalized by international standards.

Yet although not masters of their fate, neither can newspapers just assume the posture of helpless victim. To survive, and better still prosper, in the digitized information age will require a focus by newspaper management on two key strategic elements. The first concerns the successful transition of the newspaper to the converged world of online media (see the section below on the internet). The second is the modification of content to make the newspaper product more attractive. Although news reportage will continue to be a staple part of their contribution to information dissemination, newspapers have long since lost the capacity to be the first source of news. Yet the success of many niche-oriented magazines suggests that the print medium still has a role to play in providing entertainment, features, commentary and value-added journalism. Upmarket newspapers will continue to emphasize the depth of analysis and quality of their columnist journalism, while incorporating different supplements – economy, finance, literature, the arts – to boost sales on specific days of the week. Certain genres of coverage – such as sport, culture and lifestyle – now occupy greater space than in the past, as do stories and features aimed at women readers. Even in traditional genres, such as domestic politics, there is a tendency towards the inclusion of a more 'human interest' approach to political coverage, that emphasizes the concerns of 'ordinary voters' and the personal attributes of politicians. Coverage of popular culture, including television chat shows and reality programmes, has become an integral part of newspaper coverage, as newspapers attempt to attract young readers. Yet it is also important to sound a note of caution. Tweaking content and format in search of new readers may well be a high-risk strategy. Not only may changes in content designed to attract a younger readership fail to bring in additional new readers, but they also risk alienating older age groups that currently constitute the most faithful clientele of many newspapers, especially the regional titles.

Magazines

In contrast to newspapers, magazines were until recently in a much better state of health, even if in recent years they have not been immune to online competition from what the French call 'pure players' (i.e. magazines available only via the internet and not in print form). Indeed, the French magazine market is Europe's biggest, both in terms of revenues and advertising, while France has one of the highest levels of magazine readership in the world. Every section of French society and every leisure activity seem to be well catered for in what is a richly segmented provision in terms of target market and content specialization (Albert, 2008: 165–89). Unlike general information newspapers, which tend to aim at a broad, undifferentiated audience, magazines focus on specific sections of the population and seem more in tune with the contemporary nature of an individualistic and fragmented society (Charon, 2008: 7).

Young people are particularly avid readers of magazines, while the weakest readership is among the elderly: the opposite age profile of newspaper readers. Women read slightly more than men, but the difference is not statistically significant. The most popular magazines are those providing television listings (e.g. *TV Magazine*, *Télé Z*, *TV Hebdo*, etc.), followed by women's magazines, the two largest selling being *Version Fémina* and *Femme Actuelle*. Magazines take a significant slice – over 12 per cent – of the media advertising budget, around the same share secured by daily newspapers.

Two groups of magazine titles are, albeit in very different ways, important in terms of their political contribution. The first consists of news magazines approximating to the style of the US *Time* or *Newsweek*. France has four main weekly news magazines – *L'Express*, *Le Nouvel Observateur*, *Le Point* and *Marianne* – covering political, economic, social and cultural issues for their educationally highly qualified and socially upmarket readerships. The news magazines fill a gap left by the lack in the French media landscape of quality Sunday newspapers that in Britain, for example, have long provided a rich source of political analysis and commentary. They compete for readers not just against each other, but also with the more generalist of the business magazines such as *Le Nouvel Économiste* and *Challenges* as well as with the quality national dailies. The combined circulation of the four news magazines has grown steadily to exceed 1.5 million in 2007 (see Table 2.6).

Table 2.6   Circulation of weekly news magazines (1987–2009) (in 000s)

	1987	1997	2007	2009
L'Express	555	413	452	440
Le Nouvel Observateur	340	439	510	502
Le Point	310	288	419	412
Marianne	–	222	275	261

Source: Charon (2008: 65); Organisme de Justification de la Diffusion (2010).

The second group of magazine titles of political importance includes the photonews weekly *Paris Match* and celebrity magazines such as *Gala* which allow politicians to market themselves to audiences under conditions of 'controlled mediation'. We shall consider the contribution of these magazines in this respect in Chapter 6.

Radio

The supply of radio services has grown enormously since the 1980s as a result of technological advances and public policy initiatives (Cheval, 1997). Radio provision in contemporary France can be divided into three main categories: public service stations managed by Radio France; private commercial radio including national networks (generalist or niche in terms of content) and independent local and regional operators; and finally small, non-profit, community stations that are the contemporary embodiment of the pirate stations of the late 1970s. There is a huge diversity of radio provision nationwide, with about 900 stations sharing the frequencies allocated by the regulatory authority to the private and non-profit making sectors. France is one of the world's leading countries for the number of local radio stations, in particular for those operating on a non-profit basis. The specific number of stations varies from locality to locality, with more transmitting in urban areas. In Paris, for example, there were over 50 separate stations broadcasting in 2009. Apart from generalist networks, these included stations for ethnic minorities (such as Beur FM), religious groups (Fréquence Protestante, Radio Shalom), the gay community (Radio FG) and lovers of different types of music (Skyrock, TSF Jazz).

The principal single supplier in terms of diversity of provision is the public radio company, Radio France. Between 1945 and 1974 public service radio was organized as part of the state broadcasting corporation. When the unitary structure of this organization was dismantled in 1974, public service radio became the responsibility of a separate programme company. Funded over 85 per cent from licence fee revenue, Radio France currently manages four stations with a national reach: France Inter, France Musique, France Culture and France Info. With its mix of news, talk and music, France Inter is the company's mass audience station, while France Culture and France Musique, with their high cultural output, attract comparatively small audiences. France Info is a very popular rolling news station, with jumps in listening figures during major news events such as the first Gulf War and the terrorist attacks of 11 September 2001 in the USA. In 1996, France Info was the first European radio station to have an internet presence (Cavelier and Morel-Maroger, 2008: 55). Radio France also runs a local radio network, France Bleu, which has national programmes with local opt-outs, and Le Mouv', which broadcasts in large towns and cities and is aimed at a youth audience.

Competition for audiences across the big networks of RTL, Europe 1, NRJ and France Inter is intense. The large commercial stations also compete with each other for advertising income. In terms of attracting advertising revenue the radio sector comes well behind the press and television, with under 10 per cent of total media advertising expenditure. Alongside the provision of Radio France and the commercial stations, about 600 community stations spread across the country broadcast to local audiences. These are funded from a mix of local advertising and public subsidy provided through the Support Fund for Radio Broadcasting (*Fonds de soutien à l'expression radiophonique*), which funds small-scale installation, equipment and running costs.

Despite competition from other media, listening to the radio has until recently remained a popular leisure activity. The creation of networks such as NRJ in the 1980s led to an overall growth in the attractiveness of radio among young listeners. The music station Skyrock is popular with those under 20, while other music stations such as Nostalgie, RFM, Chérie FM and RTL2 are more listened to by older audiences. However, there are signs of a falling-off in radio listening. In 2008 the average weekly time spent listening to radio had fallen by two hours (Donnat, 2009: 4). In that year every age cohort of the French population except the over 65s had reduced their listening time in comparison with the 1997 figures. The fall was particularly marked among younger age groups: for instance, 56 per cent of 15–24 year-olds listened to the radio (almost) every day (compared with 71 per cent in 1997) and their average weekly radio usage was down to 9.7 hours (compared with 14.5 hours in 1997).

As in other countries, French radio has adapted to the arrival of the internet through the introduction of web programming and podcasts. Yet at the technical level radio is losing one of the features that distinguished it from other audiovisual media in the recent past: its portability. It faces competition from MP3 players, wifi internet, smartphones and in the near future from personal mobile television. Moreover, while digitization has had a notable impact on the production of radio content, this may well not be the case in respect of distribution. The qualitative and quantitative advantages of digitization that are so evident in television transmission are much less obvious in the radio sector. Plans were announced in 2007 to introduce an extremely expensive and technologically sophisticated digital radio transmission system that among other things would allow radio content to be readily available via various conduits, including MP3 players, computers and mobile telephones. However, in 2009 these plans had effectively been put on hold because of the high costs involved in digital switchover and no date had been given for the switch-off of analogue radio services.

Radio provides political information in the form of news, journalistic commentary, political interviews and audience phone-in programmes. Much of this output is popular with listeners, especially in the early morning slots. The journalistic quality is often of a high standard and there is no French equivalent of the high profile radio talk show hosts in the USA with their vituperative, populist approach to political debate. However, many popular stations, with their continuous diet of music, show little or no interest in news or politics. Overall, radio in France functions as a secondary medium of political information, although an extremely important one at certain times of the day.

Television

In 2009, over 98 per cent of French households had at least one television set and over 54 per cent had at least two. In 2000 the vast majority of French households were able to receive only the seven channels (including the pay channel, Canal+) available via analogue terrestrial distribution. Midway through 2009, over 70 per cent of households had at least one television set capable of receiving digital, while only 17 per cent of households – particularly those inhabited by the very elderly – depended solely on the traditional terrestrial analogue signal. The authorities reckoned that the switchover to digital, due at the end of 2011, was on course for a successful outcome. The highly restricted supply of the three state channels of the early 1980s had become a distant memory from a prehistoric age of broadcasting.

For many viewers digital is the passageway to multi-channel television, funded through the three main revenue streams of the licence fee (public channels only and in decline in real terms), commercial advertising and viewer subscription. Digital television is available via four platforms: terrestrial, ADSL, satellite and cable. Of these, the terrestrial platform is by far the most popular: 43 per cent of French households (11.5 million) accessed digital television via the terrestrial platform in mid-2009, up from only 16 per cent two years earlier. In contrast, in mid-2009 ADSL was available in just over 17 per cent of households (4.6 million), digital subscription satellite in just under 15 per cent (3.9 million), digital cable in under 7 per cent (1.8 million) and free digital satellite in just over 4 per cent (1.1 million). Access to the subscription-based cable and satellite platforms had hardly altered in the two years between 2007 and 2009.

By the time of full switchover it is clear that the majority of households will access digital television via the terrestrial platform. This came on stream after lengthy delays only in 2005. One of the major reasons for the delay was the opposition of TF1, itself for a long time involved in the ownership of one of the competing satellite platforms. Though formally the objection of TF1 to the roll-out of the terrestrial platform focused on the issue of technical standards, in practice the company feared losing advertising revenue to other channels on a national platform where it would be only one of several content providers. Accustomed to being the hugely dominant commercial player in the analogue era, TF1 recognized that it needed to make significant adaptations if it were successfully to meet the more competitive conditions of the digital age.

The early movers into digital were the satellite and cable distributors. In contrast to some other Western European countries and despite an ambitious state-led cable project announced by the Socialist government near the start of Mitterrand's first presidential term, cable has never been a major means of television distribution in France. In 2010, over nine million households, particularly those in large towns and cities, were able to receive the services of Numericable, which has a virtual national monopoly in the cable operator business. However, only just over three million households – about 12 per cent of the national total – actually took out cable television subscriptions and just under half of these were for old-fashioned analogue services.

For about a decade, starting in 1996, there was competition in digital satellite distribution between the two giants Télévison Par Satellite (TPS) and CanalSatellite (a third distributor, AB Sat, is a minor player through its BIS Télévisions package). CanalSatellite was part of the Canal+ group, while TPS was initially jointly owned by TF1, M6 and France Télévisions. The greater experience of the Canal+ group in pay-TV distribution and viewer subscription management was an important factor in the battle between the two big satellite distributors, as was the group's hold over programme rights in areas such as the French football club championship, Ligue 1. After a war of attrition for subscribers, the two companies finally merged in 2007, although the merger was in reality more of a takeover of TPS by CanalSatellite, now known as CanalSat.

Finally, there are various distributors of ADSL television packages, including Orange, SFR, Alice, Darty and Free. This platform has allowed telecommunications operators to move across into broadcasting as distributors and, in the notable case of Orange, as a content provider. Orange has created its own film and sports channels, distributed only on its own networks. Orange Sport, for instance, has obtained exclusive transmission rights for some games in Ligue 1. Orange also has the most diversified broadcast provision on mobile telephones. In 2008, the regulatory authority approved another major innovation as part of digital switchover: personal mobile television which, it was argued by its advocates, would in the future bring numerous television channels to handheld devices in excellent image quality.

The most obvious consequence of digitization on the supply side has been a significant increase in the distribution of television content, with a plethora of channels available on the top cable, satellite and ADSL packages: by the end of 2009 a total of 225 digital television services (excluding local channels) had been given some form of formal recognition by the regulatory authority. Among thematic channels, sport and film were the main areas of programming, followed by documentary and music outlets. Traditional broadcasting companies such as France Télévisions and M6 had launched their own niche channels to trade on their established brand image, while many new digital channels had also come into existence.

At the end of 2009 viewers on the terrestrial platform could receive 18 free national and nine pay-TV channels, as well as some local channels. These included the established channels previously available via analogue: TF1, France 2, France 3, Canal+ (unscrambled programming only), France 5, M6 and Arte. In addition, viewers could receive France 4 (aimed at the 15–34 age group), an array of generalist private channels, two rolling news channels (i-Télé and BFM TV), musical channels (for instance, Virgin 17) and a youth channel (Gulli). The pay-TV channels included Canal+, Canal+ Cinéma, Canal+ Sport, Eurosport France and the rolling news channel LCI. Of the 11 original pay-TV channels on the terrestrial platform, two had given up their franchises by the end of 2009: AB1 and Canal J. The overwhelming majority of households who accessed digital television via the terrestrial platform were content with the diet of the free channels, whereas on the other platforms viewers were more likely to take out a subscription package: a different form of 'digital divide' in terms of viewer usage of multi-channel television provision.

For the regulatory authority the implementation of digital terrestrial television was also seen a means to facilitate the development of local/regional channels. Historically, French television has been highly centralized geographically. As part of its remit, France 3 broadcasts different regionally oriented news programmes nationwide and thus serves alongside the regional press and local radio as a significant source of non-metropolitan news for provincial audiences. The regionalization of French television is, however, not as developed as in Germany or Spain: this reflects the lower status of the region within the French political system, the absence of strong regionalist political parties and the original institutional development of television in France, with strategic decision-making based in Paris. With the arrival of digital terrestrial, initially 18 local channels, previously available in analogue, received authorization to broadcast on the new platform. An additional seven new channels were created in the greater Paris region. In early 2009, 35 local channels were broadcasting in different parts of the country and calls for tenders had been put out with the aim of increasing that figure to above 50. Nonetheless, even in the more variegated and segmented provision that has resulted from the implantation of digital television, the main channels in terms of both supply and demand are still national.

Overall, the television sector in the digital era is characterized by strong competition for audiences, revenue, programme rights and product, both across distribution platforms and among content providers. In increasing the number of specialist channels aimed at particular niche markets, the spread of digital television further segments broadcasting supply and has inevitably led to a reduction in the market share of any single channel. The major losers in terms of audience share are the traditional big players from the analogue era. Consumption patterns were initially slow to adapt to the increase in supply. However, with the routinization of multi-channel television following the rollout of the terrestrial platform, viewing patterns shifted. Whereas in 1998 the seven national generalist channels had a combined audience share of over 95 per cent, this had declined to 91 per cent in 2002, 83 per cent in 2007, 77 per cent in 2008 and was under 70 per cent in January 2010. None of the new channels is by itself a major player in the digital landscape, although some have very respectable audience shares. For instance, in January 2010 among house-holds that could receive their services, TMC had an audience share of 3.1 per cent, W9 had 2.7 per cent and Direct 8 had 1.8 per cent. More importantly, the new channels have cumulatively taken audiences away from the traditional analogue providers (see Table 2.7).

Table 2.7   Audience shares of national television channels (as % of total)

Channel	2004	April 2009	April 2010
TF1	31.8	26.3	24.3
France 2	20.5	16.2	15.7
France 3	15.2	12.2	10.5
Canal+	3.8	3.6	3.6
France 5 (pre-7 p.m.)	6.7	2.9	3.0
M6	12.5	10.7	10.4
Arte (post-7 p.m.)	3.7	1.6	1.7
All other free channels available on the digital terrestrial platform	n/a	14.5	19.7

Source: Médiamétrie (2010).

The newcomers have also eaten into the share of advertising revenue obtained by the traditional channels. The advertising market in television was long skewed in favour of the two leading commercial channels, TF1 and M6, who obtained much higher proportions of television advertising than their share of the audience. In 2002, for example, TF1 had a 53 per cent share of the television advertising market for a 32 per cent audience share, while M6 had a 20 per cent share of television advertising for a 14 per cent audience share (Chupin *et al.*, 2009: 86). In 2008 the TF1 group had a 33 per cent share of the television advertising market, while M6 had 17 per cent: a combined total of 50 per cent compared to 56 per cent the previous year. The combination of a cyclical crisis in media advertising in 2008–9 and increased competition from the new free digital channels on the terrestrial platform had an adverse impact on the revenues of TF1 and M6. Even the gradual suppression of advertising on the public channels from 2009 onwards (see Chapter 4) – a policy measure designed to help TF1 and M6 – failed in the short term to have the desired effect, with the other digital terrestrial channels being the main immediate beneficiaries of the new policy. Thus, while in 2007 the advertising receipts of the new free channels on the digital platform totalled €260 million, by 2008 this had increased to €541 million and by 2009 to €888 million. Finally, increased competition across the television industry is also evident in the area of programme rights, especially in audience-pulling genres such as sports and film.

The huge increase in the amount of television content provison has not, however, been matched by an overall growth in audience consumption. The average length of total television viewing in 2008 compared with 1997 remained stable at around 21 hours per week. This global figure, however, masked some differences across generational cohorts. In particular, there was a marked decline among the 15–24 age group, down from an average of 18 to 16 hours per week. It is possible that as this generational cohort grows older there will be an overall drop in the amount of time devoted to television viewing.

National television is by far the main mass medium of political information. This is not surprising in the light of television's social implantation. Virtually every household has at least one television set; a basic core output is available 'on tap' at no additional cost to users on top of the annual licence fee; television viewing is a well-established leisure activity; the visual qualities of the medium make its content easily accessible; and viewing some output is a ritual event in the daily routine of many citizens. Surveys continue to put television well ahead of radio, the press or the internet as the public's primary source of national and international news. For instance, in February 2007, during the run-up to the presidential election campaign, 59 per cent of voters put television as their primary source of political information compared with 17 per cent for radio, 10 per cent for the national press, 7 per cent for the regional press, 6 per cent for the internet and 1 per cent for free newspapers (Vedel, 2008: 64). By the start of 2010 these figures had not altered substantially: television was the primary source of national and international news for 57 per cent of citizens, followed by radio (20 per cent), the press (14 per cent) and the internet (8 per cent) (La Croix, 2010). Thus for the French citizenry as a whole, television was a more frequent primary source for national and international news than radio, press and the internet combined. In this regard it should be noted that while their hold over audiences is under threat in the digital communications environment, the main evening news programmes of the national free-to-air channels TF1, France 2, France 3 and M6 still attracted a combined total of around 18 million viewers on a daily basis in 2009. However, news consumption patterns are changing. Among the 18–24 age group the internet (19 per cent) was the second most important source of national and international news after television (63 per cent), while for all those under 35 the internet came ahead of the press (La Croix, 2010).

The internet

Prior to the arrival of the internet France had experimented with its own national computerized information distribution network, Minitel, which was launched by the state postal and telecommunications service in 1982 and quickly gained the reputation of being an extremely successful online service, especially for financial and business transactions. However, as a purely national service Minitel was never going to prosper against the global reach of the internet.

The internet was slow to take off in France after its entry into the mediated public sphere in the early 1990s and by the end of the decade France was well behind other countries such as the USA, Denmark and Finland in respect of domestic internet usage. At the start of 1998, Prime Minister Lionel Jospin's government launched a governmental action programme for the information society in what proved a successful attempt to ensure the implantation of high-speed broadband networks in France (D'Almeida and Delporte, 2010: 374). The take-up of broadband over the next ten years was impressive.

At the end of 2009, France had 34.7 million internet users aged 11 or above (65 per cent of the relevant population). At the same time almost 17 million households had domestic internet access (over 62 per cent of the total), with most having high-speed broadband connections via ADSL or cable. Consumer take-up of broadband was helped by the popularity of 'triple play' offers (internet, television and fixed line telephone), with relatively cheap monthly subscription rates. Internet usage is particularly widespread among the young and declines as one moves through the generational cohorts. In 2008, 57 per cent of the 15–24 age group used the internet (almost) every day, compared with only 4 per cent of those over 75. The internet is also more used by the highly educated and better off. This contrasts with television which is a medium of the elderly and less highly educated. There is, therefore, still a digital divide in French society with regard to both internet availability and usage.

While the spread of the internet has had an impact on all traditional news media, it has posed a particularly acute problem for newspapers. By making information instantly available to users, the internet is often the first port of call for audiences seeking up-to-date news about moving events in real time. This is an area in which newsprint newspapers cannot hope to compete – indeed it could be said that this is simply an extension of the problem of being 'first with the news' that newspapers have had to face since the arrival and spread of radio (1920s–30s) and television (1950s–60s). In addition, for a growing number of people the internet is a more attractive and user-friendly source of information than newsprint newspapers. This is particularly the case with certain sections of society, notably the young.

The internet also provides information in a non-linear fashion, which allows users to augment and deepen their information search at will. News sites provided by internet portals such as Google and Yahoo!

provide new – and from newspapers' perspective highly unwanted – competition for consumers and advertising revenue. To many the internet's combination of visual and audio text, its interactive functions, its accessibility for users on the move via mobile phones and other handheld devices and its capacity to allow users to be producers and not just consumers of information make newsprint newspapers look tired and out of date. The expansion of internet reach into domestic households has also led to advertising revenue – both brand and classified – moving away from the established media, as advertisers chase changing patterns of media usage among their target audiences in, for example, the purchase of goods and services.

The initial response by many newspaper executives to the advent of the internet was simply to publish an online replica of the hard copy newspaper (or in the most extreme cases to do nothing by pretending that the internet did not exist!). Initially the internet was regarded simply as another means of content distribution. This strategy quickly revealed its limitations as it became clear that a huge swathe of linear text was not the way to attract users to a newspaper's website. There has certainly been a growth in the quality of the web presence of French newspapers in both national and regional markets, with a concomitant reorganization of newsrooms to incorporate both newsprint and online versions of the journalistic product. Several newspaper companies have invested significant resources in creating multi-faceted websites that serve to propagate the newspaper brand, while at the organizational level newsrooms are increasingly integrated in the production of both newsprint and online versions.

One of the most successful online media ventures in France is the website Le Monde.fr, which provides archival resources, discussion sites for users and links to other relevant websites. In 2007 *Le Monde* launched lepost.fr, a website aimed at younger readers, which has proved successful in terms of user hits but has sustained significant financial losses. Newspaper titles are also seeking to distribute content via mobile telephones and tablet devices such as the iPad. For instance, in 2009 a digital version of *Libération* was available to iPhone users for a monthly subscription of €12 (compared with €1.30 per day for the newsprint version). News magazines embraced the web early and with enthusiasm, creating electronic versions of their titles (Charon, 2008: 66). In contrast, *Le Canard enchaîné* refuses to publish its content on the web and prides itself on its status as a newsprint newspaper.

A major issue facing newspaper management in the online sector is whether to charge the user for services through the creation of 'paywalls' or to provide content for free. There is evidence that young people in particular have become accustomed to not paying for access to certain services (e.g. the downloading of music) and that this is creating a new relationship between provider and user in the online world. Some newspapers such as *Le Monde* charge users for access to at least some of their services (e.g. access to their archives), but allow other content to be accessed for free. This so-called 'freemium' model (a mix of free and premium content) may be one way forward for newspapers and it is certainly one that many French press groups are actively considering (Rieffel, 2010: 74). Another possibility is that newspapers will increasingly try to secure advertising funding for their online services so as to reduce, or better still eliminate, the direct costs of website access to the consumer. The issue of how to monetize web-based content is a major problem for press groups in France as in many other developed societies, with evidence that users may be willing to pay for value-added information in certain fields (e.g. in financial news) or for quality journalism, but are not willing to pay for general and political news, which can be accessed somewhere else on the web at no direct cost to the consumer. Established media organizations that fully embrace the potential of the internet can reasonably hope to enjoy success in terms of usage, but the big question in France as in all other advanced democracies is whether a viable business model for newspapers on the internet can be found.

The internet is clearly not just a new means of distribution for traditional content controlled by the established media organizations: it is in itself a new medium. For instance, it has given rise to new types of journalistic content that originate from outside of the mainstream media and to new modes of interaction between user and content provider. In certain respects the internet brings some notable advantages for information provision. It allows ordinary citizens to contribute to the production process through submission of photos and video footage (YouTube, Dailymotion, Flickr) as well as text. It has facilitated the emergence of a range of social, alternative and participatory media, including Facebook and Twitter. It permits access for a wider variety of sources than in the past and should, therefore, help create a more level playing field between traditional official sources and more marginal sociopolitical actors in terms of news coverage. It allows journalists to publish information and opinion across a range of websites and in different formats. The internet can thus be seen to democratize information production and distribution.

Critics, however, also point to potential drawbacks. For instance, the internet may deprofessionalize the activity of journalism, with the result that there is now widespread concern among journalists about their occupational role. Journalists' traditional professional status based on claims to authority, expertise and legitimacy has been undermined by the rise of new practices of news gathering and distribution. Blogs, at their worst, become sites of unsubstantiated rumour and gossip where the rules of ethical journalism do not apply. Stories may circulate very quickly in the blogosphere and gain traction with public opinion even when the revelations subsequently prove to have no basis in fact. The veracity of information then becomes an important issue. In contrast, one major advantage that some (though certainly not all) press outlets have in the eyes of the French public is their relative credibility as suppliers of accurate information. These enjoy a strong brand image which is already serving them well in the online world. It is not surprising, therefore, that some newspaper and news magazine websites such as Le Monde.fr, Le Figaro.fr and L'Express.fr feature among the most popular in terms of usage.

In addition, several new independent websites have been created outside of the traditional mainstream media, with news content available only (or principally) via the internet. Rue 89 (www.rue89.com/), Bakchich (www.bakchich.info/), Mediapart (www.mediapart.fr/) and Arrêt sur images (www.arretsurimages.net/), as well as citizen news websites, such as Agoravox (www.agoravox.fr/), provide additional sources of news, information and comment for their users. These web-based news sites try to provide a different perspective on news items from the mainstream media, focus on particular topics of interest to their users and, in the case of Rue 89, make significant use of contributions not just from professional journalists, but also from experts (e.g. academics) and ordinary users. They are currently niche players in the direct provision of online news to the public, coming well behind the general portals such as Google News and the websites of the mainstream offline media. Moreover, like the web versions of established media outlets, their commercial viability has not yet been secured. These sites are, however, frequently cited by mainstream media and they have become an integral part of the world of online journalism in France.

The internet is a particularly attractive medium for politicians and other sources, because it allows them the possibility of bypassing the gatekeepers and filters of mainstream news media. However, while many political actors have established their own website, the internet is still not a major provider of political information for the mass electorate. Partly this is due to the fact that the internet is still not a universal medium (the digital divide). In addition, the web remains a 'pull' technology where users actively have to search out information – in contrast to television which is a 'push' technology. While in the 2007 presidential election the internet played a more significant role than had been the case in 2002, its use was still the preserve of a minority (Vedel, 2008: 71). According to survey evidence, in 2009–10 those who predominantly used the internet as their main source of political information (supplemented by television) constituted about 10 per cent of the adult population in France (Vedel, 2010). They were mainly young men with a low interest in politics.

Conclusion

Domestic news media markets in contemporary France are characterized by hyper-competition for audiences and revenue. Media consumers are less loyal than in the past to any particular media outlet, while the young are a particularly difficult clientele to attract and retain. New technology poses an economic challenge to the established mainstream media, notably digital channels in the television sector and the internet in the case of the press. Finally, traditional journalistic practices are having to adapt, sometimes reluctantly and frequently with considerable tension, to media organizations' need to have both an online and offline presence.

The impact of new technology on the production, distribution and reception of content is the most notable feature of the contemporary media landscape. Handheld computers, internet broadband connections, flat-screen televisions, DVD players, games consoles, MP3 players, multi-functional mobile phones and tablets have become part of the communications and entertainment world of a large number of French citizens. Many of the new technological devices both allow for greater portability than in the past and embrace different functions. Thus, in the space of a decade or less, fixed pieces of equipment dedicated to a specific function (television screen, radio receiver, phone handset) have been largely replaced or at least complemented by mobile multifunctional devices (Donnat, 2009: 2).

As we saw in Chapter 1, in the past the arrival of a new medium did not result in the marginalization, far less disappearance, of pre-existing media. Instead, these adapted to the new situation in terms of content, while still retaining their specificity in terms of mode of audience use. For instance, newspapers altered their content to respond to the challenge from radio and then television, but at the end of the twentieth century the physical form of the newsprint newspaper was as recognizable as it had been over a hundred years earlier.

Has this situation now irrevocably changed? Have digital media in general and the internet in particular radically altered the French media landscape so that it is not just reasonable but necessary to speak of a paradigmatic shift in its central features? Certainly, on the supply side, there is ample evidence of the impact of the contemporary digital era of multimedia convergence. For instance, the web versions of newspapers cannot be reduced to on-screen versions of the newsprint version – they have come to represent a very distinctive media product. With its mix of constantly updated text, video material, graphics, links to other websites and user-generated content, the web version of a newspaper is a radically different entity from the newsprint version. Moreover, the internet is itself a medium of information and communication separate from the traditional mainstream media.

On the demand side, change is also happening fast, albeit with differential impact across society. Some users have altered their media consumption habits in relatively minor ways: they still read their regional newspapers in hard copy, listen to radio programming on a dedicated radio receiver and continue to watch on a television set the output of generalist channels that have existed for many years. In contrast, for other sections of society, media consumption is already very different from a few years ago. The young, in particular, have grown up with a screen culture, the dematerialization of content and the routinization of broadband internet. They have become accustomed to using different media on a multi-task basis. For this generation in particular, accessing web content via a smartphone while on the move is as much a part of their routine as sitting in an armchair and reading a newsprint newspaper is for their elders.

3 MEDIA PLURALISM

- Configuration of media ownership
- Does ownership matter?
- Media ownership rules
- Media proprietors and Sarkozy
- Political pluralism in the press
- Political pluralism in broadcasting
- Conclusion

Pluralism in the media is often analysed under two headings: external and internal. External pluralism concentrates on the number and range of different outlets operating in a particular media sector or across sectors. Here the focus is on diversity of supply, with particular attention being paid to the issue of ownership concentration. Internal pluralism refers to the range of different views disseminated in any particular media outlet. In this case the focus is on diversity of content, especially but not exclusively in the spectrum of political views disseminated. There is no simple correlation between pluralism in supply on the one hand and diversity of content on the other. In France, as in many other advanced democracies, different sets of rules have been put in place as part of media policy to try to achieve both objectives.

The expansion of the French media in recent years, notably in the broadcasting and online sectors, has opened up the possibility for greater pluralism in supply. At the same time it has also given established media companies the opportunity to consolidate and extend their existing stakes both within and across different market sectors. Some concentration of media ownership can be defended on the grounds of delivering desirable economies of scale and scope. However, from an economic perspective excessive concentration may result in a lack of competition, while from a sociopolitical standpoint it may militate against diversity of content. Structural rules on media ownership both within and across different media sectors have been in place for many years in France in an attempt to secure an acceptable level of external pluralism.

With regard to internal pluralism, individual newspaper titles, news magazines and news websites are under no obligation in this regard. They are free to disseminate politically partisan opinions and to be as one-sided as they like in their editorial content. In contrast, radio and television are supposed to ensure the expression of different views across the political spectrum and to avoid partisanship in their news coverage. This means that the broadcast media are the object of significant regulatory supervision in the sensitive area of political content provision, whereas the press, magazines and news websites are subject to no specific oversight in this respect.

This chapter begins with an examination of external pluralism in the contemporary French media through an analysis of the configuration of ownership, both within and across different media sectors. The second section considers the issue of why ownership matters, while part three focuses on current rules on media ownership. This is followed by a section on the nature of the links between media proprietors and President Sarkozy. Part five focuses on pluralism in the press, while the final section deals with the expression of political pluralism in the broadcasting sector.

Configuration of media ownership

Sectoral concentration

The first level at which ownership concentration may be evident is within a particular media sector. There is still a lot to be said for examining patterns of concentration within distinct sectors. For instance, when used in a historical framework, such an approach can show important elements of continuity and change in ownership over time. Moreover, even in an age of technological convergence, it remains the case that some leading companies are still best known for their presence in a single sector, whether it be newspapers, magazines, radio or television. In addition, a sector-specific approach recognizes that traditional boundaries between media retain their importance for many audiences, who in accessing content do not simply substitute one medium for another. Finally, in France, ownership regulations continue to be applied within media sectors and not just across them.

Any assessment of the extent of ownership concentration in the French press first needs to differentiate between the national and regional newspaper markets. With regard to daily national newspapers, three leading press groups had a combined 70 per cent market share in 2002 (Ward, 2004: 8). While at first sight this may seem a high level of concentration, the corresponding figures for Germany (87.4 per cent) and the UK (70.6 per cent) were higher still. Moreover, ownership across the national newspaper market in France was reasonably diverse, in that there was no significant concentration of titles in the hands of any single press group: in 2002 the leading group had 26 per cent market share, followed by 24 per cent for the second group and 20 per cent for the third (Ward, 2004: 8). In 2010 this picture had not changed radically: the main national newspaper group was the Amaury company, which owned both the sports daily, *L'Équipe*, and the popular daily, *Le Parisien/Aujourd'hui en France. L'Équipe,* one of the major sports dailies in Europe, is associated with popular sporting events, notably the annual Tour de

France cycle race. Its biggest-selling issue was on the day after France won the World Cup in 1998. The Amaury group was followed by Socpresse (*Le Figaro*) and Le Monde group (*Le Monde*). No press group owned more than one national daily title in what the French authorities officially call 'the politics and general news press' ('*la presse d'information politique et générale*').

In any event, it must be remembered that in the contemporary French media landscape the national newspaper sector is dwarfed in circulation terms by the market for regional newspapers (see Chapter 2). Thus, potentially the main ownership concentration issue in the French newspaper industry is at the regional level. In 2002 the top three regional newspaper groups had a combined nationwide market share of 46.7 per cent, which indicated a level of 'moderate concentration' (Ward, 2004: 9). Based on a cohort of the top 20 selling papers, the leading regional press group had a 16.9 per cent market share, followed by 16.4 per cent for the second group and 13.4 per cent for the third. In short, in 2002, no single press group owned lots of daily regional titles nationwide. Some restructuring of the regional press market has since taken place, with the result that by 2010 four main regional press groups – Est Bourgogne Rhône-Alpes, Hersant Média, SIPA Ouest-France and Sud-Ouest – dominated the market in different parts of France, with some cross-shares across the groups (Chupin *et al.*, 2009: 109). In the past few years, therefore, there has been a notable increase in concentration in the regional newspaper market across the country as a whole.

For a reader in any particular French region, of course, it is not nationwide concentration of regional titles but rather possible concentration at the regional level itself that is of concern. In this respect the restructuring of the regional newspaper sector simply consolidated the pre-existing practice whereby in any particular French region a single daily newspaper title frequently enjoys a de facto monopoly position and is usually well able to protect its territorial fiefdom against potential competitors (Martin, 2002). Although they do not constitute a monopoly in the strict sense of the term, since they may still be in competition with smaller local papers, the national dailies and in the larger towns local editions of free newspapers, these big regional titles have secured a strategic position in their respective sub-national markets, frequently absorbing previously independent papers into a powerful regional press chain. The Ouest-France group, based in Rennes, is a good example of this tendency, with its dominant position in Brittany, parts of Normandy and the Pays de la Loire. Pacts have also been made between different regional newspapers not to penetrate into one another's established circulation area. In short, while concentration of the regional newspaper market across France as a whole may well be only moderately high, in any particular region it is likely to be very high indeed.

It is striking that since the withdrawal of Socpresse from the regional market after 2005, the main newspaper groups in the national and regional markets are quite different. There is remarkably little shared ownership across these two newspaper markets and certainly nothing to compare with the national/regional crossover shares of the Trinity Mirror or Daily Mail and General Trust groups in the UK. Similarly, since the Lagardère group pulled out of the regional newspaper market in 2007 to concentrate on its other media holdings, there are only minor examples of crossover in ownership between the newspaper and magazine sectors in France, notably ownership of the national daily *La Croix* by the Bayard Presse group and of the Sunday newspaper *Le Journal du Dimanche* by Lagardère.

In the broadcasting sector there is reasonable diversity of ownership at both national and sub-national levels. In addition to the public company, Radio France, three commercial groups dominate radio nationwide: the RTL group (RTL, RTL2 and Fun Radio); the NRJ group (NRJ, Chérie FM, Nostalgie and Rire et Chansons) and Lagardère (Europe 1, Europe 2 and RFM) (See Table 3.1).

Table 3.1 Market share of leading radio groups (late 2008)

Radio France	21.7
RTL	19.1
NRJ	15.4
Lagardère	14.6

Source: CSA website

In television the dominant players since the economic liberalization of the sector in the 1980s have been the privatized TF1 owned by the Bouygues group, the public channels, especially France 2 and France 3, now organized in the single company France Télévisions, and the commercial channel M6. The arrival of new digital channels has led to a reduction in ownership concentration in the television sector as other players have entered the market for the supply of programming at both national and local levels.

Cross-media diversification and vertical integration

The second level where ownership concentration needs to be considered is across different media sectors and along the value chain of production, content and distribution. Technological convergence and public policy decisions have facilitated the potential movement of media companies across previously distinct sectors, opening up opportunities for cross-sectoral ownership, corporate mergers and the formation of strategic alliances. The importance of combining ownership of content with control of the means of distribution to audiences has become a constant refrain of media company management. There seem to be clear economic gains to be made in the digital era by companies with a controlling interest in the various stages of content production, programming and distribution (Murdock, 2000: 38). Yet for several media companies in France, cross-media diversification and vertical integration have proved difficult in practice.

For many years after the Liberation the possibility of ownership across press, radio and television was effectively excluded by the maintenance of the state monopoly in broadcasting. Only after the abolition of the monopoly in 1982 was the possibility of cross-media ownership opened up to private companies. In the 1980s and 90s several newspaper and publishing groups seized the new opportunity to extend their business interests out of their core market into the potentially lucrative broadcasting sector, taking a stake in radio and television in the hope that the synergies obtained would lead to economies of scale and scope (Doyle, 2002). The Sud-Ouest newspaper group, for instance, had three local radio stations in the mid-1980s. Overall, however, private radios owned by press groups were not commercially successful, with several newspapers encountering problems in their attempt to diversify into this new market. A similar story was also apparent when press groups moved into television. For instance, the powerful Hersant newspaper group, which owned the national titles *Le Figaro* and *France-Soir* at the time, held a major stake in the national commercial channel La Cinq between 1987 and 1990, before finally selling its share in the face of disappointing financial results.

In the contemporary media landscape the main French group with ownership shares across different media sectors and along the value chain of production, content and distribution is Lagardère. Lagardère's media interests are organized around six areas of activity. It is the biggest magazine publisher in France, with *Elle*, *Paris Match* and *Télé 7 Jours* among its many titles, is a major player in radio and is also involved in television – albeit in a minor fashion – through ownership of thematic channels such as Gulli, Canal J and Virgin 17, as well as having an ownership stake in the subscription channel Canal+ and the digital satellite company CanalSat. In addition, it has ownership interests in television production (Lagardère Entertainment), the provision of digital services (Lagardère Digital France) and advertising (Lagardère Publicité) (Charon, 2008: 46–7).

At its height, just after the turn of the millennium, Vivendi was a leading exponent of cross-media diversification with stakes in the music industry, mobile telephony, television and film production. Currently the Canal+ group is an important player in television channel ownership (including Canal+ Cinéma and Canal+ Sport), programme distribution (CanalSat) and film production, acquisition and distribution (Studiocanal). However, the group has no presence in either radio or the press. On a smaller scale the Bolloré group runs a digital television channel, Direct 8, and owns the free newspapers *DirectSoir* and *DirectMatin*. At the regional level, the Ouest-France group has an ownership stake in local television and radio, different internet websites, a publishing house and the national free newspaper *20minutes*.

In comparison with the media markets of other major EU states, France has no equivalent of a company on the scale of Murdoch's News Corporation in the UK, Bertelsmann in Germany or Berlusconi's Mediaset in Italy, all of which have extensive cross-media interests within their respective countries. The financial weakness of national newspaper companies in France has in general prevented them from being successful major players in other domestic media sectors, especially national television; indeed, the lack of significant cross-media diversification by national newspaper groups remains striking. In contrast, several regional newspaper companies have moved to take a stake in local television channels that have come on stream as part of digital switchover, with the result that cross-media concentration is more of a problem at the sub-national level. There has been even less movement in the opposite direction: in general the newspaper sector has been insufficiently attractive for broadcasting groups to wish to move across to take an ownership stake in the press, although TF1 has a minority shareholding in the French version of the free newspaper *Métro*.

Does the internet have a radical impact on the configuration of ownership in the news media through its capacity to allow new, smaller-sized companies to enter the market? For domestic players the answer is probably not, with the possible exception of the local level where community websites may play an important information and communication function. Significant resources are required to manage a website, with the result that in general the established mainstream media have an in-built competitive advantage in establishing and maintaining a strong internet presence because of their existing expertise in content production and distribution, despite some competition in recent years from independent news websites. At the start of 2010 leading groups in terms of audience internet usage included familiar names from the mainstream media such as Skyrock, *L'Équipe*, Lagardère Active, M6, France Télévisions and NextRadioTV. For instance, France's largest social networking site, Skyrock.com, was the creation of Pierre Bellanger, who founded Skyrock radio in the 1980s. Like the radio station, the website is very popular among the 15–24 age group.

Transnationalization

Media ownership in contemporary France is largely dominated by domestic enterprises. Nonetheless, some foreign companies, accustomed to operating on a transnational basis, do have ownership stakes in the French media, particularly in the magazine sector. The most important of these is the German group Bertelsmann, which is the only company to have developed a significant presence across the media sectors of press, radio and television in France. Via its French subsidiary Prisma Presse, Bertelsmann is the second largest magazine publisher in the country, covering a range of different magazine genres. Its magazine titles include *Télé Loisirs*, *Femme Actuelle*, *Prima*, *Voici*, *Gala*, *VSD* and *Capital* among many others. Through its dominant share in the RTL media group, Bertelsmann also has an important ownership interest in the national free-to-air commercial channel M6, various thematic television channels linked to M6 and the national radio station RTL.

The Italian company Mondadori, part of Berlusconi's Fininvest media group, is the third most important company in the French magazine sector, having taken over in 2006 the titles owned by the British media group EMAP. Mondadori France publishes a range of magazine titles including *Télé Poche*, *Télé Star*, *Biba*, *Closer*, *FHM* and *Grazia* among others. On a smaller scale than either Bertelsmann or Mondadori, the leading Belgian magazine publisher Roularta owns the news magazine *L'Express* and the financial weekly *L'Expansion*. In the cable business, UK and US private equity companies have an ownership stake in the French cable operator, Numericable. Finally, because the internet is simultaneously a local, national and global medium, its growth has allowed major non-domestic players such as the news aggregator Google News and the social networking site Facebook to establish a growing presence in France.

Power of conglomerates

A particularly interesting aspect of media ownership in France is that many of the companies that own a stake in the media are conglomerates rather than pure media concerns. Ownership of media outlets often forms part of a broader portfolio that includes industrial and/or commercial sectors. Indeed, frequently their media interests do not constitute the core business of the conglomerate. More particularly, several media outlets are owned by groups that have a business interest in fields such as arms manufacturing, aerospace, luxury goods, construction, transport and retail (see Table 3.2). In this respect France differs markedly from the UK, Germany and Italy, where the major media companies are (almost) exclusively focused on media-related activities.

Table 3.2 Media ownership as part of conglomerate

Company	Areas of non-media ownership	Media ownership
Bouygues	Construction, mobile telephony	TF1
Lagardère	Defence, aeronautics	Magazines, Europe 1, Canal+ (minority share)
Dassault	Military aircraft	*Le Figaro*
Pinault	Retail	*Le Point*
LVMH	Luxury goods	*Les Echos*
Bolloré	Energy, transport	Direct 8 thematic channel, free newspapers
Rothschild	Finance	*Libération*

Source: author

Does ownership matter?

Does it matter who owns the media, how much they own or what nationality they are? Is concentration of media ownership a problem or a solution? What is at stake in the political and policy debates on media ownership? In this section these questions are discussed under three analytic headings: economic arguments, sociopolitical concerns and commercial conflicts of interest.

Economic arguments

From an economic standpoint the media are regarded as an industrial or business sector similar to any other, such as automobile manufacture or retail distribution. From this perspective the nationality or political leanings of media owners are much less important issues than the impact of ownership concentration on market competition. Ownership concentration may have beneficial consequences for the media. For example, as in the case of any market, consolidation may result in efficiency gains from economies of scale and scope and as a result of new synergies. There are clear economies of scale (advantage of size) and scope (advantage of diversified supply) for companies that have a significant share of a specific media market (Doyle, 2002: 45–65). It may even be argued that as far as ownership in a single media sector is concerned, there is a strong potential for additional economic efficiency gains through a relaxation or liberalization of regulations on concentration. From an economic perspective, therefore, in single media sectors, big may well be beautiful, since consolidation gives rise to a more cost-effective use of administrative, technical and editorial resources.

In addition, large media companies are better able to overcome high barriers to market entry and establish new media products and services. Ownership concentration may help a media sector secure new sources of investment to rise to the opportunities presented by technological and commercial developments. 'Risky new media markets require venture capital and market power in order to launch new products' (Collins and Murroni, 1996: 58). Finally, for national companies to compete effectively in European and global markets, critical mass size may well be crucial. This is a particular concern in France where President Sarkozy has argued that the country does not possess media companies capable of competing successfully in transnational markets to achieve export success. Concentration may thus allow France to develop its own national media champions, able to operate more effectively in non-domestic markets (see Chapter 7).

Economic arguments can also be employed to support concentration of ownership *across* sectors. Essentially the case here is based on the view that the operations of different media industries such as the press and broadcasting involve the performance of similar or related functions, notably the collection, editing and dissemination of information, news and entertainment. Economic gains can be made from the transference of skills across sectors. Technological convergence may further reinforce the case for allowing more liberal cross-media ownership patterns than in the past, since it can be argued that as the barriers between traditionally distinct media sectors break down, the synergies are likely to be even greater. Critics have pointed out, however, that ownership concentration may not produce the economic benefits claimed by its supporters. For example, Doyle (1999) has emphasized an absence of operational synergies between television broadcasting and newspaper publishing, apart from the possible but by no means certain benefit from the opportunity to cross-promote products.

More important still are those economic arguments that emphasize the negative aspects of ownership concentration, whereby far from being beneficial or merely neutral, concentration may actually be economically harmful. These arguments stress the undesirable effects that arise from the establishment and abuse of monopoly or dominant market positions, as a result of which the market imperfectly reflects consumer preferences. The economic concern is that in a concentrated market there will be insufficient competition to protect the interests of the consumer. Large media companies are capable of taking over or driving out smaller companies and may engage in uncompetitive practices, including predatory pricing and cross-subsidy of products, which make it difficult for competitors to enter or survive in the market (Meier and Trappel, 1998: 46).

Sociopolitical concerns

A sociopolitical perspective on the issue of media ownership argues that an assessment of the economic costs and benefits of concentration in terms of consumer welfare is too narrow in scope. A sociopolitical approach seeks to widen the terms of the debate away from an emphasis on purely economic variables by arguing that the media are qualitatively and even quintessentially different from other industrial and business sectors since they deal in the production and distribution of information and cultural products. The media play an essential sociopolitical role in informing citizens, increasing democratic knowledge and promoting debate about values, policies, and the means and ends of politics. The sociopolitical concern is that in a concentrated market there will be inadequate diversity in editorial content, that some voices will be over-represented and others under-represented and that a single way of looking at the world may come to predominate at the expense of alternative versions.

This does not mean that media concentration is necessarily indefensible from a sociopolitical perspective. Indeed, some advantages may flow from a certain concentration of resources. Large media companies, for example, are more likely to have the personnel and financial backing to devote to extensive coverage of news and current affairs. In driving down costs, a market with a multiplicity of competing outlets may result in none of them having sufficient resources to devote to specific news beats (such as foreign correspondents) or to certain types of coverage (such as in-depth current affairs programming). Extensive coverage of a prolonged international event, such as the Middle East conflict, can stretch the resources of even a major news organization. From a sociopolitical perspective, therefore, big can sometimes be desirable and even essential.

In contrast, concentration would be regarded as harmful if it had a deleterious impact on levels of pluralism and diversity (Feintuck, 1999: 76). There is no simple link between pluralism of ownership on the one hand and diversity of content on the other, and so ownership regulations designed to ensure the former cannot guarantee to secure the latter (Lancelot, 2005: 14–16). Nonetheless, there must be a danger that the more ownership is concentrated in fewer privately owned companies, the less likely it is that a range of opinions will be given means of expression via the media. The potential for the abuse of ownership power increases in proportion to any growth in media concentration, as does the risk of a narrowing of views and arguments placed into the mediated public sphere. The potential problems for editorial pluralism and diversity of content are thus exacerbated if cross-media diversification leads to a country's previously distinct media markets being dominated by a very small number of companies. Therefore, despite the lack of a clear relationship between ownership pluralism and content diversity, a case can still be made for the retention of regulations on ownership as part of a broader regulatory framework, including regulation of content and protection of editorial and journalistic independence, designed to promote diversity of opinions and the free exchange of ideas.

Commercial conflicts of interest

Under conditions in which much of the private sector media are owned by companies with wider industrial and business interests, media ownership is an important issue because of the possibility of conflict between the profit maximization of the company's non-media activities on the one hand and the capacity of its media outlet(s) to report on those activities freely and without bias on the other. For example, it is likely to be difficult for TF1 news staff to cover in a wholly dispassionate manner the investment decisions and business performance of the Bouygues group in the telecommunications and construction sectors. Bias may have an impact on the news agenda, with stories about the Bouygues group's activities being given more (or less) coverage than merited by the normal application of the channel's news values. It may also influence the framing of such stories, so that the activities of the Bouygues group are reported sympathetically rather than neutrally or even critically. At worst, news coverage may amount to little more than a publicity puff for the parent company. This was said by some critics to have happened in 2009, when TF1 news gave highly positive coverage to the Bouygues group's project to construct the Tour Signal in the business sector of La Défense on the western outskirts of Paris.

This type of media bias does not require overt and explicit proprieto- rial (or even managerial/editorial) interference. Instead, socialization proc- esses within the newsroom, whereby staff internalize the values and culture of the media organization, have an impact on journalists' behav- iour that often translates into a willingness to conform. It is likely that a culture of self-censorship will exist in newsrooms when it comes to coverage of the business or industrial activities of the media company's parent group. For instance, one of the fears of journalists working for the daily financial newspaper *Les Echos* was that after its takeover by Bernard Arnault in 2007 it would be difficult for them to cover impartially the activities of Arnault's luxury goods group, LVMH. Simi- larly, it is not clear that *Le Figaro* can be relied on to cover in a balanced fashion the activities of the Dassault group with regard to the market for military aircraft sales.

Media ownership rules

Regulation to prevent unacceptable levels of media ownership concentra- tion and the abuse of dominant market positions has long been accepted as a legitimate component of public policy in France as in other advanced democracies. Key technical questions for policy-makers to address have included how to define relevant markets, what are the optimal means to measure the market dominance of a company within and across different media sectors (e.g. by advertising share, financial turnover or audience figures) and whether there is a need for sector-specific structural limits on media ownership in addition to general competition rules. A more fundamental political concern is how to balance economic/industrial considerations, which may favour media concentration, against the pur- suit of the democratic goals of pluralism and diversity, which may be best promoted by anti-concentration measures. French policy-makers have sought to address three objectives in the formulation and implementation of regulatory policy on media ownership: first, to maintain and promote competition in national media markets; second, to ensure adequate levels of external pluralism of supply; and, third, to provide conditions for the emergence and sustainability of domestic companies capable of competing in transnational markets. Since these objectives are not necessarily mutu- ally compatible, there are inevitably cross-cutting tensions at the heart of policy-making in this field.

Among member states of the EU, the details of regulatory regimes concerning media ownership vary from country to country. There is no single overarching piece of EU legislation on this issue (Levy, 1999: 50–8), aside from general competition rules that have undoubtedly had a significant impact on the structure of Europe's media industries. In the digital era, competition policy has been particularly influential in its application to prospective mergers between leading European media companies in their attempts to control markets (Harcourt, 2005).

The first issue for national policy-makers within the EU to address is whether there is any need for sector-specific regulation over and above the competition rules that are applied to all markets for goods and services. The case for such minimal regulation is largely based on three arguments (Green, 1995). First, additional regulation is unnecessary in an age where scarcity of resource has been replaced by media plenty. From this perspective, ownership provisions to ensure pluralism and diversity are out of date, since the attainment of these highly desirable goals is now sufficiently guaranteed by the proliferation of outlets in the marketplace. Second, regulation has become ineffective and unenforceable in an era of technological convergence and transnational communications. In the digital age, sector-specific structural rules no longer make much sense. Put most simply, the internet has rendered media ownership restrictions null and void.

The third argument is founded on the view that national restrictions might disadvantage the emergence of large multimedia conglomerates capable of competing in an increasingly interdependent global media market (Humphreys and Lang, 1998). While the maintenance of a competitive domestic market tends to support limits on concentration, the formation of national champions to compete in global markets may require precisely the opposite – a significant concentration of resources. This argument has found strong resonance in France in recent years among those pushing for a liberalization of ownership rules (Giazzi, 2008). Yet while outside of the magazine sector the absence of a powerful French media giant at the European and global levels is evident, it is much less certain that the reason for this state of affairs is to be found in the national regulatory regime. An official study for the French government published in 2005 – the Lancelot Report – argued that anti-concentration rules, including those designed to limit vertical integration between production and programming, were not the main cause of this French deficiency. Instead it pointed the finger at the under-development of the French advertising market compared to that of France's EU competitors and the importance in France of advertising that takes place outside of the media, such as direct marketing, mailings and public relations (Lancelot, 2005: 46–7). The forum on the press (*États généraux de la presse écrite*) set up in 2008 to provide policy advice to the Sarkozy presidency on reforming the newspaper industry also argued that current anti-concentration legislation was not an obstacle to the creation of powerful multimedia groups (États généraux de la presse écrite, 2009: 53).

The opposing case – in favour of specific anti-concentration rules – argues that there is no simple correlation between the expansion of media supply on the one hand and greater pluralism in ownership and diversity of content on the other: ownership in media markets still needs to be regulated if they are to function in the interests of the consumer and more especially the citizen. The Lancelot Report agreed with this line. It argued that while the structural rules regarding media ownership in France were complex, incoherent, ineffective and out of date (Lancelot, 2005: 70–4), they were still necessary in the interests of ownership pluralism and content diversity. It is likely that in the near future this will continue to be the official French position: an unwillingness to abandon structural rules altogether, combined with a recognition of the need to update them for the new conditions of the digital age.

As well as being subject to general competition rules, therefore, the French media are the object of specific structural regulations in terms of ownership. These were included in the 1986 communications statute and have been updated on several occasions since. Their application falls within the remit of the regulatory authority for broadcasting, the CSA, which monitors mergers and issues concerning cross-media ownership. For example, shareholders in a broadcasting company have the obligation to report to the CSA when their holding exceeds 10 per cent. However, the CSA has no remit to intervene if changes of ownership, even major ones, take place within the rules, as when RTL replaced Suez in the ownership of M6 in 2004.

The details of the structural ownership rules are as follows. First, in the televison sector in particular there are limits on the percentage share of a media company that an individual person (or company) may own. For instance, in the case of a national television service (i.e. one covering an area of more than ten million inhabitants) the upper limit is 49 per cent if the average annual audience of the service exceeds 8 per cent of the total television audience. This latter ceiling was raised from 2.5 per cent in 2008 in a controversial move piloted through parliament by a close supporter of Sarkozy, Frédéric Lefebvre. The legislative change was seen by critics as designed to favour the interests of TF1 and M6 in the developing digital terrestrial market. If a person/company owns more than 15 per cent in one national television service, then they may not own more than 15 per cent in a second one; if they have more than 5 per cent in two such services, then they may not own more than 5 per cent in a third. In addition, foreign (i.e. non-EU) interests are limited to a maximum 20 per cent share in a terrestrial radio or television service and in newspapers. Governments of both right and left have been keen to ensure that significant sections of the national media remain wherever possible in French hands.

There are also upper limits applied to the market share allowed to companies in distinct media sectors. In the press sector a company is not allowed to have more than 30 per cent of total newspaper circulation. There are no such limits in the case of magazines. In the broadcasting sector the limits placed on ownership are measured by both number of franchises and audience share. In national television a company may not own more than one analogue franchise or seven digital franchises. In radio the maximum aggregate audience is 150 million for analogue services and 20 per cent of the potential total audience for digital services. Finally, cross-media ownership rules are based on a 'two out of three' formula, applied in both local/regional and national markets. For example, at the national level a company may not exceed two of the following: holding a franchise for terrestrial television services reaching more than four million viewers; holding a franchise for one or more radio services reaching more than 30 million listeners; publishing or controlling one or several daily newspapers with a total circulation share of over 20 per cent.

Media proprietors and Sarkozy

One of the interesting aspects of the debate on media pluralism during the Sarkozy presidency has been the close nature of the interlinkages between the President and leading media proprietors. Well before becoming President, Sarkozy had cultivated close personal ties with various private sector media bosses, several of whom have their home and/or company headquarters in the upmarket Paris suburb of Neuilly-sur-Seine, the President's original political base. Media moguls close to Sarkozy include Arnaud Lagardère (Gadault, 2006), head of the Lagardère group; Bernard Arnault, owner of the daily financial newspaper, *Les Echos*; Vincent Bolloré, owner of the television channel Direct 8 and the free newspapers, *DirectMatin* and *DirectSoir*, as well as chairman of the board of directors of Havas, one of the world's largest advertising and communications companies; and Martin Bouygues, owner of the main free-to-air commercial television network, TF1. In addition, Serge Dassault, owner of the conservative daily *Le Figaro*, is a parliamentary senator in Sarkozy's UMP (Rocco, 2006).

Sarkozy's critics have made much of the closeness of his connections with media bosses, pointing out, for instance, that it was Bolloré who lent the President his yacht for a few days of well-publicized relaxation immediately after the latter's election victory; that Lagardère once referred to Sarkozy as 'not a friend but a brother'; that Arnault and Bouygues were both witnesses at Sarkozy's marriage to his second wife, Cécilia; that Bouygues is also the godfather to his son by Cécilia; that Laurent Solly, a member of Sarkozy's presidential campaign team, left after the 2007 election to take up the post of vice-chairman of TF1 and then head of TF1 Digital; and that several media proprietors were among the guests at the celebration party at the Fouquet's restaurant on the night of Sarkozy's presidential triumph (Mamère and Farbiaz, 2009).

Since their media ventures are often part of larger commercial and industrial conglomerates that bid for state contracts in France (e.g. Lagardère in the defence sector, Dassault in military aircraft production and sales and Bouygues in construction), or whose interests are subject to state regulation (for instance, Bouygues and telecommunications), or that have business ventures in overseas countries where the French state exerts political influence (e.g. Bolloré in Francophone Africa), it is in the interests of these media proprietors to maintain a good link with the President. All are dependent on at the very least the benign neutrality of the French state towards their business interests and, more usually, on the state's active cooperation through supportive regulation or even direct procurement orders for their products (Chupin *et al.*, 2009: 110).

It is also in Sarkozy's interests to keep on good terms with these media proprietors so as to maximize his chances of obtaining favourable coverage in their outlets. It is then a simple step to envisage a relationship based on mutual exchange: positive news coverage for Sarkozy and his government in return for state decisions sympathetic to the companies' wider corporate as well as media interests. As one commentator succinctly, if rather crudely, remarked: 'The Dassault group needs the President of the Republic to sell its planes. The President needs *Le Figaro* to sell his policies' (Portelli, 2009: 114). It is certainly true that the structural links between Sarkozy and media proprietors form an integral component of a holistic approach on the part of the President to news management (see Chapter 5) and that they have sometimes had an impact on news content. For instance, under pressure from its owner, Arnaud Lagardère, the news staff of *Le Journal du Dimanche* pulled a story that Sarkozy's wife, Cécilia, had failed to vote in the second round of the 2007 presidential election. Generally, however, Portelli's charge is an over-simplification of the way in which news agendas are formed and issues framed; media owners do not simply determine news content even in their own outlets (Musso, 2009a: 397).

Political pluralism in the press

There is no regulatory requirement for individual newspaper (or news magazine) titles to strive for internal pluralism or diversity of viewpoints in their political coverage. On the contrary, French newspapers are free to editorialize, to adopt strong political positions and to support whichever political parties and candidates they choose to in election campaigns. Yet because newspapers are free to be politically committed does not mean that they necessarily exhibit consistent and high levels of partisanship in practice.

In their comparative study of the media and politics in developed capitalist democracies, Hallin and Mancini use the concept of political parallelism to analyse the nature of the relationship between the press and the political sphere (2004: 26–30). A press system characterized by external pluralism, where each newspaper title closely articulates the views of a particular political party or social group, will also exhibit a high level of political parallelism; conversely, the more balanced or neutral the press content and the less close the ties between newspaper titles and political parties, the lower the level of political parallelism. Hallin and Mancini put forward various complementary indicators by which to assess how strongly political parallelism is embedded in the media system in general and the press in particular. In this section we shall apply three of these indicators to the case of the press in contemporary France: first,

organizational connections between the press and political actors –
newspaper titles may (or may not) have formal institutional ties with
political parties or social groups; second, the partisanship of a newspaper's readership – there may (or may not) be a strong overlap between the
readership of a title and voter support for a particular party/leadership
figure; and finally, newspaper content – the editorial line and news
framing of the newspaper title may (or may not) explicitly back a
particular political orientation or party.

If one applies the first of these indicators to the press in contemporary
France, it is clear that no major daily newspaper – including the elite
opinion-formers *Le Monde*, *Le Figaro*, *Libération* and *Les Echos* – is
either owned by or has close organizational links with a political party or
other formal political organization. This was not always the case. When
immediately following the Liberation there was an explosion of new titles
coming on to the market, party political newspapers were strongly in
evidence. In the period since the end of the Second World War, therefore,
the early postwar years represented the high point of external pluralism
and political parallelism in terms of the range of different newspaper titles
organizationally affiliated to a political party. In the 1950s, however, these
papers began a process of decline as readers came to use papers more for
entertainment and general information than for purposes of political
identification. The Christian Democrat daily *L'Aube* folded in 1951, the
Socialist Party daily *Le Populaire* gave up the ghost in the 1960s and the
Gaullist Party daily *La Nation* disappeared in 1974, although it had
survived until that year only thanks to a hidden subsidy from the Gaullist
government.

For a long while there was one notable exception to this general rule:
L'Humanité, the official daily newspaper of the French Communist Party.
The editor of *L'Humanité* was a member of the party's politburo, the
party exercised critical surveillance over the contents of the paper, and
there was a high level of party membership among journalists. However,
in the final years of the twentieth century the collapse of communism
internationally, which meant the end of subsidies from the Soviet Union,
and a huge drop in electoral support for the Communist Party in France,
which translated into declining circulation figures, threw the paper into a
financial crisis that substantially altered its organizational link with the
party. In 2000–1 the paper was officially separated from the Communist
Party and its ownership opened up to new stakeholders (Eveno, 2008:
129). As a sign of change, the paper was even forced to accept minority
ownership stakes being taken by TF1 and the Lagardère group. With this
change in the status of *L'Humanité*, the last organizational link between
political parties and a major national newspaper title effectively disappeared from the French media landscape.

Second, in terms of the political preferences of their readerships,
individual newspaper titles tend to be characterized by diversity rather
than uniformity. This is most obviously the case with the regional dailies.
The readership of any particular regional newspaper is of necessity
politically heterogeneous because of the lack of choice of titles in any

particular regional market. However, it is also true – albeit to a lesser degree – of the national dailies: the readership of Le Monde comes from across the political spectrum, Le Figaro has some readers who support the left, albeit a minority, and Libération can count among its readers a small number who voted for Sarkozy in 2007.

Finally, in terms of content and editorial line, newspaper titles are frequently reluctant to identify too closely with a particular political party or elite politician. Again, this is most obvious in the case of many regional dailies. Their powerful sales position within particular geographical markets encourages regional titles to downplay any strong party political views for fear of alienating sections of their readership and thus compromising sales figures. Commercial self-interest trumps any inclination towards political partisanship. At the national level, daily newspapers that adopt an editorial line too overtly sympathetic to a single political party or orientation may run the risk of market failure. This was the case, for example, with Le Matin de Paris, which was launched as a new national daily supporting the Socialist Party in 1977, but ceased publication at the beginning of 1988 having failed to carve out a market niche for itself in competition with Le Monde and Libération.

This does not mean that national newspapers have refrained from adopting a partisan stance, notably during election campaigns. Le Monde, for instance, offered its support to Mitterrand in the 1981 presidential election, although this did not prevent the paper from turning against him, especially during a second presidential term that was particularly sullied by revelations of scandal (Collard, 2008). Le Monde was also suspected of being in favour of Balladur in the run-up to the 1995 election and was very critical of Chirac both before and during his two presidential terms. In the 2002 election it was resolutely anti-Le Pen prior to the second round, as were all the main national titles, while in 2007 it gave lukewarm support to Royal. In 1995 Le Figaro had some difficulty in choosing between the two mainstream conservative candidates, Balladur and Chirac (Moores and Texier, 1997: 193), in 2002 it was arguably more anti-Jospin than pro-Chirac and in 2007 it supported the candidacy of Sarkozy. In 1995 Libération was lukewarm in its support for Jospin, but in 2007 was against Sarkozy.

Yet despite these examples of newspapers declaring themselves more or less explicitly for or against a particular candidate in presidential election campaigns, many titles are often reluctant to present themselves as too closely or unconditionally tied to a particular political leader or party both during and outside of campaign periods. This is not just because of the danger of alienating readers, potential or actual, although that is clearly an important factor. It is also because much of contemporary political debate is – or at least seems to be – less amenable to satisfactory framing in terms of traditional partisan divisions. Issues such as the socioeconomic impact of globalization, climate change or EU constitutional reform often cut across historic left-right dividing lines. In addition, firm electoral loyalties and pronounced ideological convictions are now less strongly demonstrated by many voters than in the past.

For branding purposes as well as from a historical association with particular sets of values, some newspapers continue to identify themselves in terms of certain political, economic and cultural ideas: *Le Figaro*, for example, is a socially conservative and economically liberal title, while *Libération* is socially liberal, economically centre-left and supportive of postmaterial values such as environmentalism and minority rights. The readers of these newspapers are perfectly familiar with the general world view of their favoured title and many read it to have their opinions (and even prejudices) reflected back to them in its columns. Yet every newspaper now has to be careful of how its brand values influence the stance it takes in terms of partisan political engagement, both during and outside of election campaigns. Too close an association with a particular political party or leadership figure may have negative consequences for the financial bottom line.

This does not mean that all French press titles have somehow morphed into outlets marked by a commitment to internal pluralism, striving for impartiality and balance in their political content – far from it. On the contrary, one can still find several examples of newspapers and news magazines that are highly supportive of a particular political outlook and its personification in a specific leadership figure – witness the strong support for President Sarkozy provided by *Le Figaro* under its editor-in-chief Etienne Mougeotte, formerly director of programmes at TF1. Among the weekly news magazines, *Marianne* has been a consistently vocal critic of Sarkozy, while *Le Point* and *L'Express* have been accused of being overly sympathetic to the President (Portelli, 2009: 111–12). In addition, there remains a strong tradition of 'opinionated journalism' across much of the press sector, with individual journalists showing support for or opposition to particular parties, policies or individual politicians. Yet it is also the case that many press titles have to be careful how they articulate editorial support for, and criticism of, political leaders and parties, if they are to retain readers. The overall result is a complex picture of political parallelism in the contemporary French press, ranging from some editorially partisan titles (some national dailies, some news magazines) at one end of the spectrum to a marked reluctance to display overt and committed political leanings (most regional dailies) at the other. Moreover, even those titles that still adopt a partisan position editorially often show some internal pluralism in their commentary pages, for example by publishing the views of different political parties and social groups.

Political pluralism in broadcasting

Internal pluralism is a key objective in the political output of the broadcasting sector, where the ideal of equitable coverage has long been enshrined in regulatory provisions as well as being part of the journalists' code of professional practice. One of the responsibilities of the CSA is to monitor the amount of time allocated by broadcasters to different political actors in news coverage and to candidates and parties during election campaigns, with the findings made public on a regular basis on the authority's website (www.csa.fr). In 2002 and 2007, for example, the CSA scrupulously monitored the quantity of broadcast coverage given candidates in the presidential and parliamentary campaigns. Political commercials are not allowed on French radio or television either during or outside of campaign periods. Instead, broadcasts are allocated to parties and candidates according to rules that place a premium on equitable treatment.

There is no evidence of overt and intended partisan bias with regard to the amount of coverage given the major parties, notably the UMP and the PS, on radio and television news. Indeed there has been a formally institutionalized degree of pluralism in the allocation of time accorded the parties of the mainstream opposition on the one hand against that given the government and the parties of the parliamentary majority on the other. Until recently the rules stated that outside of election campaigns political figures from the parliamentary opposition should receive at least half the time given to government ministers and figures from the parliamentary majority combined. Nonetheless, charges of partisan political bias continue to be levelled, especially concerning television news output. Some of this appears to be ritualistic shadow boxing between the parties of mainstream right and left as part of their attempts to raise an issue that may resonate with public opinion. François Bayrou's attack on media bias in the run-up to the 2007 campaign, made with some brio in an interview on TF1 news, certainly raised his profile as a serious presidential candidate among the electorate.

Within the context of this stopwatch approach to securing internal pluralism, one important issue that came on to the agenda early in the Sarkozy presidency was the status of the President in the official calculations. In the past, presidential appearances were not included in the regulatory authority's framework since the President was regarded as the head of state and therefore not deemed to be involved in the cut-and-thrust of party politics. However, in the light of Sarkozy's hyper-occupation of broadcast media space after his presidential victory in 2007 (see Chapter 5), opposition parties quite understandably condemned what they regarded as a flagrant gap in the procedures of the CSA. After pressure from the Constitutional Council, the rules were changed in 2009 so that interventions by the President and his advisers that are 'in terms of context and content relevant to national political debate' would now be taken into account in the official calculations (CSA, 2009a). The new rules specify that political figures from the parliamentary opposition must receive at least half the time given to appearances by the President, government ministers, the parliamentary majority and presidential advisers combined.

A concern on the part of broadcasters and regulators with achieving 'stopwatch pluralism' between the major political forces of government and opposition should not be undervalued in the context of a broadcasting system that historically was for many years used by the governing party in a crude partisan fashion. Yet it clearly only scratches the surface of how both to ensure pluralism and avoid bias in radio and television's political coverage. For instance, one charge frequently made against broadcasters is that the alternative and oppositional views of minor parties are frequently squeezed out. Smaller parties, such as the Greens, often complain about the amount of coverage they receive – testimony to the difficulties of defining and then operationalizing the concept of equity in what is still in many respects a fragmented multi-party system. In the long run-up to presidential elections, for example, the broadcast media may decide in advance who are the major candidates and skew coverage accordingly. In 2002 the media focus was on the anticipated second round run-off between President Chirac and Prime Minister Jospin. In concentrating on this aspect of the contest between the two heavyweights of right and left, the broadcasting media – along with the press and opinion pollsters – failed to appreciate the challenge from Le Pen and so played their part in contributing to the thunderbolt result of the first round that saw Jospin unexpectedly eliminated by the leader of the extreme-right. A similar critique of the broadcast media's focus on the competition between Sarkozy and Royal – condemned as a 'stifling bipartism' ('*bipartisme étouffant*') – was made with reference to coverage of the run-up to the 2007 contest (Reymond and Rzepski, 2008: 74).

Another problem in terms of a stopwatch approach to internal pluralism arises in how broadcasters cover an issue where there is a high degree of consensus across the main parties of right and left. To a significant extent this is what happened in the referendum campaign for the ratification of the EU constitution in 2005, even if the Socialist Party was internally split on the issue. Broadcast media coverage of the campaign focused disproportionately on the 'Yes' camp, since this was the choice of many of the mainstream political and economic elites, as well as of leading media commentators. The decisive victory of the 'No' vote showed that much of the campaign coverage had failed to reflect the concerns of a majority swathe of public opinion. As a result, critics talked of a lack of pluralism and of a democratic deficit in the coverage of the mainstream media (Maler and Schwartz, 2006). This was in marked contrast to much of the referendum-related content on the internet, where supporters of a 'No' vote were particularly vocal.

The main defect of the stopwatch approach, however, lies not so much in the difficulties associated with its application, but in its inherent limitations as a guarantor of internal pluralism and a safeguard against bias. For instance, the concern with monitoring time allocation tells us nothing about the tone and style of coverage. This is where the qualitative concept of 'directional balance' comes in (Norris *et al.*, 1999). In general, it would be difficult to demonstrate a significant and consistent difference in journalistic tone between news items or interviews featuring politicians of the government and parliamentary majority on the one hand and those representing the mainstream opposition on the other. In contrast, in the 2002 presidential contest there was a distinct, if perhaps understandable, lack of directional balance in television coverage of Le Pen's candidacy in contrast with that of Chirac between the two rounds of voting. Le Pen and Chirac may have received roughly equal time in news coverage, but they were by no means equally treated either in news reports, where Le Pen's candidacy was routinely vilified, or television interviews, where the journalists adopted quite distinct inquisitorial styles and were clearly more hostile towards the leader of the extreme-right (Kuhn, 2004).

Finally, if internal pluralism in political coverage is to be fully achieved, then it could be argued that there should be no bias in the construction of the issue agenda or the framing of issues by the broadcast media. Neither 'stopwatch' nor 'directional' balance is sufficient. In addition, and most importantly, the issues focused on by the broadcasters must not consistently advantage or disadvantage one party or leadership figure over the others. Internal pluralism at this level is notoriously difficult to achieve. Even during election campaigns, when broadcasters are particularly on their guard and content is closely monitored by the regulator, intense competition takes place between parties and candidates to raise their favourite issues which they hope will be picked up and highlighted by the news media. To some extent, therefore, the resources and professionalism of a particular candidate may give him or her a competitive advantage in setting the media's campaign news agenda. As a result, what at first sight may appear as media bias in favour of a particular candidate may be due not to partisanship on the part of editors and journalists but rather to the capacity of politicians to impose themselves and their favoured issues on the media agenda and have the latter framed in a sympathetic fashion.

Sometimes the 'background news' agenda may put a candidate severely on the defensive, as happened to Jospin in 2002 when the overwhelming media focus on the issue of insecurity directly benefited Chirac and allowed Le Pen to surf on a series of television news items concerning petty crime and an apparent breakdown of law and order in French society (Kuhn, 2005b). In the 2005 EU referendum, much of the 'background news' coverage, with its emphasis on the allegedly negative consequences of liberal EU policies on French employment, actually worked to the benefit of the 'No' vote, whatever the imbalance of the official campaign coverage in favour of a 'Yes'.

In short, the task of ensuring internal pluralism and equity in broadcast news and political coverage is immensely complex. It certainly involves achieving a reasonable stopwatch balance between mainstream parties of left and right, taking into due consideration the time allocated the government and, under Sarkozy, the President. It also includes a mechanism to provide a fair platform for the views of minor parties, without at the same time overstating their importance. It embraces a level playing field in terms of qualitative aspects such as the tone and style of reporting. Finally, in an ideal world, neither the mediated campaign agenda during elections, nor the news agenda in general, should unduly and systematically favour one party or candidate in terms of the issue terrain – although it is hard to see how this can be consistently achieved in practice. Little wonder that the operationalization of the concept of internal pluralism should so often prove a minefield for broadcasters both during and outside of election campaigns.

Conclusion

Diversity of media supply (external pluralism) and of political content (internal pluralism) are widely regarded as essential features of a healthy democratic public sphere. While from an economic standpoint it is important that a particular media market does not become overly concentrated if competition is to be assured, from a sociopolitical perspective pluralism in ownership is generally regarded as more likely than monopoly or oligopoly to create the necessary conditions for diversity of content to flourish. Yet some concentration of media supply may well be considered economically desirable, especially if a strong commercial presence is to be secured in transnational markets. In drafting rules on media ownership, therefore, a satisfactory level of external pluralism in and across domestic media markets may be just one objective for policy-makers.

While newspapers are under no obligation to practise internal pluralism and are free to be as partisan in their political commitment as they wish, in practice commercial self-interest often acts as a constraint on full-blooded political engagement. National dailies in particular often include commentary pieces from across the mainstream political spectrum. In contrast, broadcasters are highly regulated on the question of internal pluralism in their representation and coverage of politics. Yet even operating in a highly rule-bound environment and professional culture that emphasize the importance of fairness and diversity, broadcasters do not find it easy to achieve the goal of internal pluralism, especially the further one moves away from the simple criterion of equitable time allocation among mainstream political views.

4 MEDIA POLICY AND REGULATION

> - The importance of politics in media policy-making
> - Media policy during the Sarkozy presidency
> - Media regulation
> - Conclusion

The media are vitally important information providers, entertainment industries and sources of employment. In the light of their political, cultural and economic significance, it is not surprising that they have long been the focus of various public policy provisions. This is still the case today. The French state continues to regard various aspects of media structures and operations as legitimate areas for policy intervention, from complex rules on media ownership to the Hadopi law introduced in 2009 to tackle the thorny issue of internet piracy. Indeed, since the election of Sarkozy to the presidency in 2007, major policy initiatives have been undertaken in both press and broadcasting sectors that will leave their mark on the French media landscape for many years to come. In its examination of media policy and regulation, this chapter begins with a section on the enduring importance of politics in the policy-making process. The second section examines the formulation of media policy during the Sarkozy presidency, focusing on recent government reforms in the press and television respectively. The chapter concludes with a section on media regulation, including an overview of the role of the regulatory authority for broadcasting, the CSA.

The importance of politics in media policy-making

In Chapter 2 we looked at some of the main formative influences that have had an impact in shaping the essential features of the French media landscape of the early twenty-first century: notably, technological advances, economic factors, changing sociocultural patterns and processes of transnationalization. Not surprisingly, these different variables have also made a major contribution to setting the media policy agenda in contemporary France. All the different actors involved in the policy-making process have to take due account of changes in the technological, economic, sociocultural and transnational spheres in the formulation and implementation of policy decisions. From this perspective, policy-makers can frequently be seen as responding to features of the media environment that are beyond their control; indeed, policy options are often influenced by developments that have not been anticipated by policy-makers. Thus, both the direction and pace of change may leave policy-makers involved in a process of 'catch up', as existing policies are seen to be inappropriate to new conditions, impossible to enforce or no longer regarded as desirable. This is particularly evident in the case of new communications technology, the introduction of which often necessitates a re-evaluation of policy as previous sets of responses are superseded by technological advances, sometimes of a radical nature.

Moreover, while these different variables have an objective reality, they are also used in the discourse of different policy actors who seek to play up (or down) their importance to further their own particular interests. For instance, nobody can deny that the spread of the internet has had a major impact on the contemporary media landscape in France. The exact extent of that impact, its precise nature and any desirable public policy initiatives are, however, all open to debate. The perception of different actors and the 'spin' they seek to give to changes that affect their interests become an integral part of that policy debate.

Thus, while technological, economic, sociocultural and transnational variables undoubtedly influence the agenda and issue-framing of media policy, they do not impose their own irrefutable logic on the policy process in some independent fashion. Policy outcomes are not inevitably determined by impersonal extraneous forces; rather they are the product of a process of conflict, cooperation, lobbying and negotiation by different actors in the policy arena. These actors pursue their own particular interests and/or claim to speak on behalf of the public interest, mobilizing arguments and resources to support their case. It is important, therefore, to emphasize the political dimension in media policy-making. In the case of contemporary France, this is most obviously manifested in the large measure of control exercised by the political executive over the policy-making process.

For instance, historically, governmental intervention has been central on the supply side in the broadcasting sector, with certain initiatives such as the satellite and cable projects of the late 1970s and 1980s being directly managed by the state. In similar fashion, market entry by commercial interests into broadcasting was the result of a political decision taken by the Socialist government in the early 1980s, while the privatization of TF1 in 1987 was also primarily motivated by political considerations. In 2008, President Sarkozy announced the withdrawal of advertising from public television and in 2009 he pledged greater state financial support for the press – two politically inspired initiatives. Sarkozy could have chosen not to change the funding mechanism for France Télévisions and to leave the newspaper industry to make the painful adjustment to a new economic model under its own devices. Instead he decided that new policy measures were required. These two recent initiatives by the political executive once again demonstrate that change in the structures and functioning of the French media landscape are not simply the product of technological shift or wider global developments over which national policy-makers have no control. On the contrary, political decisions made by national actors have a real and tangible impact.

The process of media policy-making in France usually involves input from a range of different actors, although of course their capacity to influence policy decisions varies enormously. These actors include:

- the President and his advisers at the Elysée;
- relevant government ministries, most notable the Prime Minister's Office and the Ministry of Culture and Communication;
- media and communication organizations, including press groups, commercial broadcasting companies, public service broadcasters, independent production companies, telecommunication companies and the film industry;
- the EU;
- the regulatory authority for broadcasting;
- the French parliament, notably the relevant specialist committees;
- special interest lobby groups, think-tanks and assorted experts;
- the Constitutional Council.

Three points are worth noting about this list. First, it has expanded over time as a result of political changes (e.g. growing intervention from the EU), institutional developments (such as the establishment of a regulatory authority for broadcasting) and changes in the media (including new outlets and content providers). Second, since media policy-making is overwhelmingly an elite process, the list omits any reference to public opinion. The public's participation in media policy-making is at best indirect and of marginal influence. Moreover, media policy rarely features as an issue during presidential and parliamentary election campaigns. Finally, in general the most important actors in media policy-making are the political executive, most notably the President, and the leading media companies.

During the Fifth Republic a powerful presidency, usually supported by a stable and coherent majority in parliament, has been established at the apex of the policy-making process. The President has generally been able to impose his will on the various legislative initiatives in the media field. For example, the decision in 1974 to abolish the ORTF was made by President Giscard d'Estaing, while the initiative to set up two commercial television channels in the mid-1980s came from President Mitterrand. Sometimes the President has been willing to delegate power to one of his ministers. During de Gaulle's presidency, for instance, the Minister of Information, Alain Peyrefitte, was responsible for the 1964 broadcasting statute that led to the establishment of the ORTF (Institut Charles de Gaulle, 1994). In 1969, President Pompidou was initially content to allow his Prime Minister, Jacques Chaban-Delmas, to introduce a major reform of the newsrooms at the ORTF, but then regretted the initiative and subsequently brought broadcasting policy within the presidential domain. Since the early 1970s the guiding hand in media policy formulation has generally emanated from the Elysée and the least one can say in this respect is that the Sarkozy presidency is no exception to this rule.

In formal terms the government also plays a leading role in the process of media policy-making. Not only has it benefited from specific powers such as control of the level of the licence fee for public broadcasting, but it also enjoys an important policy position through its dominance of the legislative process. Legislation promoted by government has been particularly important with reference to the broadcasting sector. For example, traditionally one of the most important policy functions performed by government has been overall control of market entry into broadcasting. Frequency scarcity meant that the allocation of spectrum to broadcasters had to be managed, and in practice strategic policy decisions were made by government in conjunction with the President. As a result, for most of the twentieth century, the government acted as a gatekeeper, effectively determining who was (and who was not) allowed to broadcast radio and television programmes originating from within the state's territorial jurisdiction.

The leading policy-making role of the government comes to the fore during periods of executive cohabitation, when the Prime Minister, government and parliamentary majority all come from a different political family to the President. In these circumstances, responsibility for media policy moves from the President and his staff at the Elysée to the Prime Minister and his office at Matignon. The first cohabitation government led by Jacques Chirac introduced a major reform of broadcasting in 1986, that included the privatization of TF1. The most recent cohabitation government (1997–2002) led by Lionel Jospin introduced legislation in 2000 designed to strengthen public service broadcasting in competition with commercial operators and reduce its dependence on commercial advertising.

Alongside the political executive, media companies constitute the other important set of policy actors, lobbying decision-makers at national and supranational levels to promote their corporate interests. Their media outlets may act as public commentators on the media policy process and can be used by their owners and management to campaign for or against a particular policy option. For example, in the 1980s the Hersant group used its regional and national newspapers, including *Le Figaro*, to express opposition to the Socialist government's proposed anti-concentration legislation in the press. More usually, these companies lobby politicians from the position of a political actor that enjoys privileged insider status in the policy-making process. Large media companies in particular have expertise and resources they can mobilize to exert an impact on policy-making, as was evident in the role played by TF1 in influencing Sarkozy's reform of public television. Conversely, media companies may lack influence in the policy process because they are out of favour with the political executive, as has been the case with the public broadcasting organization France Télévisions during the Sarkozy presidency.

Media policy during the Sarkozy presidency

It is clear that the media landscape in France is being transformed by the switch to digital technology and the spread of the internet. The media policy initiatives taken by the political executive during the Sarkozy presidency have been strongly influenced by advances in new information and communication technologies and in particular by the impact these have had on the traditional media sectors of press and broadcasting. In seeking to organize and manage the transition to the digital age, the authorities have started out from the basis of considering the situation of existing media outlets in these two sectors. Thus, two of Sarkozy's highest profile initiatives in the area of media policy have targeted the press, particularly the newspaper industry, and public television respectively.

The press

To appreciate the rationale for the policy intervention of Sarkozy in the press it is important to keep four points in mind. The first is the undoubted crisis in the newspaper industry (see Chapter 2), the origins of which long predated both the accession of Sarkozy to the presidency and the arrival of the internet. National press groups had been undercapitalized since the postwar reconstruction of the industry, while the economic difficulties facing newspapers, especially national dailies, had been an increasing source of concern for several years prior to Sarkozy's election (Muller, 2005; Tessier and Baffert, 2007). In particular, it was clear to many commentators that the French press was in a structurally weak position to face the challenges and exploit the opportunities of rapid technological change. In short, when Sarkozy came to office, the French newspaper industry was in an objectively problematic situation, with the disappearance of some newspapers a clear possibility.

Second, since the reforms undertaken shortly after the Liberation in 1944, press groups have habitually looked to the state for assistance. Close structural links have developed between newspaper companies on the one hand and government ministers and state officials on the other. Press groups have become important lobbyists for their industry and have been routinely incorporated into the policy-making process, defending their particularistic economic and industrial interests at a time of major challenges to the sustainability of their enterprises. Their representative organizations fulfil an insider advocacy function for the newspaper industry. Moreover, the principle of state involvement – practised by governments of both right and left – far from being regarded as undesirable, has been seen as beneficial, even necessary, by many in the newspaper business. In the eyes of some commentators a dependency culture has been built up, whereby newspapers look to the state to help resolve their difficulties rather than fostering a culture of entrepreneurial independence. At worst, newspapers may feel that they have the right to be bailed out by the public purse and that the state has the obligation to provide them with assistance. In short, French newspapers have a close relationship with the state that is not replicated in many other Western European democracies, including Germany and the UK.

Third, since the postwar reconstruction of the newspaper industry the state has been more than willing to be actively involved in matters concerning the organization and functioning of the press. The idea that the state has a legitimate role to play as a patron for the press has been accepted by a wide cross-section of political elites. The clearest manifestation of state involvement is to be found in the system of financial assistance provided for newspapers to supplement their income from advertising and sales. This system of state aid has the avowed objective of fostering pluralism among newspaper titles and encouraging access for readers to a range of news outlets. Historically, state aid to the press has taken the form of both direct financial support and indirect subsidies (such as preferential postage rates), with the latter historically the more important of the two: for instance, €847 million of indirect aid and €163 million of direct assistance in 2007, excluding the €110 million spent on the state subscriptions to the Agence France-Presse news agency in the same year. Although it is difficult to make exact calculations, it has been estimated that prior to the Sarkozy reforms state aid accounted for around 10 per cent of the total turnover of the French press (Albert, 2008: 59) and higher in the case of some daily newspapers. As a think-tank report commented in 2006, with state aid amounting to nearly one third of income from sales, 'France is without doubt the country in the world where the press is the most massively assisted' (Institut Montaigne, 2006: 50).

Against this background, it is reasonable to ask how effective and desirable the long-standing system of state aid to the press has been in practice. In the past, criticisms of state aid have focused both on the principle and the practicalities of its operation. The objection on principle is that such aid has unjustifiably distorted the mechanisms of the free market, making newspapers less likely to take risks, to be dynamic and entrepreneurial, and to respond to changing social and economic circumstances. In general this objection has not been very strongly held among French policy stakeholders. In 2006, an independent think-tank with economically liberal leanings, the Montaigne Institute, did propose the abolition of all direct state assistance, though only at the end of a period of three years during which a massive injection of state funds would be made in return for essential modernization measures taken by the industry (Institut Montaigne, 2006: 96–7). Indirect state aid, notably to help newspaper distribution, would continue, although the think-tank argued that the amount could be reduced over time as volume sales increased. In the French context such a proposal appeared to many to be unacceptably radical.

Criticism has been more commonly directed at the way in which the system has functioned in practice. In this context, the key question has been: has state aid helped newspapers with a weak financial base but a significant information function? The answer, according to critics, was that it had not, or at least not well enough. To avoid possible charges of political bias and at the same time not alienate powerful press groups that benefited from the arrangements in place, the system of aid has been politically neutral. However, it has been argued that this concern with neutrality and formal equity, however understandable it may be, has thrown state aid off course. By appearing to help all, state aid to the press has been too indiscriminate, not differentiating between the needy and the already well-off. Indeed, the system may even have been perverse, with unintended consequences running counter to the principles that underpinned its operation: it may actually have helped the better off newspapers. For example, the mechanism of postal aid helped only those papers with a big postal distribution; these tended to be the papers that were already commercially successful. A paper may have been receiving 80 per cent of its income in advertising and still be eligible for state assistance. Thus, state aid was available and of great benefit to newspapers that were already prospering in the marketplace. At the same time, the system was limited in scope. For example, there was no state aid, either in the form of subsidy or preferential loans, to help in the foundation of new newspapers. Overall, therefore, the system tended to favour the status quo rather than encouraging new initiatives.

These three elements – the serious crisis in the newspaper industry, the insider access of press groups to state officials and the postwar tradition of state involvement in the press – all pointed towards some form of public policy intervention during the Sarkozy presidency to address the serious contemporary problems of the French newspaper industry. There is, however, one further element that needs to be included in this explanatory background: the values of the President himself. Sarkozy could have decided to make a break with the practice of state intervention and allow market forces to determine the fate of newspapers. He chose not to do so. Why? The first reason lies in the complexity of the President's ideological value system. Although often presented as a politician steeped in the Thatcher-Reagan neo-liberal mindset, in fact Sarkozy is an ideological chameleon, capable of changing his discourse to suit the prevailing conditions (Marlière, 2009). Second, Sarkozy has a close interdependent relationship with several media proprietors, many of whom are owners of major newspapers (see Chapter 3). Third, he wants to build up powerful 'national champions' who can compete in transnational media markets. Finally, there is the fear that if French newspaper titles were to go under then the 'news gap' might well be filled by media outlets over which the state has potentially less control. In 2008, for instance, 85 per cent of internet access in France passed via Google, which was draining away increasing amounts of advertising revenue from the French press (États généraux de la presse écrite, 2009: 4).

The crisis in the French press met with a policy response from Sarkozy within the first two years of his presidency. In the autumn of 2008 he established a forum on the press (*États généraux de la presse écrite*) composed of representatives from across the industry to make policy recommendations. It consisted of four working groups, made up for the most part of leading media executives and news managers. Each group focused on a specific aspect of the problem: the future of journalism; the industrial model of publication, distribution and financing; the shock of the internet; and relations between the press and society. The forum was given a short time – less than three months – to undertake its discussions and make its recommendations, indicative not just of the perceived gravity of the crisis, but also of Sarkozy's policy style of prioritizing action over sustained reflection. In fairness to the President it was also the case that several official reports had already examined the problems of the press in the recent past.

The findings of the États généraux de la presse écrite were published in January 2009 and the key recommendations were subsequently taken up by the Sarkozy government. The forum argued for modification of the system of state aid, drawing attention to the perverse impact of subsidies, which 'structure behaviour in a conservative logic instead of encouraging the renewal of supply' and 'which do not necessarily encourage social dialogue' (États généraux de la presse écrite, 2009: 62). The forum also proposed a single fund for the modernization of the press, consisting of four 'baskets' corresponding to the four types of need identified by the working groups: the maintenance of pluralism; distribution; restructuring; and innovation, creation and development.

In response the state agreed to commit about €200 million of extra aid per year for three years on top of the significant financial assistance already provided to the press sector. A large proportion of the additional subsidy was allocated to improving distribution networks – with a significant planned increase in household delivery and the freezing of postal tariffs – as well as additional assistance to modernize printing works. To avoid discrimination between online and print journalism, electronic newspapers would henceforth benefit from state assistance and a new status of online press publisher was created by legislation. In addition, a new legal framework for the exercise of intellectual property rights for journalists across different media platforms was announced so that journalists working in an online capacity would not be disadvantaged. Finally, it was agreed to give every French teenager on their eighteenth birthday a year's free subscription to a newspaper of their choice for one day per week: newspapers cover the cost of the free copies, while the state finances their delivery. In a separate development, at the start of 2010, the French government considered the possibility of levying a tax on the advertising revenues of Google and other internet portals. In short, the key recommendations of each of the four working groups were quickly translated into public policy.

By the standards of other advanced democracies this policy response to the problems of the newspaper industry was both wide-ranging and financially generous. However, this does not necessarily mean that it is properly focused or guaranteed to succeed. First, some aspects of the old postwar model in publishing and distribution, including chronic overstaffing, have not been satisfactorily addressed for fear of the industrial unrest that might ensue. Second, some of the policy responses, such as improvements in the home delivery system, look anachronistic in an age when many citizens, especially the young, are becoming accustomed to access their news and information online. Indeed, in financial terms the vast bulk of state expenditure is being used to address problems in the newspaper sector such as printing and distribution that preceded the transition to the digital age, rather than preparing the industry for the current and future 'shock of the internet' (Plenel, 2010: 87–8). Finally, as newspapers haemorrhage revenue, even large amounts of state aid will not necessarily guarantee the vitality of the press as a whole, nor the survival of any particular title. In short, despite the huge amount of public money being mobilized, the state's restructuring policy may prove to be limited in scope, ill-directed and ineffective. More still needs to be done in policy terms on how to save professional journalism (a particular information function) rather than simply protect the newspaper industry (a particular set of structures and practices). Yet it is not clear how the policy process, dominated by established newspaper professionals with an attachment to traditional organizational modes of behaviour, can achieve this.

Television

Prior to his policy initiatives in the press, the President had intervened spectacularly to announce a sweeping reform of public television that was to have an impact well beyond that of the public service provider France Télévisions. At his first presidential press conference in January 2008 Sarkozy stunned the assembled audience of journalists with the revelation that he intended to remove commercial advertising as a funding stream for public television. This initiative became part of a broader reform – the biggest policy shake-up in broadcasting since the 1980s – that finally became law in March 2009. The two main objectives of the reform were to facilitate the company's transition to an enterprise that fully embraced all distribution platforms linked to digital technology and to foster a renewal of public service programming in the competition for audiences with private sector providers. The three main provisions of the new legislation were as follows:

- the establishment of a single organizational entity (*enterprise commune*) to manage the digital channels and online services of public television;
- the withdrawal of commercial advertising from France Télévisions, initially in the period between 8 p.m. and 6 a.m., and extended to the rest of the schedules by the end of 2011 when full digital switchover was due to take place;

- the appointment of the chief executive (*président directeur général*) of France Télévisions directly by the President.

Although defended by its proponents as a forward-looking piece of legislation, in these three key aspects the reform actually returned public television to an earlier age of French broadcasting. First, the establishment of a single company re-established the institutional arrangements that existed prior to the 1974 Giscardian reform and completed a process of moving towards the reconstruction of a unitary public television organization that had begun in 1989 (Cour des comptes, 2009: 60). The public channels incorporated in this reorganization include France 2 (generalist), France 3 (generalist/regional), France 4 (youth), France 5 (educational) and France Ô (overseas departments and territories). The argument in favour of this change was that in a more competitive and fragmented media landscape the services of public television required better coordination to ensure a strong public service presence against an expanding array of generalist and niche-oriented commercial channels and new content providers. This was a powerful argument that received wide acceptance among relevant policy stakeholders, including the top management of France Télévisions. The main difference between the new organizational set-up and that of the Gaullist ORTF was that the new framework did not include public radio, whose local and national services continue to be organized in a separate company, Radio France.

Second, the withdrawal of commercial advertising from France Télévisions took public television back to the financial arrangements of the 1960s when the ORTF was funded almost exclusively from licence fee revenue. In stark contrast to the BBC's domestic television services, public television in France had been part funded from commercial advertising since 1968. The contribution of advertising as a share of public television's finances grew substantially in the 1970s and 1980s and then fell back after 2000. In 2004, for example, advertising accounted for just over 29 per cent of public television's total revenue, down from nearly 39 per cent in 1998.

Nonetheless, in 2007 advertising still accounted for about 30 per cent of total revenue for France Télévisions and its withdrawal represented a major financial challenge for the company's management. This was particularly the case as the level of the licence fee in France (€118 in 2009) is low compared to that of most other European broadcasting systems and President Sarkozy had previously shown no inclination to increase the licence fee significantly to help make up for any financial shortfall. Instead, the 2009 reform introduced new taxes on internet service providers and phone operators on the one hand and on the advertising turnover of private television channels on the other to plug the financial hole. Since it was not legally possible to allocate the revenue from these taxes directly to France Télévisions, this component of the organization's revenue is now directly allocated out of general state funds. As a result, public television would now be funded in part from licence revenue (around €2 billion in 2009), in part directly from the state budget

(€450 million) and in part from advertising (€350 million). Increases in the level of the licence fee were now tied to the general rate of inflation in the economy. Ironically, with the downturn in media advertising in 2008–9 as a result of the economic crisis, France Télévisions may well have benefited financially in the short term from these new funding arrangements (Cour des comptes, 2009: 81–3).

This central aspect of the reform was defended by President Sarkozy on the grounds that because of their dependence on advertising revenue for an important part of their income stream, the programme output of the public channels was insufficiently differentiated from that of their commercial rivals, with the tyranny of the ratings influencing both the substantive content of programming and the allocation of programmes to particular time slots (Risser, 2004). To remedy this situation, Sarkozy proposed that France Télévisions should be liberated from its dependence on advertising to become a French-style BBC.

Was the President's allegation accurate? Certainly it was fiercely contested by the management of France Télévisions who argued that their output was substantially different from that of their commercial competitors. The regulatory authority came to a similar conclusion. While in some programme genres it could be argued that there has been considerable similarity in content between public and private providers, it is clear that in other areas public television has explicitly chosen not to compete with its commercial rivals and has scheduled what might be regarded as more stimulating and challenging output in genres such as documentaries, serious drama and political programmes. Moreover, despite the popularity of some reality television shows with audiences in recent years, including *Loft Story*, the French-style *Big Brother* first shown on M6 in 2001, the public channels have steered clear of investing in this prime-time genre as they do not regard it as falling within the terms of their public service mission.

The withdrawal of advertising predictably caused uproar when it was first announced. Yet in political terms the initiative was shrewdly calculated since the opposition parties of the left, including the Socialist Party, had long campaigned against the perverse impact of advertising on programming without ever going so far as to legislate for its abandonment. Indeed, the abolition of advertising on public television had been included in the Socialist-Communist manifesto way back in 1972. The broadcasting trade unions were similarly put on the back foot – opposed to advertising on public television in principle, but fearful of the consequences of its withdrawal in practice, notably on levels of employment within the industry. Some television professionals welcomed the change, arguing that it would remove the pressure of the ratings system and open up new possibilities for cultural creativity. The problem in the eyes of those opposed to this aspect of Sarkozy's reform was not the principle of the initiative – there is clearly nothing unacceptable in having an advertising-free public service provider of television content – but rather the government's reluctance to raise the level of the licence fee and the problematic nature of the proposed additional revenue streams.

Finally, the President regained direct responsibility for the appointment of the chief executives of the two public broadcasting companies, France Télévisions and Radio France, with the regulatory authority reduced to exercising a purely consultative role (Saint-Cricq and Gerschel, 2009). This direct mode of appointment returned public broadcasting to the era prior to Mitterrand's 1982 reform that first established a regulatory authority for broadcasting, one of whose powers was to appoint the heads of the public broadcasting companies (Dagnaud, 2000). Successive reforms of broadcasting since 1982, introduced by governments of both right and left, had maintained the role of the regulatory authority as the source of appointment to the top managerial posts in public broadcasting (see Chapter 1).

Why did Sarkozy propose a return to the status quo ante 1982? He defended the policy shift on two grounds. First, he argued that since the President enjoyed the power of appointment of the chief executive in other spheres of the public sector such as the railways, it was logically coherent that he should enjoy a similar power in the case of public broadcasting. Second, the Elysée alleged that the existing system of appointment by the regulatory authority was essentially hypocritical in that while it appeared to transfer power away from the political realm and so depoliticize the process, in reality the regulatory authority had with one notable exception always bowed to the wishes of the political executive with regard to those selected (Cotta, 2008). Reassigning responsibility for the appointment of the heads of France Télévisions and Radio France directly to the President would, it was claimed, simply bring the legislation into line with prevailing practice and thereby make the process more transparent. Such a view rather depressingly presupposes that in France the regulatory authority can never secure a satisfactory degree of operational independence from the political executive. In the eyes of Sarkozy's critics, however, the clear danger was that in sidelining the regulatory authority, the President was asserting personal control over the appointments process with a view to having sympathetic incumbents in place in these key posts well ahead of the 2012 presidential election.

The 2009 reorganization of public television was motivated above all by political concerns. It formed part of a series of reforms undertaken by Sarkozy following his presidential election victory. He campaigned on a platform of 'quiet change' and was at pains after his election to give expression to his desire for reform across a broad range of domestic and foreign policy areas. Television is an area where the impact of change can be quickly seen by voters. Both Giscard d'Estaing and Mitterrand introduced broadcasting reforms near the start of their presidential terms and so in paying attention to reform in this area Sarkozy was maintaining a Fifth Republic tradition of presidential interventionism and executive power.

There was also an element of revanchism in the President's concern to reform France Télévisions. On various occasions during the 2007 campaign and before, Sarkozy had complained about the supposed inefficiencies of the public broadcasting organization and the allegedly discourteous attitude shown to him by some of its journalists, notably on the regional channel France 3. As President he did not seek to develop a fruitful working relationship with the chief executive, Patrick de Carolis, who was not generally regarded as a Sarkozy supporter. De Carolis had not been consulted or even briefed in advance of the controversial reform measures and learned about the proposal to drop advertising while watching the presidential press conference on television (Berretta, 2010: 57). In contrast, Sarkozy enjoys close relations with several media bosses in the private sector, including Martin Bouygues, the owner of TF1 (see Chapter 3). In the run-up to the 2008 presidential press conference, TF1 actively lobbied the President and his immediate entourage in favour of the type of reform that Sarkozy subsequently announced (Musso, 2009b: 97–100). This led to charges in the press that the reform of public television had been motivated primarily by a desire to help the large established private channels prosper in the more competitive digital environment.

Certainly the withdrawal of advertising from public television seemed expressly designed to bolster the balance sheets of the generalist channels TF1 and M6. The audience share of TF1, for many years France's most popular channel, has been in decline since the introduction of digital terrestrial television in 2005: from 31 per cent market share in 2007 to 27 per cent in 2008 and below 25 per cent in 2010. However, this is not the only problem it faces. Its programming is increasingly regarded as old fashioned by certain sections of the audience, notably the young, while the cyclical downturn in the advertising market as a result of the economic recession hit the channel badly. In this context a political decision to stop advertising on France Télévisions must have looked like a quick fix solution to the TF1 management. At the same time, all commercial channels in France stand to benefit from the introduction of additional advertising breaks in programme schedules and an increase in the permissible length of time devoted to advertising – from six to nine minutes per hour on average over the day for terrestrial channels. The resultant virtuous circle for commercial television was the possibility on the supply side to increase the number and length of advertising breaks, including during prime-time schedules, coupled with greater demand from advertisers, who can no longer place their advertisements on the public channels.

Challenges for public service broadcasters

In the short term the management of public television will be concerned primarily with the impact of the new funding regime on programming. Yet important as it may be, this is not the only issue on the agenda of public broadcasters in France. Three others are worth noting here, since they have policy and regulatory implications. These are: the distinctive role of public service broadcasters in a multi-channel competitive market; the transition from public service broadcasting to public service communications media; and the importance for public service broadcasters of reflecting the ethnic diversity of contemporary French society.

First, there is the question of the mission of public service broadcasters in a media landscape increasingly dominated by private providers and market concerns. At one level this is simply about public broadcasters' securing audiences in a more competitive market – not in itself a new issue. The expansion in the supply of programming as a result of digital switchover, especially via the terrestrial platform, will inevitably lead to a reduction in the audience share of public television. Yet even without the financial imperative of securing commercial advertising revenue it will be impossible for public television simply to isolate itself from audience-driven market pressures. In part this is because the political case for the continued existence of a licence fee system to fund public television is dependent to some extent on the success of the programme output of its mainstream channels, notably during prime time, in attracting mass audiences. While it is true that not all public television output is obliged constantly to aim simply for high ratings or to attract a particular sociodemographic section of the audience, it still remains the case that consistently low ratings make public broadcasters vulnerable to criticism from viewers, sections of the media and political elites.

In short, France Télévisions will have to face up to the dilemma that all public broadcasters have to negotiate in a system characterized by market competition and audience fragmentation: what is the distinctive contribution of the public service provider? If public broadcasting increasingly emulates the management practices and resembles the output of commercial rivals, then the defence of a specific public service component in broadcasting and communications on the grounds of its particular contribution to the achievement of socially desirable objectives is severely weakened, along with the claim to a secure source of public funding (Iosifidis *et al.*, 2005: 11). Conversely, if France Télévisions retires to a small public service ghetto of 'worthy' broadcast ouput, it runs the risk of losing more viewers and so the case for public funding via the licence fee is again undermined. With its strong emphasis on educational and cultural programming, the 2009 reform seems to push France Télévisions in this latter direction. The possibility in this scenario is that public television in France becomes a less central part of the broadcasting system, playing a supporting and complementary role in a landscape where the tone is increasingly set by commercial operators.

Second, there is the question of the transition from public service broadcasters to public service communications media. The public broadcasting organizations in France do not enjoy a status or legitimacy in their national media landscape equivalent to that of the BBC in the UK. In part this is because the experience of the 'government model' in the formative years of its development prevented public broadcasting from developing a tradition of political independence that would allow it to foster a positive relationship with civil society and embed itself in popular consciousness as a national icon (Hallin and Mancini, 2004: 30-3). In addition, the break-up of the ORTF in 1975 drove a wedge between the provision of public radio and television services. Even after the implementation of the 2009 reform there is no single public broadcasting organization in France. Moreover, whereas since the John Birt reforms of the early 1990s the BBC has regarded news and information provision as a central, defining component of its mission, this has been less true of French public broadcasters. Thus, while the contemporary BBC regards itself not just as a *broadcaster* but as a major public service *communication* actor, embracing radio, television and online services, Radio France and France Télévisions are still in many respects traditional suppliers of radio and television programming respectively. The online provision of news and related information and educational services by French public broadcasters is underdeveloped compared to that of the BBC. Yet – and here we return to the funding issue – a successful transition from broadcaster to multi-platform communications operator requires a stable and secure financial foundation that may be currently lacking in the French case.

Finally, there is the capacity of public broadcasters to reflect the reality of a multi-ethnic and multicultural republic through their employment practices and programme content. French public broadcasting has long lacked role models from ethnic minority communities, while much programming fails to take adequate account of the variegated ethnic composition of French society. This is a difficult issue for French media policy stakeholders since it forms part of a much broader and highly contentious sociopolitical debate on how the tradition of universal republicanism can be reconciled with greater cultural pluralism. Anglo-American notions of multiculturalism are widely rejected among French political elites, as they are seen as promoting group loyalties that break the bond between the individual and society, between the citizen and the state. This has led in the past to an under-representation of ethnic minorities in public broadcasting, both in appointments and in programme content.

In recent years there has been growing awareness of the need for all broadcasters, not just the public providers, better to reflect contemporary France's ethnic and cultural diversity. In 2006 much publicity surrounded the appointment of Harry Roselmack as the first black presenter on the main evening television news programme of TF1. While such an appointment was open to charges of tokenism, the CSA has begun to address the issue of under-representation in a more comprehensive fashion, putting pressure on broadcasters to ensure that in their news coverage and fictional programming the diversity of French society is better reflected. The regulatory authority has also pledged to assess the implementation of appropriate policies by broadcasters in this area. The first CSA report on diversity in French television programming, published in 2009 (CSA, 2009b) showed evidence of a quantitative and qualitative under-representation of ethnic minorities, with about 90 per cent of on-screen representation accorded to 'people seen as white' ('*personnes vues comme blanches*'). The main exception to this general rule was not surprisingly in musical entertainment programming. The under-representation was even worse in genres that were especially related to the daily life of French society, such as drama and news output. It was only thanks to foreign content, such as US-produced fiction and international news stories, that greater diversity in ethnic origins was evident in these two important programme genres. In short, French television as a whole, including the public channels, still has a lot of work to do in terms of adequately representing the ethnic diversity of contemporary French society.

French public broadcasters are certainly not exceptional among their European counterparts in having to face up to these challenges. However, in the French case what makes the situation particularly difficult for public service broadcasting organizations is the combination of the hostility of an interventionist President and the lobbying influence of commercial broadcasters on government policy. The current political climate in France is scarcely conducive to the well-being of public broadcasting institutions or the values they aspire to represent.

Media regulation

Regulating media content has long been an integral part of public policy. The French state imposes rules on media with regard to their content, both to restrict some types of material and to promote others. No medium is simply free to publish what it likes. For instance, there is a legislative ban on hate speech, making racial defamation and provocation to racial hatred or violence punishable by criminal law. In 1990, legislation was introduced to incorporate a ban on Holocaust denial; it is illegal in France to claim that the Holocaust did not take place. France also has strong legislation to protect individual privacy. This in part explains why French newspapers largely abstain from covering the sexual improprieties of their political elites (see Chapter 6). Because of their audience reach in society the news media have a particular responsibility to comply with these and similar legislative provisions.

In comparison with the broadcast media, the press and the internet are subject to a minimal degree of content regulation. The press, for instance, has a right of reply provision that gives individuals the right to respond to newspaper coverage that they deem to have been unjustifiably critical of them. Yet since the 1881 reform, the basic premise has been that in peacetime newspapers are free to publish what they wish as long as their content does not infringe general legislation. There is no statutory regulatory authority monitoring the activities of the press in France, nor a self-regulatory body along the lines of the UK Press Council. Some newspapers monitor their own behaviour in line with general journalistic codes of professional ethical practice. In addition, some titles, such as *Le Monde*, also employ an ombudsman (*médiateur*) who acts as a conduit for comments and complaints from readers and passes judgement, published in the newspaper, in cases of disagreement between readers and newsroom staff. With regard to the internet, the 2009 Hadopi law established a public regulatory agency, the High Authority for the

Distribution of Works and the Protection of Rights on the Internet (*Haute autorité pour la diffusion des œuvres et la protection des droits sur Internet*), with the specific objective of targeting the sharing of peer-to-peer files where this constitutes a breach of the author's intellectual property rights (*droits d'auteur*). However, this controversial legislation addresses the conditions under which content is distributed rather than the substance of the content itself.

In contrast to the press and the internet, the broadcasting sector has always been subject to extensive and detailed regulation (Dagnaud, 2000). Content regulation in broadcasting can be explained with reference to its historical legal status as a state monopoly, its ease of accessibility and the alleged power of radio and television to influence audience attitudes and behaviour. Broadcasting is regulated by the CSA, which was established in 1989. The board of the CSA consists of nine members – three appointed by the President, three by the Chairman of the National Assembly and three by the Chairman of the Senate. Each member is appointed for a non-renewable six-year term, with one third of the board renewed every two years. Appointments to the CSA are generally informed by party political considerations as well as by professional competence and the Council currently has a strong bias towards the right. Nonetheless, the authority has survived several alterations in government between left and right – no mean feat in a domain traditionally marked by high political controversy – and, while one should not overstate this, its existence prior to the 2009 broadcasting reform had to some degree constrained the freedom of manoeuvre of President and government to interfere directly in the management of public broadcasting.

Among its many functions, the CSA:

- manages and allocates radio and television frequencies;
- delivers authorizations to broadcast to radio and television services distributed by terrestrial transmission: for instance, it has taken an active role in the encouragement of the development of digital terrestrial television;
- ensures the respect by all operators of the laws and rules and can sanction those who are in breach of them;
- advises on the appointment of the heads of the public radio and television companies;
- supervises the respect of political and trade union pluralism over the airwaves;
- organizes the official broadcast campaigns for certain elections (presidential, parliamentary, etc.);
- watches over the protection of young viewers and listeners: since 1996, at the behest of the CSA, French television channels have implemented a classification system for programmes deemed suitable for different age ranges among minors;
- promotes the representation of the diversity of French society in programming;

● gives an opinion to the government on proposed legislation concerning broadcasting.

The CSA has no power of censorship; nor can it impose a programme
on a television channel or radio station. The monitoring of programme
output is done at the time of transmission, never in advance. All
broadcasters have to respect some content regulations, for instance with
regard to political pluralism (see Chapter 3). In addition, those services
wholly or part funded from advertising are regulated with respect to the
type and amount that may be included in their scheduling. For instance,
television advertising for products containing alcohol was banned by the
1991 Évin law. Advertising on behalf of hypermarkets and big chain
stores (la grande distribution) was allowed on terrestrial television only
from the start of 2007 following pressure on the French authorities from
the EU.

Broadcasting regulation in France has to conform to the provisions of
relevant EU directives, notably those contained in the 2007 version of the
original 1989 Television Without Frontiers Directive, the aim of which
was to create a single European broadcasting and audiovisual market by
allowing the free flow of programmes within the EU (Negrine and
Papathanassopoulos, 1990). Nonetheless, much French broadcasting regulation is still driven by national concerns. Such regulations are often
designed to promote rather than prohibit certain types of content. Radio
stations, for example, have to transmit a certain quota of French language
songs in their music output (currently 40 per cent for generalist stations,
of which half should be for new talent or new productions) and this must
be achieved in the hours of 'significant listening' (heures d'écoute signifi-
catives). Since exposure on radio is linked to sales and download of
music, this regulation has an economic as well as a cultural objective: to
boost the French music industry in the face of Anglo-American competition.

More generally, the imposition of production and transmission quotas
on French-produced television programmes and feature films, along with
guaranteed subsidies from broadcasters to the French film industry, has
long been an integral part of the television sector's regulatory structure
and is undoubtedly the product of the lobbying power of different
stakeholders, such as the film industry and domestic production companies, in the national media policy community (Dagnaud, 2006: 185–214).
The primary beneficiary of quotas and subsidies has been the domestic
film industry rather than independent television production – testimony to
the higher status given to film over television in cultural policy circles and
to the clout of the film industry as an 'insider' pressure group.

Content quotas have been defended in national and international policy
fora on the grounds of cultural protection – now relabelled as 'promotion
of cultural diversity' – in the face of unfair international competition
dominated by the US entertainment and film industries. Such quotas can
be regarded as the policy outcome of either a half-digested interpretation
of media imperialism theories or a perfectly understandable desire to

protect French artefacts in an interdependent global cultural market. They can also be seen as a form of economic protectionism, providing support to internationally uncompetitive domestic sources of production, or as a defensible concern with maintaining a national production base in an important area of the global media economy.

Through the use of content regulation there has been a strong and concerted attempt to maintain a distinct French identity to the French broadcast media. Has this ensured their distinctiveness when compared to the media of other European nations of similar size? The answer in the case of television is open to question. For instance, in terms of the amount of imported programming shown on television schedules, French television has not been especially exceptional or distinct when compared to that of the UK or Germany. However, in fairness to the French authorities it could be argued that without regulatory constraints on content the amount of domestic product shown on French television might well have been significantly lower, as French companies took advantage of the financial savings to be made through a policy based on cheap imports. If so, then regulation does to some extent allow for a certain amount of cultural and economic protectionism.

Public service broadcasters are subject to very specific content regulations, with greater obligations in terms of programming than their commercial competitors, for instance with regard to the provision of specific programming for religious and political expression. Indeed, one of the main strengths of public service broadcasting in the past has been as a showcase for domestic product in a society where elites across the political spectrum have traditionally valued the importance of national cultural dissemination and have regulated to protect and promote national cultural product in broadcasting. Following the 2009 reform of public television, the operating conditions (*cahier des charges*) imposed by the government on France Télévisions were made more specific than in the past. The television company was given objectives and even quantifiable targets in terms of programming across a whole range of genres: culture, music, drama, science and education, sport, film, fiction, documentaries, youth, news, Europe and religion. As under previous regulatory regimes, the proportion of output of European origin across its channels had to be at least 60 per cent and of French origin at least 40 per cent, while the company also had to devote a slice of its budget to European, notably French, film production. These very specific regulatory conditions were designed to strengthen the difference between public and private sector television channels and, one suspects, to facilitate the audience maximization strategies of the main private sector companies such as TF1.

What of the future? As national borders become more porous in the face of global technological change, corporate transnational ownership strategies and liberal WTO and European regulations, a defensive national regulatory strategy in broadcast content will become more difficult to deliver. This will be true whether the success of such a strategy is evaluated in cultural or economic terms. In an age of multi-channel television, segmentation of supply and audience fragmentation, there will also be increasing pressures on the financial bottom-line for network operators and content providers. French product will have to compete to secure its privileged position on domestic television. Finally, the expansion in the number of broadcast outlets and new content distribution platforms through technological shift undermines some of the traditional arguments for state regulation of broadcast content such as spectrum scarcity and possibility of market failure, while also making effective regulation technically more complex. In theory, more outlets should result in a reduced need for content regulation by state officials (apart from the area of consumer protection). Yet it is also the case that the regulatory tradition in French broadcasting is well implanted, while various lobby groups have a vested interest in the continuation of content regulation to protect their particular spheres of activity, especially in the face of external competition. While the future details of content regulation in the broadcasting sector are difficult to predict, what is clear is that the state will continue to play a central role in determining the rules, in close association with powerful media groups and industry players: politics will continue to play a vital role in this aspect of media policy-making.

Conclusion

Different variables influence the process of media policy-making: techno-logical, economic, cultural and transnational. Media policy, however, is not simply determined by technological factors or global developments: politics matters, and particularly the input of national actors, notably the President and powerful media companies. Initiatives taken by President Sarkozy in the press and television are good illustrations of the continued importance of politics in media policy-making. In particular, Sarkozy has been a highly interventionist President who has dominated the media policy-making process. A long-standing integral part of media policy has been regulation of content. While the press and internet operate in minimally regulated environments, in the case of the broadcasting sector the French state continues both to prohibit and encourage certain types of content for cultural and economic reasons. The practice of state regula-tion, embodied in the work of the CSA, has survived into the digital age.

5 THE POLITICAL EXECUTIVE AND NEWS MANAGEMENT

- A legacy of government censorship and control
- The French executive as a 'primary definer' for the news media
- A fragmented executive
- Competing sources and compliant journalists
- News management under President Sarkozy
- Conclusion

All political executives in western democracies now pay close attention to news management. In an information environment characterized by the 24-hour news cycle and a glut of competing media outlets, journalists have a voracious appetite for fresh primary material. At the same time, a wide range of sociopolitical actors have professionalized their activities as sources for the news media. Any political executive, therefore, has to work hard in its attempts to exert a determining influence on both the structure of the news agenda and the framing of issues. Sometimes it will push for an issue to be put high on the media agenda and framed in a way that advances its partisan interests; at other times it is desperate to keep an issue out of the mediated public sphere and to limit any damage that may occur if, despite its best efforts, critical reporting does take place. The initial objective of the political executive is to retain as much proactive control of the news management process as possible, with the secondary aim of achieving a variety of mutually reinforcing goals: to maintain, or better still improve, its electoral popularity; to retain the confidence of its supporters in parliament and across the country; to seize the initiative from its political opponents; to manage public expectations regarding executive policy initiatives; to convey the impression of being in control of events; and to reinforce its authority at the heart of the political system.

This chapter examines the news management activities of the political executive in contemporary France. Using examples largely taken from the Chirac and Sarkozy presidencies, the chapter argues that the executive's capacity to act as a 'primary definer' for the news media is considerable, particularly in the light of the significant attention paid to this area of activity by President Sarkozy. While fragmentation of the core executive continues to pose problems for effective news management, the nature of the journalistic culture in France, especially among broadcasting journalists, means that the French executive is normally subject to less adversarial contestation from the news media than is the case in Anglo-American democracies. Nonetheless, in seeking to impose its version of events in the mediated public sphere, the French executive does not command and control the news agenda. It has to mobilize its resources, compete with other sources and hope that unanticipated events do not blow its news management strategy off course.

The chapter is structured as follows. Part one examines the legacy of governmental censorship and control of news output in both press and broadcasting sectors. The second section considers the applicability of the concept of 'primary definer' to the news management activities of the French executive. Part three focuses on executive fragmentation as a barrier to effective news management, while the following section covers the areas of source competition and the professional culture of journalists. The final section examines news management by the political executive during the Sarkozy presidency.

A legacy of government censorship and control

There is a long history of censorship and control of the news media by the state authorities in France, most notably under monarchical and authoritarian regimes prior to the establishment of the Third Republic in the latter part of the nineteenth century and during both world wars in the twentieth. Moreover, even after the end of the Second World War, and more precisely in the 25-year period between the Liberation in 1944 and the end of the de Gaulle presidency in 1969, the political executive had frequent recourse to direct forms of repressive intervention in both the press and broadcasting sectors to prevent the media from reporting on certain events, issues and political figures and to delimit the boundaries of coverage where it did take place.

Newspapers, magazines and books were, for instance, heavily censored during France's involvement in the Algerian war of independence (1954–62). Censorship was employed to bolster morale at home, to win the hearts and minds of the French public in support of government policy and to prevent opposition to the official perspective on the conflict from becoming too vocally persuasive. The leftish intellectual weekly, *France-Observateur*, was suppressed repeatedly, as was the Communist daily, *L'Humanité*. Talbott writes that 'no government tried to establish a formal apparatus of censorship. But each did its best to prevent the press from publishing certain kinds of information, especially allegations or revelations of the use of torture. Nothing was more likely to invite the attention of the authorities than charging the army with misconduct' (1981: 106–7).

The relationship between the government and the press during the Algerian conflict cannot, however, be explained simply in terms of top-down censorship. First, many newspapers were perfectly content to promote the official line on the war, even at the cost of ignoring reports of torture committed by the French military in Algeria. These papers engaged in selective self-censorship, not as a pre-emptive move to avoid being censored by the authorities, but rather because they were prepared to act as a media conduit for the official perspective on the conflict. This might have been because they were in genuine sympathy with the official line on the war or, even if they had doubts on this issue, because they did not wish to alienate that section of their readership which backed the government's position. Second, the government was not always successful in ensuring that censorship was effectively applied against those sections of the press that sought to present a different agenda from the official one. Alternative and oppositional views of the conflict did feature in the French press, qualifying the official perspective or even countering it head on. Finally, it should be noted that political interference was not confined to suppressing articles sympathetic to the cause of Algerian independence or hostile to the French military. When after the establishment of de Gaulle's Fifth Republic official government policy changed to one of support for self-determination for the Algerian people, the French government put pressure on the press to refrain from giving the oxygen of publicity to the viewpoint of hardline defenders of the cause of French Algeria (*Algérie française*).

During the Fourth Republic, official control of broadcasting worked especially to the detriment of the Communist Party and General de Gaulle. For different reasons both were regarded by the ruling political parties as destabilizing and hostile political actors who potentially stood to benefit from the overthrow of a regime that faced severe problems of economic reconstruction at home and controversial military involvement in colonies abroad. To try to minimize their impact on electoral opinion and the policy agenda, de Gaulle and the Communist Party were for long spells denied access to state radio during the 1950s, while the latter were also the victims of Cold War anti-Communist propaganda broadcasts. Under Guy Mollet's Socialist-led coalition government (1956–7), measures were taken to suppress anti-government views in news broadcasts. With the political system fighting for its life over the handling of the Algerian issue, the temptation to use state radio as the mouthpiece of government policy was overwhelming. As a result, the official perspective on the conflict dominated state radio coverage.

After the establishment of the Fifth Republic in 1958 the Gaullist government strictly controlled broadcast news content to ensure that it would support the realization of their electoral and ideological objectives. The Gaullists argued, with little hard evidence or much sense of conviction, that since most of the press was against them, it was reasonable in the interests of political pluralism across the media as a whole that television should be in their favour. For the Gaullists, television thus became indispensable in the construction of a popular consensus in support of the new institutions. Thus, in the key formative years of the new regime, television news was subject to strict and direct government control (Bourdon, 1990; Chalaby, 2002). One aspect of the relationship between the authorities and television was the practice of partisan appointments to key managerial and editorial posts. In addition, the Ministry of Information was used to set the agenda for the main evening television news programme on France's one and only television channel. The consequences of this Gaullist control of television were evident in the way in which in the early years of the Fifth Republic political opponents were largely kept off the air, while government ministers were constantly seen celebrating the success of Gaullist policy initiatives. The role played by state television during the 1968 'events', when in the early days of the protest the medium largely ignored the outpouring of dissent, was a perfect illustration of its institutional subordination to the Gaullist state during de Gaulle's presidency.

Yet in retrospect, 1968 also marked the beginning of the end of the era of naked government manipulation and control. This change of emphasis was driven by the political recognition that such an authoritarian approach had by the end of the 1960s become counterproductive in terms of audience opinion formation. Since many viewers no longer regarded television news as politically independent, its credibility for the provision of a balanced and impartial version of events was open to question. Following the resignation of de Gaulle from the presidency in 1969 the state ceased directly to control and censor television news output, while the Ministry of Information no longer determined television's news agenda. Instead, the political executive began to disengage from the crude Gaullist 'command and control' model of news media management.

A gradual, uneven, but irreversible shift in the executive's relationship with television news started during the early years of the Pompidou presidency (1969–74), with an important reform introduced by Prime Minister Chaban-Delmas in 1969 that gave the newsrooms of the two state television channels a high degree of functional autonomy. The impact of this organizational change, notably on the more widely viewed first channel, was to create a sense of critical distance between televison news output and the government. Many Gaullist parliamentarians never fully accepted the 1969 reform and even the President soon dissociated himself from his Prime Minister's initiative. Pompidou still considered the journalists working at the ORTF to be 'the voice of France' ('la voix de la France') and therefore to have a special official responsibility in their news reporting.

On coming to office in 1974, President Giscard d'Estaing specifically rejected the idea that journalists employed in state broadcasting had some sort of official status that differentiated them from their press colleagues. Yet for the political executive television still remained far too important a medium of political information and agenda-setting simply to be left in the hands of professional news editors and journalists. The President and government continued therefore to try to shape both the agenda and the framing of the medium's news output. During the Giscard d'Estaing presidency (1974–81) they sought to do this largely through the appointment of politically sympathetic journalists to key editorial posts. During the 1980s the abolition of the state monopoly, the expansion in the supply of radio and television and the creation of a regulatory authority introduced important structural changes to the broadcasting landscape. In terms of news management the response of the political executive was to continue to adapt its mode of interdependence with the broadcasting media: patronage, influence, pressure and intimidation were all part of the armoury deployed by Presidents Mitterrand and Chirac.

The French executive as a 'primary definer' for the news media

All political executives in advanced democracies enjoy the benefit of three key assets that guarantee them privileged access to the news media on a routine basis as an official source: significant organizational resources in terms of finance and personnel; extensive insider knowledge and policy expertise across a range of political issues; and a high degree of legitimacy conferred through the electoral process. This combination of organizational resources, expert knowledge and political legitimacy thus gives the French executive a strong, frequently dominant, position compared to other sources in the process of news management.

One way of theorizing this power of the French executive as an official source centres on the concept of 'primary definer'. This model places the news media in a subordinate and secondary role to major power-holders in society – including the political executive – in the task of agenda construction. According to this account, the organizational demands and professional values of the news production process 'combine to produce a systematically structured *over-accessing* to the media of those in powerful and privileged institutional positions'. In turn, this 'permits the institutional definers to establish the initial definition or *primary interpretation* of the topic in question' (Hall *et al.*, 1978: 58, original emphasis).

The concept of primary definition can therefore be explained with reference to two features of developed political communication systems: first, the routinization of the news production process in an age of sophisticated mass communications technology and highly bureaucratic media organizations; and, second, the legitimacy which is conferred on certain individuals, groups or institutions as authoritative sources of information because of their social status, technical expertise, economic power and/or political position. The process of news production inevitably makes significant use of official sources, that are themselves geared up to provide information in ways that the media find user-friendly. These official sources normally enjoy good formal and informal links with news editors and journalists. They are generally perceived by the media as a regular and reliable source of news copy and this position allows them to influence the media agenda and issue coverage. At the same time, because they possess some form of authority, primary definers are usually essential sources of information if the media are to have a complete account of events. Whereas many individuals and groups in society are excluded or marginalized in the process of news construction, primary definers enjoy a privileged insider position. A presidential press conference, television interview or intervention at an international summit guarantees substantial media coverage because of the nature of the source, irrespective of the content of the message.

The President and his advisers ('the Elysée'), the Prime Minister and his staff ('Matignon') and the other government ministries are key primary definers for the contemporary French media. Across a range of domestic and international issues their input makes a significant contribution to agenda construction and the framing of issues. To help ensure that the official version dominates media coverage, the political executive is helped by a range of support staff and official bodies, including political and communication advisers, public relations personnel and governmental information agencies. The political executive's perspective on events, therefore, usually has little difficulty in being articulated in mainstream media outlets.

How helpful is the idea of primary definer in explaining the nature of the interdependence between the political executive and the news media in contemporary France? Before we consider this question analytically, let us briefly consider two examples of news reporting, both taken from the early period of Chirac's second presidential term (2002–7). The first concerns the issue of road safety, which Chirac had just announced as a high political priority. In the autumn of 2002, French television gave particular prominence to this issue, with the news programmes of TF1, France 2 and France 3 running 554 stories on road safety compared to 123 during the same period in 2001 – a jump in news coverage wholly out of proportion with any increase in the number of road accidents (Séry, 2003). The altered news emphasis was thus not being shaped by any quantitative change in the number of incidents taking place in the real world. Both in the number of stories devoted to this theme (agenda structuring) and the nature of the coverage (issue framing), French television news in effect acted as a publicist for the potentially controversial measures – including speed cameras – introduced by the government. On this occasion the executive acted as a primary definer for the news media, or to put it another way, the media took their cue from the government.

In sharp contrast, a few months later, during the heatwave of the summer of 2003 that resulted in thousands of premature deaths among the elderly in particular, the government's news management strategy found itself flailing in response to a crisis situation. In substantive terms, ministers and state officials frequently provided inadequate and inaccurate responses to journalists' questions; in symbolic terms, the government got its communication signals woefully wrong. One of the iconic television images of the summer of 2003 was that of the health minister, dressed in a sports shirt and clearly speaking from his holiday location, appearing on the main evening news programme on TF1 to talk about the crisis. Whatever the validity of the minister's verbal comments, the overall image conveyed to the concerned viewer was wholly inappropriate. During the crisis the French government failed effectively to manage news coverage of the deteriorating health situation (the political problem) and its response (the policy solution). In addition, by not returning to France from his holiday in Canada, President Chirac missed an opportunity to engage in a mediatized act of symbolic communication – the head of state as father figure showing his concern for the welfare of the nation's most vulnerable citizens. These two contrasting examples should alert us to the difficulty of making sweeping generalizations about the power of the French executive to function as a primary definer in news media management. In the first example (road safety) the government was in proactive mode and largely in control of the story, while in the second (the heatwave) it was in reactive mode, responding to events outside its control and clearly without a contingency plan as to how to deal with the media's desire for information.

Analyses of government news management in western democracies point to three potential problems that a political executive may face in its attempt to structure the media agenda and frame issues (Schlesinger, 1990). First, core executives (and their parliamentary support) are usually internally divided and so do not speak to journalists with one voice. Second, there is competition among a range of sources in the process of news definition – the executive does not have a monopoly as an official source. Finally, the media are not simply passive recipients of information from sources. Journalists frequently challenge the official version of events and subject it to critical scrutiny. How relevant are these three problems for the political executive in France?

A fragmented executive

Let us begin our analysis of the executive and news management by focusing on selected features of the political system of the Fifth Republic that have influenced the executive's capacity to act as a primary definer for the news media. In particular, this section emphasizes the division and fragmentation of the French executive, which it is argued are largely built into the governing structures of the system and which have in the past contributed to a certain model of news management, irrespective of the political persuasions or partisan affiliations of key office-holders such as the President and Prime Minister.

The first notable aspect of the political system in this respect is the mix of presidential and parliamentary logics embedded in the institutional framework of the regime. At the apex is an executive dyarchy consisting of a President and a Prime Minister, the former directly elected as head of state and the latter appointed by the President as head of the government, which is in turn constitutionally responsible to parliament (Elgie, 2003: 95–128). When the President and Prime Minister come from the same political party or coalition, their working relationship may well be close and relatively harmonious. However, this is by no means guaranteed.

Presidential-prime ministerial disharmony may still occur even when both office-holders come from the same political party, as in the case of the highly publicized hostile relationship between President Mitterrand and Prime Minister Michel Rocard, both Socialists, between 1988 and 1991 (Huchon, 1993).

Executive cohabitation exacerbates the likelihood both of substantive disagreement over policy and of conflict being symbolically manifested in the public domain, as was the case in the first 'short cohabitation' between President Mitterrand and Prime Minister Chirac (1986–8) and in the latter months of the 'long cohabitation' between President Chirac and Prime Minister Jospin (1997–2002). In both these cases the President and Prime Minister went on to be competing candidates in the presidential elections that brought the periods of cohabitation to an end. The closer the political cycle came to these elections, the more any pronouncements from the Elysée and Matignon in the war of press releases were interpreted by the media as part of the upcoming campaign battle. In short, while presidential-prime ministerial relations in the Fifth Republic have not necessarily been characterized by constant mutual hostility and resentment, the framework of the regime undoubtedly institutionalizes greater potential for conflict at the top than is formally to be found in the executive arrangements of most other advanced democracies, with potential consequences for the coherence of its news management activities.

Second, the French executive as a whole is prone to a high degree of structural fragmentation which has a notable effect on its pretensions to function as a unified authority. Indeed, the fissiparous nature of the central governmental apparatus led a major study of policy coordination in France to relinquish the term 'core executive' in the singular in preference for the notion of 'core executives', so as better 'to emphasize the plurality of inner core authorities' (Hayward and Wright, 2002: 21). In similar fashion, Elgie illustrates his thesis regarding the myth of the strong French state by pointing to the 'unavoidable conflicts within the government' which can itself be regarded as 'a conglomeration of competing Ministries' (Elgie, 2003: 80). It is clear, therefore, that the French executive is far from being a monolithic entity, acting with a unified will and a single sense of purpose; rather, it is divided and segmented. The fault lines are rarely ideological. Sometimes they reflect the normal turf war between ministerial departments; sometimes they are underpinned by divisions over policy; and frequently they involve personality clashes fuelled by political ambition.

The third relevant feature of the political system has been the coalition nature of many Fifth Republic governments. The multi-party nature of electoral competition means that these governments have frequently included representatives from different political parties. A classic recent example is the Jospin government of the 'plural left', which had ministers drawn from no fewer than five different political formations (Willerton and Carrier, 2005). In the run-up to national elections there has been an in-built imperative on the part of each governmental party to differentiate itself from its 'competitor-partner' so as to maximize its electoral score and increase its potential for political leverage after the election. This was clearly demonstrated in the 2002 presidential contest, when each of the parties of the 'plural left' put up its own candidate, with devastating consequences in the first round for the left in general and Jospin in particular (Gaffney, 2004).

Finally, in contrast to some other western democracies it is not the norm in the Fifth Republic for the Prime Minister to combine the function of head of government with that of leader of the majority party. In 1997, for instance, Jospin made it clear on being appointed to the premiership that he did not wish to continue as leader of the Socialist Party (Victor, 1999: 40). Neither Edouard Balladur in 1993, Jean-Pierre Raffarin in 2002, Dominique de Villepin in 2005, nor François Fillon in 2007 enjoyed the luxury of having to make this particular choice, since none of them had held the status of majority party leader prior to being appointed to the premiership. This is not just a technical point concerning the formal division of labour between the head of government on the one hand and the leader of the majority party on the other. Rather it represents another potential source of political and communication discord at the heart of the political system. At various points in the history of the Fifth Republic the leader of the majority party has been in a position of rivalry and even outright conflict with the Prime Minister and/or the President: three notable examples are Chirac as leader of the Gaullist Party towards Prime Minister Raymond Barre and President Giscard d'Estaing between 1976 and 1981 (Giscard d'Estaing, 2006); Chirac towards Prime Minister Balladur between 1993 and 1995; and Sarkozy as leader of the UMP towards President Chirac and Prime Minister de Villepin between 2005 and 2007.

Executive dyarchy, experiences of cohabitation, ministerial turf wars, coalition government and the career rivalry engendered by presidential ambitions – the structures and functioning of the political system of the Fifth Republic contribute to a picture of division and disunity that makes coordination of executive news management both highly desirable and at the same time extremely difficult to achieve. The significant degree of pluralism and competition among official executive sources often gives rise to confused and conflicting messages and severely undermines any top-down 'command and control' news management strategy. Instead, coordination in French executive communication has tended to remain loose at best, despite attempts in the past to impose coherence by the Prime Minister's office (Schrameck, 2001: 71; Ambiel, 2005: 76–7).

The two most obvious manifestations of this fragmentation in executive communication are, first, when government ministers deliberately leak against each other through the media and, second, when they unintentionally contradict each other about an aspect of government policy. In early 2005, for example, the Minister for Foreign Affairs (de Villepin) placed critical remarks about the stewardship of the Prime Minister (Raffarin) into the public sphere, thereby positioning himself as a prospective candidate for the premiership in the event of the latter's dismissal by the President, which indeed took place later that year.

Unintentional contradiction at the heart of government has also been in evidence. For instance, in 2002, at the very moment when the Prime Minister was assuring the nation of his intention to hold to the President's promise to lower taxes and at the same time reduce the financial burden on business, the Minister of Finance argued in an interview given to the financial newspaper *Les Echos* that the two measures were not simultaneously compatible. The Prime Minister's office had apparently not been forewarned of the minister's remarks and so had to engage in a subsequent damage limitation exercise with journalists (Ambiel, 2005: 126).

Competing sources and compliant journalists

A second potential problem for the French executive in the process of news management is that it faces competition from a range of other actors who are also seeking to influence agenda construction and issue framing. The Elysée, Matignon and government ministries are not the only primary definers for the media. Some of the other actors, such as minor political parties and fringe pressure groups, may lack the necessary resources to make a sustained impact as a primary definer: they do not have the necessary media capital. This is not the case, however, with many other actors who function as official sources for the news media and who frequently put forward a definition of events not just different from, but in opposition to, that proffered by the executive.

Within the state apparatus, for instance, the Higher Judicial Council (*Conseil supérieur de la magistrature*) has during the Sarkozy presidency often been a vocal critic of judicial reforms proposed by the government and has used the news media as a channel to transmit its views and redefine the framing of the issue. The presidents of the regional councils are not just important political actors at the sub-national level, but also official sources on a range of socioeconomic and political issues for regional media outlets in particular. If the president of a region comes from a different political formation to the executive in Paris, then competition to set the news agenda on issues related to the region is almost guaranteed. Since 2004, for example, the majority of regional councils have had presidents from the main opposition party at the national level, the PS. Some of these regional political bosses, including Royal in Poitou-Charentes, are also major figures on the national political stage, further amplifying their power as a news media source. Much the same can be said in respect of mayors of large towns, who are not just important sources for local/regional media outlets but are also frequently important political figures in national politics and as such important sources for the national media (Le Galès, 2008: 212–13). Other actors regularly used by the news media as official sources include mainstream political parties, major pressure groups, think-tanks and independent expert bodies. In short, while the national political executive may often hope to dominate the field as an official source for the news media, it cannot expect to do so as of right, far less exercise a monopoly.

The final problem that western political executives may face in their attempts to manage the news lies in the attitudes and behaviour of journalists. One aspect of the interlinkages between elite politicians and journalists in contemporary France is their functional proximity. Although their educational and professional paths may be quite different, they operate in a relatively closed world in which they get to know each other well (Ferenczi, 2000–1; Masure, 2009). Indeed, affairs of the heart, including marriages, between politicians (male) and journalists (female) are not uncommon: Dominique Strauss-Kahn/Anne Sinclair, Jean-Louis Borloo/Béatrice Schonberg and François Baroin/Marie Drucker are some recent examples of the personal interlinkages between the two milieus. Perhaps the highest profile relationship of this type is that of Bernard Kouchner, the Minister of Foreign Affairs under Sarkozy, and Christine Ockrent, a former news anchor and currently occupying a top position at the French international news channel, France 24 (see Chapter 7). In this context it is hardly surprising that Sarkozy sought solace with a female journalist from the conservative daily *Le Figaro* when his marriage with Cécilia was in difficulty in 2005, while in the summer of 2007 the then leader of the Socialist Party, François Hollande, was photographed with a journalist from *Paris Match* in the weeks following his split with his former partner, Royal.

In the interdependent relationship between the political executive and journalists the professional cultural norms of the latter are particularly important. Journalistic cultures vary across different western societies and professional roles 'can range from neutral transmitter of politics to interpretative or even openly adversarial styles of news reporting' (Pfetsch, 2008: 88). Traditionally in France journalists have manifested a high degree of deference towards elite politicians, leading to a relationship that in the eyes of some commentators is based on overly close cooperation, collusion and even connivance (Carton, 2003). Carton's study reminds us that much of the interdependence between politicians and journalists on a daily basis is backstage rather than front, informal rather than formal, and covert rather than overt. One commentator has called the result of this interdependence an uncritical, reverential style of journalism (*journalisme de révérence*) (Halimi, 2005: 17–48).

In much of the mainstream, media deference on the part of journalists to elite politicians remains more of a feature of occupational norms and behaviour in France than in Anglo-American democracies where a journalistic tradition of critical watchdog and 'Fourth Estate' thinking is more firmly implanted (Neveu, 2001). The majority of French journalists remain less distant and less autonomous in their relationship with elite politicians than their counterparts in the UK and USA. Journalistic deference is especially notable in the broadcasting sector. For instance, French television interviews between leading politicians and broadcast journalists often seem tame compared to the cut-and-thrust of their equivalents in other western democracies. In France, elite politicians are frequently given a platform from which to deliver their views, with the journalists posing questions but rarely putting the politicians on the spot or challenging their version of events.

The French President in particular is frequently treated with kid gloves in formal television interviews on the major networks, being fed 'soft' questions rather than subjected to rigorous interrogation. Frequently, more than one journalist is involved in the interview and in practice the President's advisers decide which journalists will be selected, often choosing the news anchors of the main free-to-air networks. These journalists are generalists and lack the specific expertise (e.g. in economic matters or foreign affairs) to ask probing questions even if they were minded to do so. Going head-to-head with the main evening news anchors from TF1 and France 2 can hardly be considered a trial by fire for an experienced politician such as Sarkozy, as was evident in the televised interview from the United Nations in New York in September 2009 when the two interviewers – Laurence Ferrari (TF1) and David Pujadas (France 2) – failed to probe the President on economic and foreign policy issues.

Journalists may even be given advice regarding the subjects 'on which the President would welcome the opportunity of speaking' (Hayward and Wright, 2002: 93). When in the annual ritual of the 14 July interview in 2000 the television journalists moved away from the agreed terrain to ask some potentially tough questions about allegations of financial wrongdoing at City Hall during Chirac's period as Mayor of Paris, the President refused to respond. Interestingly, the journalists did not pursue the issue: 'It is not part of French culture to ask the same question five times. If the President will not reply, he will not reply' (Hayward and Wright, 2002: 93). Only occasionally are the rules of polite engagement infringed, as when Patrick Poivre d'Arvor, the TF1 news anchor at the time, asked Sarkozy prior to his first G8 summit meeting in 2007 if he did not feel like a 'nervous little boy going into the big boys' playground'. It was reported that Sarkozy had not appreciated the way in which the question had been framed by the interviewer.

What explains this journalistic subordination in broadcast interviews? One possible reason might be thought to lie in the institutional status of the President as head of state rather than head of government. In the Gaullian tradition the President of the Fifth Republic is supposed to be above party political conflict. Yet the US President is also the head of state and embodiment of the nation, but this does not stop the American broadcast media from on occasions adopting a critical stance towards him in interviews. Nor is the reason to be found in explanations based on overt political control. The public-private division in the ownership of the broadcasting media is not an important factor either: there is little appreciable difference between the journalists of TF1 and those employed by France Télévisions in their interviews with the President.

One factor might simply be fear on the part of television journalists that they may end up being pushed to one side within their news organization if they step out of line. Another explanation might be sympathy on the part of the journalist towards the politician, either out of political conviction or opportunistic careerism. A quite different explanation, however, may lie with audience expectations. The politician is an elected representative of the Republic and a certain formal courtesy, even hierarchical deference, on the part of the journalist is simply part of the cultural protocol. It is not that French television journalists are incapable of being assertive, as has been clear in interviews with Jean-Marie Le Pen, where the leader of the National Front has been subjected to a tougher style of questioning than that accorded politicians of both mainstream left and right. Nor is it that French audiences are averse to critical journalistic commentary: there is a market for a range of mocking media treatment of politicians, including cartoon books (*bandes dessinées*), newspapers such as *Le Canard enchaîné*, the satirical puppet-based sketch show *Les Guignols de l'Info* on Canal+ and user-generated content on the web. Yet in the context of a formal television interview with mainstream political leaders, most notably the President, French journalists often prefer to pull their punches. While in terms of content the audience is not best served by this practice, it may be that an adversarial relationship between journalist and political leader in a formal television interview would quite simply not be acceptable to many French viewers.

This rather cosy relationship between elite journalists and the political executive in broadcast interviews sometimes (but by no means always) sharply contrasts with those televised occasions when politicians are interviewed directly by members of the public. In April 2005, President Chirac met with representatives of the nation's youth in a television programme on TF1 as part of the referendum debate on the proposed ratification of the EU constitution. Chirac was clearly discomfited by the content and tone of the young people's questions to him, eventually declaring with considerable bafflement and exasperation that he did not comprehend their critical attitude towards Europe: 'I don't understand you' ('*Je ne vous comprends pas*'). In this programme Chirac looked quite obviously ill-prepared for a substantive debate and symbolically out of touch with the concerns of this important tranche of the electorate.

News management under President Sarkozy

The victory of Sarkozy in the 2007 presidential election has had striking consequences for the news management activities of the political executive. Sarkozy has dominated media coverage not just of domestic politics, but also of those European and international political issues, such as the global financial crisis, in which France has been closely involved as a policy actor and which tend to be covered by the French media through a predominantly national prism that focuses on the key leadership role of the President. His efforts to manage the media have been the subject of considerable journalistic attention and critical commentary (Duhamel and Field, 2008; Veillet, 2009), including a study where his highly mediated public profile earned him the appropriate title of *le téléprésident* (Jost and

Muzet, 2008) and two books that have compared his relationship with the media in France to that of Silvio Berlusconi in Italy (Musso, 2008; 2009b).

Sarkozy's mediated omnipresence is the result of the combination of four analytically distinct but in practice interrelated and overlapping types of media content: first, top-down political communication that is wholly under the control of the President and his advisers, such as formal, set-piece speeches, televised addresses to the nation, the official Elysée website with its text and imagery (www.elysee.fr/) and the President's own Facebook page; second, two-way public communication between the President and journalists or the President and members of the public, including television news interviews, press conferences and broadcast debate programmes with audience participation; third, professional journalistic reportage and commentary about the President available via a range of traditional outlets in the press, radio and television, as well as on the online sites of these established mainstream media; and finally a range of alternative, participatory and social media content on the internet, including independent news websites, political blogs, citizen journalism and user-generated content. From the perspective of the political executive, the more one descends this categorical hierarchy, the less control can effectively be exerted over the mediation of its message in the public sphere.

Sarkozy's reputation for close attention to proactive news management long preceded his 2007 election victory (Artufel and Duroux, 2006). For instance, in the period immediately following Chirac's second presidential victory in 2002, after a campaign that had placed crime and public insecurity at the heart of the election agenda, Sarkozy in his new role as Minister of the Interior orchestrated a series of police raids on suspected criminals. These highly mediatized events were designed to help support his image as a strong 'law and order' politician, to boost his popularity with the core right-wing electorate, to attract voters away from the extreme-right National Front and to reassure the public that the government was actively addressing its concerns on crime (Muzet, 2006).

The news media were for the most part willing to cooperate in these ventures, not so much out of partisan support for Sarkozy (although that was a possible factor in the case of some outlets), but rather because the stories conformed to news values of human interest, drama and topicality, while the pictures had strong visual impact. In addition, the coverage assisted the media in their exercise of self-exculpation in the face of accusations that their negative and disproportionate focus on crime stories during the election campaign prior to the first ballot had contributed to a climate of insecurity among voters and had thus in spectacular fashion aided the passage of Le Pen to the decisive second round (Perrineau and Ysmal, 2003; Gaffney, 2004).

An important aspect of Sarkozy's approach to news management in the construction of his status as a serious presidential candidate (*présidentiable*) was the way that he fostered his relationship with political reporters and correspondents as key actors in the process of news gathering and production. Sarkozy cultivated the interdependent exchange relationship, using a mix of 'hard cop/soft cop' behaviour in his interactions with journalists. He acquired a reputation for intimidation and bullying, threatening to report them to their proprietors with whom he was frequently on the closest of terms (Magoudi, 2009). Yet he was also capable of trying to befriend journalists, addressing them by their first names and frequently using the more intimate form of 'you' (*tu* instead of *vous*) as part of a process of cooption and seduction that many clearly found difficult to resist (Ridet, 2008). While in the exercise of his presidential function Sarkozy's direct contact with journalists has been reduced, his record of bullying and evidence of temperamental instability are a constant reminder to journalists of the potentially dangerous nature of the power relationship with the Elysée, which can only be exacerbated by the knowledge that their profession has become a highly precarious source of employment.

Emulating the news media strategies and techniques used by executive leaders in other major western democracies (Pfetsch, 2008), Sarkozy's professional approach to political communication in his capacity as a minister, party leader and presidential candidate was then applied to the media management functions of agenda building and issue framing undertaken by the Elysée after he became President. Sarkozy has mobilized the resources of primary definition available to the President and used (some would say abused) the supremacy of his position in a holistic, strategic approach to news management. In so doing he has adopted a largely contrasting approach towards the private and public sectors. With regard to private media, Sarkozy has emphasized an exchange style relationship with owners, senior management and news editors, while in respect of public media he has used more traditional methods of top-down control and political instrumentalization (Hallin and Mancini, 2004: 37).

Two integral aspects of this strategy have already been referred to in previous chapters, but are worth briefly alluding to again. The first is the way in which, well before becoming President, Sarkozy fostered privileged links with owners of mainstream commercial media outlets in both the press and broadcasting (see Chapter 3). In addition, some senior managers and news editors, including Nicolas Beytout (head of media at the LVMH group), Jean-Claude Dassier (head of news at TF1 until July 2009) and Jean-Pierre Elkabbach (Lagardère group and former boss of the radio station Europe 1) have been generally regarded as committed Sarkozy supporters (Quivy, 2009). These highly personal relationships with media proprietors and senior news managers would seem to give Sarkozy an inbuilt advantage in the form of privileged access to define the news agenda and influence issue framing.

Two caveats are, however, important in this context. First, it should be remembered that by no means all media proprietors wish to intervene in editorial decision-making; sometimes a media owner adopts a hands-off stance, as in the case of Edouard de Rothschild's ownership of the national daily *Libération* since he took over the title in 2005. Moreover, where owners try to interfere their intervention frequently comes up against newsroom resistance, as Dassault discovered at *Le Figaro*. Second, one should be mindful that deterministic explanations of news production that focus primarily on the dimension of proprietorial control oversimplify the way in which news agendas are formed and issues framed on a day-to-day basis. Evidence from across western democracies shows that the routine operationalization of news values may result in critical news reporting of politicians even in those outlets where owners (and top management) are favourably predisposed towards them (Schudson, 2000).

In the case of Sarkozy, the overwhelmingly critical media coverage in late 2009 of the President's attempt to have his son Jean elected as head of the public body responsible for the development of the business district to the west of Paris is a case in point, with even those media outlets generally supportive of the President reflecting the widespread indignation among his conservative electorate at the perceived abuse of presidential influence. In short, the impact of the interdependence between Sarkozy and media owners/management needs to be investigated on a case-by-case basis rather than be assumed to work consistently in the President's favour in terms of reportage and commentary. In addition, although its importance should not be ignored, this interdependence at the level of media owners needs to be seen as only one facet of a complex web of interlinkages that the President has constructed with the news media.

The second feature of Sarkozy's news media management strategy already touched upon is the reform of public service broadcasting enacted in 2009 (see Chapter 4). In contrast to his exchange relationship with commercial media proprietors, Sarkozy has sought to impose a more traditional, top-down form of political control over public broadcasting. In reasserting direct presidential responsibility for the process of appointment of the chief executives of France Télévisions and Radio France, Sarkozy was effectively sending a message to all staff, including journalists, to be on their guard. While it could be argued that this aspect of public broadcasting reform does not represent direct Gaullist-style intervention in the day-to-day operational process of news production, it undoubtedly contributes to the creation of a defensive atmosphere in the newsrooms of the public service organizations, which in the eyes of many journalists employed there are under siege and susceptible to political instrumentalization.

The resources for primary definition structurally embedded in the office of the presidency – institutional centrality, political authority and electoral legitimacy – have been fully exploited by Sarkozy since his accession to the supreme office. In so doing, he has relied on the advice of communication advisers and media consultants within his personal entourage at the Elysée. Currently an important member of the President's cabinet, Franck Louvrier began working as a communication adviser to Sarkozy in the Gaullist Party back in 1997 and has performed this function during most of the latter's subsequent political career – as mayor of Neuilly-sur-Seine, Minister of the Interior, leader of the UMP, presidential candidate and finally President. Louvrier was an integral part of Sarkozy's 2007 election campaign team (Achilli, 2006, 2007) and is one of the inner circle of advisers that meets at the Elysée to discuss and plan the day's agenda (Duplan and Pellegrin, 2008: 123–45). Another member of the Elysée cabinet is Catherine Pégard, a former leading journalist for the weekly newsmagazine *Le Point*. Other Elysée insiders with media experience, though not formally part of the President's cabinet, include Alain Minc, former chairman of the board at the influential daily newspaper, *Le Monde*, and Pierre Giacometti, former head of the opinion polling organization, Ipsos, who now runs a consultancy company that provides advice in public communication. At the end of 2009, *Le Parisien-Aujourd'hui en France* revealed that the Elysée's communication budget, which covered more than 50 staff, was of the order of €7.5 million, of which nearly €2 million related to specially commissioned opinion polls and €500,000 was devoted to the President's internet site (D'Almeida and Delporte, 2010: 316).

In many respects since becoming President, Sarkozy has tried to address the structural defects in the organization of the political executive so as to improve its efficacy in news management (and, of course, in policy-making). He has concentrated decision-making at the Elysée, sought to limit the contribution of Prime Minister Fillon and other government ministers to that of a largely supporting role and has in effect maintained his former position as leader of the majority parliamentary party, the UMP. Sarkozy has thrust himself into the public spotlight at every possible opportunity and his mediatized interventionism across a range of policy areas has led to him being frequently, if rather misleadingly, described by some commentators as a 'hyperpresident' (Maigret, 2008). Yet despite this dominant leadership role, fragmentation within the executive and in its relations with the governing majority in parliament has persisted, including conflicting messages in the news media from President and Prime Minister on key issues such as the reduction of France's budgetary deficit (Bouilhaguet, 2010). Like its predecessors the Sarkozy presidency has also seen its fair share of ministerial divisions played out in the news media. While sometimes this is simply the result of a lack of coordination of executive communication, frequently ministers and their officials have used the news media to brief against each other. At its worst this may even involve senior and junior ministers from the same department falling out in public, as happened for instance at the foreign affairs ministry between Bernard Kouchner and Rama Yade until the latter was moved in 2009.

Sarkozy has taken many initiatives designed to maintain a prominent news profile. His proactive approach to news management has been particularly important given the way he has shaped his exercise of the presidential function. In dominating the political terrain and policy agenda since his accession to the supreme office, Sarkozy has also occupied media space, going further than any of his predecessors in his efforts to manage the news agenda on a daily basis. An important aspect of this proactive approach has been the high level of presidential access to television, with Sarkozy 'going public' via television on a routine basis.

For more than the first two years of his presidency Sarkozy consistently came out top in terms of appearances on the main evening news programmes of the five principal national television channels (TF1, France 2, France 3, Canal+ and M6) (INA, 2009). This televisual blitzkrieg stood in marked contrast to the experience of his two immediate predecessors, Mitterrand and Chirac, who on the advice of their communication adviser, Jacques Pilhan, believed that appearing relatively infrequently on television amplified the impact of their message when they did speak (Bazin, 2009).

As in the early months of the Blair premiership in the UK (Kuhn, 2007), Sarkozy has also kept the news agenda moving on a fast-rolling basis in a way that has left journalists little time to follow up presidential initiatives in a sustained critical fashion. Moreover, in a break with the tradition that presidential advisers maintain a low public profile, key officials such as Claude Guéant, Sarkozy's right-hand man as general secretary of the Elysée, appeared directly on the broadcast media in the early months of the presidency to explain and defend policy proposals (Joffrin, 2008: 45). The strategic objective of all this activity was to dictate the media's framing of the new presidency.

In this context, news management served various functions: to educate voters regarding the necessity of reform measures, to explain the substance of the proposed reforms and to counter any objections from political opponents – in short, to use the technique of 'storytelling' to construct a coherent holistic narrative around the theme of reform (Salmon, 2007). Moreover, for Sarkozy, mediated presidential communication is not simply an explanatory support for policy action, but can play an important role in setting the policy agenda – a shock tactic to kick-start the policy process – as, for example, in the presidential announcement at the start of 2008 that advertising would be withdrawn as a revenue stream for the public television company. In this respect Sarkozy is not just a news manager, but a news-maker: he is a master at creating events specifically to grab media headlines.

For at least the first two years of his presidency, Sarkozy's occupation of media space was helped by two political factors, one outside and the other within his control. The first was the disarray and internal turmoil of the main party of opposition, the Parti Socialiste, following the defeat of its candidate, Ségolène Royal, in the 2007 presidential election and the subsequent resignation of the party's leader, François Hollande (Perrineau, 2008). The highly divisive struggle to succeed Hollande and the initial inability of the new leader, Martine Aubry, to impose her authority across the party significantly reduced the efficacy of the PS as a possible counter primary definer for the news media. When in November 2008 Sarkozy was briefly displaced as number one personality in television news, it was only because the French media were focusing their attention on the internecine warfare between Aubry and Royal for the leadership of the PS. The second was the President's strategy of *ouverture* (opening out), whereby opposition politicians, such as Bernard Kouchner and Jean-Pierre Jouyet, and figures from ethnic minorities and civil society, such as

Rachida Dati and Martin Hirsch, were given posts in the government and executive agencies – an initiative that both destabilized Sarkozy's political opponents by blurring traditional partisan faultlines and attracted favourable media headlines, at least in the short term.

In addition, Sarkozy has also benefited from the prevalent news media culture in France, whereby the French media, especially television news, tend to be followers rather than leaders in the process of agenda construction – they are secondary rather than primary definers. Yet as Sarkozy's term in office evolved and the 2012 presidential contest came closer, not even the best efforts of the Elysée could prevent the news media from highlighting the President's electoral unpopularity as registered in regular opinion polls, the various movements of industrial unrest that continued to plague France and the increasing sense of unease within the ranks of his party. By the spring of 2010, Sarkozy was continuing to make the news in France, but the prevalent sociopolitical conditions had made news management by the executive more difficult than at any previous period of his presidency. As a result, the Elysée had lost a significant degree of control – provisionally at least – over the mediatized framing of his presidential performance.

Conclusion

Within the historical context of presidential rule in the Fifth Republic, news management by the executive is not an invention of President Sarkozy. There is in particular a long tradition of political control of news output in the broadcasting media that stretches back over 50 years to the start of the de Gaulle presidency. Yet executive news management has altered immeasurably in the intervening period. First, the task itself has become much more complicated because of the huge expansion of broadcast and online media and the transition to a 24/7 rolling news culture. There are not just more outlets than in the 1960s, but processes of news gathering, production and distribution have been revolutionized with the advent of digital media and the internet, including the reporting of many events in (almost) real time. These developments make it considerably more difficult for the political executive to exert effective management over the news media than in the days of a single state monopoly television channel with one main evening news programme. Second, the strategic response of the executive to this more complex news media environment of necessity needs to be more multi-faceted than in the past. Aspects of top-down Gaullist-style control are still evident under Sarkozy, notably in the case of public broadcasting. However, he has also incorporated into his approach to media management elements of exchange, primary definition and storytelling in a complex web of interlinkages between the news media and the Elysée.

Since becoming President, Sarkozy has dominated news media coverage in France: not only has he been the object of more news stories than any other national politician, but to a significant extent he has also influenced the framing of his presidential tenure – for good and ill. While in terms of political power he may not be a 'hyperpresident', he has certainly rendered the presidency 'hypervisibile' (Duhamel, 2009). Sarkozy believes in the agenda-setting power of the media to shape public perceptions and has therefore devoted more time and greater attention to news management than any of his predecessors at the Elysée. This reflects his own conception of mediatized executive leadership and the importance he attaches to public communication, especially via television. It is often commented that he is the first President of the Fifth Republic whose whole life has been lived during the television age. There is therefore a strong personal element underpinning Sarkozy's news management activities; a different incumbent of the presidential office might well have behaved differently.

Yet it is also clear that in terms of news management any incumbent of the Elysée is now to a significant extent influenced, even constrained, by certain structural factors. Some of these are national – such as the institutional arrangements of the political system, the configuration of the media landscape and the specificities of the political communication culture, including the norms and values that underpin the relationship between elite politicians and journalists. Others are transnational in scope, including the growing importance of the leadership dimension in both presidential and parliamentary systems across western democracies, the transfer of news management practices across democratic political executives and the highly competitive nature of contemporary media markets. From this perspective the attention paid to news management by the current French President may be seen as largely driven by factors outside of not just his control but that of any potential incumbent of the Elysée. As a result, the French executive under Sarkozy is emulating many of the agenda building and issue framing techniques practised by political executives in other leading western democracies (Kurtz, 1998; Heffernan, 2006; Kernell, 2006; Pfetsch, 2008).

6 THE MEDIA, IMAGE PROJECTION AND CELEBRITY POLITICS

- The traditional French approach
- Politicians: from projecting an image to marketing the personal
- Mediatizing intimacy
- Sex, health and money
- Royal and Sarkozy
- Conclusion

While news management concentrates on the activities of sources to structure the news agenda and frame issues, image projection focuses on the mediated transmission of personal values, capabilities and competences in what politicians hope will be a coherent and convincing public persona to present to the electorate. In all western democracies a positive media image is important to elite politicians, as well as being an integral part of the practice of executive leadership (Helms, 2008). With the help of techniques adopted from the fields of public relations, product marketing and opinion polling, the function of image construction in a highly mediatized culture of self-promotion and symbolic communication has thus become part of the common currency of elite political activities across all advanced societies (Negrine *et al.*, 2007; Negrine, 2008). In these respects at least, contemporary France is no exception to the rule.

Yet until recently France was widely regarded as quite distinct, even exceptional, among western democracies in a key aspect of image projection: namely, the way in which a clear boundary between the private and public spheres was maintained in both politicians' mediated communication and journalists' coverage of political issues and personalities. French exceptionalism in this respect was underpinned by the norms of the national political culture, with its particular mix of Roman Catholic and secular republican values, and by the universalist rules of the one and indivisible republic that posited a certain ideal-type relationship between state and citizen based on a formal codification of the rights and responsibilities of each. It is now apparent that such a well-delineated boundary no longer exists in either the realm of political communication (content released into the public sphere under the control of politicians) or the world of journalism (information and comment mediated by journalists). Instead, recent changes in media and political behaviour, particularly associated with Sarkozy's image management and the publicization of intimate aspects of his private life, appear to constitute evidence that here too France has fallen significantly into line with the norms and practices of celebrity politics found in other western democracies (Street, 2003).

In considering the mediatization of politicians in contemporary France – including the two main contenders in the 2007 presidential election, Sarkozy and Royal – this chapter focuses on selected features of image projection and the changing public/private interface. The chapter is divided into five sections. The first outlines the traditional French approach to the management of the public/private boundary in the mediatization of elite politicians. The second section looks at the development of image projection and in particular at the way in which politicians have increasingly accepted the desirability of marketing aspects of their private lives via the media for electoral purposes. Part three concentrates on the role of the news media in these developments, in particular the factors that are underpinning a more personalized and even intimate form of coverage of politicians in the contemporary era. Section four examines three areas of media coverage where negotiation of the public/private interface has long proved particularly sensitive: sex, health and money. The final section considers the mediatizaton of Royal and Sarkozy in the run-up to the 2007 presidential contest and of Sarkozy as President after his election victory.

The traditional French approach

The traditional French approach to the management of the public/private interface in the mediatization of elite politicians was based on a shared understanding of certain practices and norms of behaviour among three sets of actors involved in the process of political information and communication: first, politicians and their support staff, including communication advisers, advertising consultants, image-makers and opinion pollsters; second, media personnel including owners, news editors and journalists; and, finally, the public as citizens, voters and media users. This understanding was based on the following elements. First, politicians did not seek to project their private lives into the public realm. Instead, they maintained a distinction between their private lives and their public careers, with the result that they did not seek to exploit the former for electoral gain. Second, the news media did not intrude into the private lives of politicians. Indeed, even where it could be argued that certain aspects of what politicians sought to retain in the private sphere might well have merited media coverage in the public interest, news outlets frequently imposed on themselves an embargo of self-restraint. In particular, the relative absence of a well-implanted sensationalist or tabloid culture among mainstream news media had notable consequences for the content, style and tone of political reportage. Moreover, apart from a few minority outlets, there was also less 'attack journalism' against leading political figures of the kind that has become a feature of mainstream political journalism in the UK and USA (Sabato, 2000). Finally, French public opinion did not consider a politician's private life to be an appropriate matter for media scrutiny or a relevant criterion in electoral evaluation. The qualities required for political office were not equated in the minds of the electorate with personal probity: for instance, sexual infidelity on the part of a politician was not seen as equatable with untrustworthiness in the public domain.

This shared understanding between politicians, news media and the public was in turn shored up by a fourth factor, namely the existence of some of the toughest privacy legislation to be found in any western society. Under the terms of a law to protect individual privacy introduced in 1970, a high level of legal protection from media intrusion was accorded the personal lives of all citizens, with politicians being among the main beneficiaries of the new legislation. In France, politicians who considered that their private lives had been infringed by media exposure could seek recompense in the courts. If found guilty, the media outlet could be fined, compelled to pay damages and forced to publish a retraction. In turn, the knowledge of the existence of this body of law had an impact on the behaviour of the news media, encouraging caution, circumspection and even self-censorship. A combination of elite political behaviour, media practices, sociocultural norms and legal provisions ensured, therefore, that France differed significantly from other western societies, including the UK and the USA, in the ways in which the private lives of politicians were mediatized into the public sphere.

The argument of this chapter is that the first two elements of this traditional approach – politicians' self-denial and media self-restraint – have to a significant extent collapsed, possibly irreparably, while the third – public indifference to politicians' private behaviour – is under some strain. Only the legal framework protecting individual privacy is still fully in place, although even here the judicial process inevitably has to take some account of changing elite behaviour, media practices and social norms in forming a judgement. As a result, there is now significant normative confusion surrounding attempts to establish an agreed dividing line between the public and the private in both politicians' mediated communication and journalists' political coverage.

This confusion is a product of mutually reinforcing changes in the interdependent relationship between the three sets of actors. Politicians pay increasing attention to – and in some cases are apparently fixated with – the mediatization of their image as part of their electoral self-promotion and at least some of them are willing to exploit their private lives to this end. At the same time, they are also keen to hold back certain aspects of their personal lives from the glare of media exposure. Sections of the mainstream news media have become more intrusive than before in revealing aspects of the private lives of politicians to public scrutiny, as competition for audiences and advertising revenue has intensified. Finally, the French public have been exposed to more information about the private lives of some of their leading politicians and this has stimulated an appetite for such information among at least some sections of the electorate.

Politicians: from projecting an image to marketing the personal

A concern by French politicians to manage their image is by no means a recent phenomenon. Back in the 1960s de Gaulle was one of the pioneers among French politicians in his systematic use of television for the purpose of symbolic image construction. For instance, during the early years of his presidency, when the political agenda was dominated by the Algerian conflict, de Gaulle was aware that his appearance on television in military uniform during crisis events sent out as clear a message to the audience as any part of his written text. In the 1965 presidential election, conventionally regarded as the first 'television election' in France, one of the opposition candidates to de Gaulle, Jean Lecanuet, is usually cited as the trend-setter in the importation of American-style image-based advertising into French campaigning (Bongrand, 2006: 51–62). Subsequent presidential elections saw the routinization of such practices, especially by the major candidates.

Mitterrand is the classic example of a French politician successfully undergoing an image makeover to meet the demands of televised presidential politics (Cole, 1994). At the presentational level his appearance was improved by wearing darker, well-cut suits and having his teeth crowned. More fundamentally, Mitterrand learnt to market himself for electoral purposes. While as the challenger in the 1981 presidential election he presented himself as representing a left-wing choice in favour of a fairer and more egalitarian society, as the incumbent in the 1988 contest he presented himself in a classic Gaullian position as the head of state above the party political fray. Symbolically he wrote a *Lettre à tous les français* ('Letter to all French people') in a literary evocation of the qualities of statesmanship and gravitas that he wished to project in contrast to the popular image of his challenger, Chirac, as partisan and opportunistic. Mitterrand's campaign posters in 1988 communicated the same consensual message: '*La France Unie*' ('France United') and '*Génération Mitterrand*' ('Mitterrand generation'). He was referred to as '*Dieu*' ('God') by his entourage, yet also affectionately called '*Tonton*' ('uncle') in popular discourse. During his 14 years in power he did not just acquire the status of an international statesman, but rather actively cultivated this image: one of the iconic photos in this respect is that of Mitterrand standing hand-in-hand with the German Chancellor, Helmut Kohl, at the monument to First World War dead at Verdun in 1984 in a powerful symbol of Franco-German reconciliation.

Like de Gaulle, therefore, Mitterrand understood the importance of symbolic imagery in the media age. The rose-laying ceremony at the graves of national heroes in the Panthéon at the start of his first presidential term and the 1988 campaign video clip showing a series of French icons across 200 years of post-revolutionary history showed Mitterrand as a figure steeped in tradition. His well-publicized identification with various architectural projects in and around Paris, including the Louvre Pyramid and the new national library, revealed him to be a man in the vanguard of the new. He presented himself at ease in the metropolitan world of the arts and culture, but also made much of his links with rural France. The mediated image of Mitterrand was, in short, complex and multi-faceted.

In their image projection, however, neither de Gaulle nor Mitterrand sought to make political capital out of their personal lives. De Gaulle's campaigning in elections and referenda focused on what he regarded as the key issues facing the country. While the strength of his views and his self-belief were rarely in doubt, he never sought to make any association between his political career and his private life in his campaigns. Moreover, during de Gaulle's presidency his wife Yvonne remained largely out of the public gaze. Similarly, Mitterrand's political image was overwhelmingly constructed around his public persona, although in his case this was an enforced choice because of the complicated nature of his long-running extra-marital relationship (see pp. 132–3). In the intervening years some other major candidates for the presidency, including Raymond Barre (1988), Edouard Balladur (1995) and François Bayrou (2002, 2007), followed this tradition of keeping their spouse and family largely out of the public spotlight.

In contrast, many elite politicians now place selected aspects of their private lives into the public sphere under conditions that they try to control as much as possible. In the 1974 presidential campaign, the youthful Valéry Giscard d'Estaing was the first major candidate to use his wife and family as an integral part of his electoral marketing in an attempt to humanize his image as a technocratic egg-head. He also tried to present himself as a man of the people by being photographed in a football strip and playing the accordion (though not simultaneously). Ironically, by the end of his presidency in 1981 he had become the subject of criticism in some media for his alleged monarchical pretensions.

In the run-up to the 2002 presidential contest Jacques Chirac benefited from the direct input of his wife, Bernadette, who pitched in to aid her husband's re-election through the publication of a best-selling book that revealed aspects of their relationship as a couple (Chirac, 2001), while she also made highly popular appearances on television chat shows. In this context Claude Chirac fulfilled a dual role. As Chirac's daughter she contributed to the image of her father as a family man, who performed the role of happy grandfather for the exclusive magazine pictures. She was also the President's communications adviser (Léger, 2007). In the 2002 campaign she controlled media access to Chirac, stage-managed photo opportunities to provide the best pictures and limited impromptu comments by the candidate in response to journalists' questions.

The mediatization by politicians of aspects of their private lives usually forms part of a broader process of political marketing, electoral positioning and image projection to create a sympathetic and well-rounded political persona with which voters can empathize. An emphasis on personal character traits – such as honesty, integrity, competence and sincerity – is combined with political statements, issue stances and policy proposals in what is designed to be an integrated electoral brand. This is then communicated to the electorate via mainstream, niche and online media and is subject to constant refinement in the 'long campaign' between elections in response to focus group feedback and opinion poll findings.

This mediatization of the personal is designed to take the politician out of the stage-managed sphere of the formal political arena, dominated by prepared speeches and planned interviews. By bringing into the public domain selected aspects of their private lives, politicians seek to display their fabricated ordinariness to voters: their favourite foods, literary tastes, superstitions and phobias are all exposed to public view. The not particularly subliminal message is: 'This is the real me; I am like you; I share your concerns; you can safely entrust me with your vote.' Yet, of course, this content is just as professionally packaged as any other aspect of a politician's media activities. Thus, the marketing of the political persona is now accompanied by the fabrication of the 'authentic person' – 'pictures of X as you've never seen them before'.

To criticize this as 'fake authenticity' presupposes that mediatization allows the possibility of the 'real person' to be shown. Yet by definition mediatization normally provides only a simulacrum of reality; the 'real person' is almost always at one step removed from the camera's intrusive presence (except when the camera is hidden, in which case the resultant images can be revealing). Most of the time, politicians, media and audiences are trapped in the illusory politics of spectacle, although perhaps it is more accurate to say that they are often willing accomplices to the maintenance of the illusion, which is usually accepted for what it is – manufactured imagery, even if, despite its transparent artificiality, such coverage does occasionally provide interesting snippets of information on the 'private person' behind the public role.

There are clear political reasons why politicians in contemporary France have been tempted to go down this route. The introduction in 1962 of direct election to the presidency by a single national constituency of voters increased media and public attention on the personal characteristics and leadership skills of candidates to the supreme office. The nationwide take-up of television during the de Gaulle presidency allowed politicians, especially among the ranks of the governing majority, to enter voters' living rooms via the 'small screen'. Thus, the advent and routinization of television as a mass medium in the 1960s ushered in fundamental changes to the nature of election campaigning and the mediatization of politics that are still in evidence today. In addition, the expansion of opinion polling further encouraged the personalization of presidential electoral competition, with respondents being asked to comment on the personal qualities of candidates. More recently, the routinization of a French version of presidential primaries has pushed further in the same direction, with candidates from within the same party having to differentiate themselves from their rivals to secure the votes of party members. Finally, in recent years there has been a considerable degree of ideological convergence across the mainstream of the party spectrum, while within parties, such as the Socialists, factionalism is now based increasingly on personal rivalries rather than sharply contrasting policy stances (Clift, 2003).

Against this background, mainstream elite politicians need to make themselves distinct from their competitors. One aspect of this 'product differentiation' is to focus on personal qualities (such as trust) that have a political currency and to project these qualities through media publicity, both controlled – for example, in books, advertising and speeches – and open – for instance, in press conferences and television interviews. Through the broadcast and online media in particular, politicians have become part of the private lives of ordinary citizens; their constant on-screen presence brings about the preconditions for the creation of 'virtual intimacy' that is such an integral feature of contemporary mediatized politics. Media-conscious politicians recognize that television is a medium of seduction as well as of persuasion and have adapted their communication strategies accordingly, while they have also wanted to exploit the communicative possibilities of online media.

Those who have failed to adapt their communication style in presidential contests have performed badly in electoral terms, with their lack of the common touch contributing to (without necessarily being the principal cause of) their first round defeat at the ballot box. Jospin's catastrophic failure in the 2002 presidential election, when he failed to proceed to the second round, is a useful example in this context (Pingaud, 2002). By 2002 Jospin's image in public opinion was already well established: he was regarded as honest, credible and competent, but also austere and rather cold. A believer in the power of analytic argument, Jospin was not particularly adept at snappy soundbite politics. Rational and didactic in television interviews, he lacked the personable qualities of a natural campaigner. The advertising specialist Jacques Séguéla, who had previously helped Mitterrand in his successful presidential campaigns, offered advice to the Socialist candidate about the content, phrasing and body language of his television appearances, including the injunction to smile more and be relaxed – but largely to no avail.

Politicians have also contributed to, as well as being affected by, the 'desacralization' or demystification of political leadership in the contemporary era. The 'heroic leadership' style of the first President of the Fifth Republic, Charles de Gaulle, now seems anachronistic in an age when voters know more about the daily lives of their leading politicians and show little deference towards them. Mainstream politicians are often regarded as out of touch with ordinary voters' concerns and disconnected from society. In response, instead of presenting themselves as part of an elite operating above the heads of the electorate, party leaders and presidential candidates now see gains to be made by cultivating their proximity to the concerns of 'ordinary voters'. For example, despite his clear fascination with luxury goods and the world of the rich, during the 2007 campaign Sarkozy appeared with several figures from contemporary popular culture in an attempt to portray himself as an ordinary man of the people.

Meanwhile, as traditional social cleavages have diminished in importance, French voters have become less unconditionally committed supporters of a particular political party, with more voters behaving like consumers in a marketplace, making their electoral choices pragmatically, based on judgements about issue salience and candidates' values. Voters, especially the young, have also become more difficult to mobilize (notwithstanding the high turnout in the 2007 presidential election). Many have become disenchanted with political elites and turned off from electoral politics. In these circumstances, politicians cannot simply rely on activating voters' ingrained political loyalties by appealing to their allegiance to a particular political tradition. Nor is it sufficient to try to persuade voters through a process of rational engagement; it is also necessary to seduce them by appealing to their emotions. In these circumstances, there may be an electoral pay-off to be gained by a politician who can present himself or herself as an 'outsider', more in touch with the concerns of the electorate. Royal did this in the preparation of her candidacy for the 2007 presidential elections, where she distanced herself from the traditional elite figures within the Socialist Party in an example of what has been called 'spatial leadership' (Foley, 2000).

Mediatizing intimacy

While one of the drivers contributing to the blurring of the public-private divide has come from the marketing activities of politicians, another is the product of changes in the news media landscape, including increased competition among outlets, the advent of a 24/7 news culture and a trend towards voyeuristic media genres. There is, therefore, clearly a media 'push' factor, encouraging the mediatization of personal intimacy by French politicians and its coverage by various media outlets in the so-called *pipolisation* (celebritization) of French politics (Dakhlia, 2008). Developments in three media sectors in particular – print media, television and online – can be linked to the changing nature of the public/private interface in contemporary political communication and journalism.

Among print media, in contrast to the crisis of general information newspapers, the strong sales figures of celebrity magazines (*la presse people*) such as *Voici* and *Gala*, competing with more established photonews weeklies such as *Paris Match* and *VSD*, are particularly noteworthy features of the contemporary media landscape (Lutaud and Dromard, 2006). The annual circulation of celebrity magazines increased from 96 million copies in 2003 to 136 million in 2008 (D'Almeida and Delporte, 2010: 356). Every week about 2.5 million people in France buy a 'celebrity' publication and more than 13 million are reputed to read them (see Table 6.1). Cover stories featuring high profile politicians frequently increase circulation figures. In turn, the popularity of photonews and celebrity magazines makes them attractive vehicles for advertisers, while allowing politicians to target sections of the electorate who are low users of general information newspapers and traditional broadcasting genres of political coverage.

Table 6.1   Weekly magazine sales figures (2009) (in 000s)

Photonews magazines	
Paris Match	611
Le Figaro Magazine	424
Le Monde Magazine	258
VSD	152
Celebrity magazines	
Closer	466
Public	428
Voici	408
Gala	268

Source: Organisme de Justification de la Diffusion (2010)

Both Sarkozy couples (Nicolas/Cécilia and Nicolas/Carla Bruni) have featured on the front cover and inside pages of Gala and Paris Match on several occasions in the past few years, with carefully arranged photos purporting to show the 'authentic persona' behind the professional politician. The French public's appetite for information about the intimate lives of their politicians has even affected the journalism of mainstream news media. For example, in the summer of 2007 the weekly news magazine Le Nouvel Observateur featured Cécilia on its front cover and devoted no fewer than ten pages to the so-called 'enigma' of France's new first lady: 'Woman of power or fragile spouse?' (Barjon and Déserts, 2007). The answer turned out to be neither.

The expansion in the supply of television in the digital age has provided those interested in politics with more sources of information, including dedicated rolling news and parliamentary channels, but it also allows the uninterested to zap across swathes of politics-free output. Traditional political debate programmes have become less common on French television since the 1990s, with such programmes no longer regarded by television management as audience pullers – rather the reverse. The decline in this genre of programming has been particularly marked in the commercial sector. Outside of election campaigns, TF1 and M6 have virtually given up on coverage of national politics except as part of news programmes. Moreover, although they may have greater regulatory obligations than their private sector competitors, even public service channels are not immune from audience-maximizing pressures.

The power of ratings in a zapping televisual culture has meant that politics has to sell itself in the competition for scheduling space with other content on mainstream free-to-air channels. In terms of style of coverage broadcasters are constantly looking at new ways of covering politics to attract the kinds of audiences that advertisers desire. These commercial pressures on television scheduling have encouraged politicians to appear on non-traditional programme formats such as television chat shows in an attempt to flesh out their image and get their message across in a less adversarial setting than political debate programmes. In the 1990s and early 2000s chat shows such as *Tout le monde en parle* (*Everybody is Talking About It*), *On ne peut pas plaire à tout le monde* (*You Can't Please Everyone*) and *Vivement Dimanche* (*Roll on Sunday*) welcomed politicians onto their programmes, but only on condition that they refrained from discussing the politics of the public realm (issues and policies) and instead concentrated on aspects of their private lives (Neveu, 2005).

Alongside chat shows, the other development in television's political coverage worthy of note has been the increased attention to process journalism, whereby politics is presented as a narrative, drama and spectacle, with recognizable dramatis personae and a plot constructed around the theme of personal ambition and human emotion. One manifestation of this trend is the popularity of 'behind-the-scenes' (*coulisses*) type programmes, where issues are presented through a focus on the 'human' side of politics and the emotional consequences for the protagonists.

In his extended essay *La fin de la télévision* (*The End of Television*), Missika outlines what he regards as the essential characteristics of political information in the current stage of television's development (Missika, 2006). These include: the rise of 'infotainment' (i.e. a mix of information and entertainment) content and genres in contrast to a more serious, rational form of news; a focus on the wings and backstage of politics, on the tactics and strategies of politicians; and a tendency towards a more intimate, personal and emotional register in reporting. Missika argues that when these three tendencies of what he calls the 'post-television' era are combined, it is possible to understand why the politician as a person – 'their private life, their character, their crises, their sexuality, their money, their children, their property – has become a news topic of the first order' (2006: 86).

Other academic researchers have written about the explosion in the 'television of intimacy' in France since the early 1990s (Mehl, 1996), evident in various television reality shows, including France's first version of the *Big Brother* format, *Loft Story*. The growth of reality television in its different forms has allowed and even encouraged audiences to engage in a voyeuristic relationship with a show's participants, as certain psychological traits are revealed before the cameras (Jost, 2009). In this context of the de-privatization of the sphere of intimacy via television, it is tempting for media executives and politicians to see a mutually beneficial gap in the market. A political version of a reality show to be screened on TF1 and entitled *36 Heures* (*36 hours*) was mooted at the start of Chirac's second presidential term. While the project was finally blocked by the government, the fact that the concept was considered marketable by TF1 management and that some leading politicians expressed an interest in participating indicated the extent to which both media and political elites were willing to consider 'politainment' genres (i.e. politics as entertainment) for their own respective ends of audience maximization and electoral outreach.

Finally, there is the multi-faceted impact of the internet to change both rules and practices. The trend on the part of politicians towards the mediatization of their private lives has been amplified by the routinization of the internet as a medium of political communication and information, and in particular by the increased popular use of social media websites and the spread of new forms of content, such as the blog. The 2007 presidential election was the first in which the internet played a major role – including official candidate websites such as Royal's *Désirs d'avenir* (*Hopes for the Future*) and an array of political blogs (Vedel, 2008). The blog allows a politician to bypass the traditional intermediary filters and journalistic gatekeepers of the mainstream news media. In terms of process, the production of the blog is fully under the control of the politician as source and the resultant output can be put into the public sphere without any intermediation. With regard to content, the nature of the blog allows for a mix of public and private information to be disseminated at will: politicians may not only give their views on public events, but can also control the release of more personalized information, including elements of their private lives if they so choose.

There is, however, also the possibility of 'blog backlash', with politicians open to information about their private lives being put on the web by their political opponents, journalists or amateur bloggers. This happened to Royal in the 2007 presidential campaign, when information about her property holdings and alleged tax avoidance originated on the internet and then became a story in the mainstream news media. While the accuracy of the information was contested by the candidate, the capacity of a blog for spreading rumour and gossip – as well as accurate information – is a new potentially destabilizing element that politicians now have to incorporate into their rebuttal communication strategy.

In 2010, a blog on the website of the Sunday newspaper *Le Journal du Dimanche* provided unsubstantiated revelations of the alleged extramarital affairs of both President Sarkozy and his wife Carla Bruni. The news story quickly circulated the globe and was picked up by mainstream media across the world – except in France. The French media's reluctance to run with the rumour was influenced not just by the privacy legislation and the fear of political reprisals (although both these factors would undoubtedly have weighed heavily), but also by journalists' suspicion as to whether the allegations were accurate. Ironically the Elysée's heavy-handed response to the rumour – the possibility of an international plot to destabilize the President was raised by one official – did dominate mainstream news headlines for a few days and allowed the French media to allude in cryptic fashion to the original revelations.

Sex, health and money

It is important to remember that politicians' public relations activities are centred not just on image projection and self-promotion, but also on image control and self-protection. In western democracies the three main areas of news coverage where the public/private interface may potentially lead to contention between politicians and the news media concern sex, health and money. How in recent years have these topics been dealt with by the French media?

Part of the traditional normative accord between journalists and politicians in France is that sexual relationships, including marital infidel-ity, belong to the private sphere and are off-limits to media coverage, even if a propensity for sexual infidelity on the part of a politician may well be hinted at in some media content. The most notorious example of media reticence in the face of a politician's extra-marital affair was Mitterrand's relationship with his mistress, Anne Pingeot, and in particular the product of their union, their daughter Mazarine. It has been argued that not only did several journalists know about the existence of Mitterrand's illegiti-mate daughter well before this information was revealed to the public, but that some journalists even cooperated with the Elysée in keeping the information a secret (Chemin and Catalano, 2005: 109–25).

Throughout her childhood and teenage years Mazarine thus inhabited a shadowy world in which her status was hidden to many, partly disclosed to some, and fully revealed to only a select few (Pingeot, 2005). It was not until November 1994, when Mazarine was already nearly 20 years old and Mitterrand had been head of state for 13 years, that the President's private secret was made fully public by *Paris Match*, with the requisite photos to illustrate the shocking news (Chemin and Catalano, 2005: 225–43). By this time Mitterrand was coming to the end of his second seven-year term in office, was in the advanced stages of the cancer that would kill him barely over a year later and was seeking to control how his life and career would be represented and evaluated after his death. Towards the end of his second presidential term his reputation had become sullied following revelations about his wartime association with the collaborationist Vichy regime. The revelation of Mazarine's existence, so long zealously protected by Mitterrand, now became part of his bid to impose on posterity a positive framing of his legacy.

Accustomed to detailed and salacious media coverage of the sexual indiscretions of their own politicians, Anglo-American audiences may be tempted to regard respect by the French news media for this aspect of Mitterrand's presidential tenure as a commendable feature of French journalism. Was this not a private matter with no public interest? Yet before one rushes to praise the restraint of the French news media in this respect or the desirable impact of strong privacy legislation, two caveats are worthy of note. First, neither Anne nor Mazarine were simply elements of Mitterrand's private life: both benefited from accommodation and security protection paid for out of the public purse. State funds were thus involved in the protection of Mazarine's privacy. The existence of Mitterrand's 'second family' was, during his time at the Elysée at least, a matter of legitimate public interest. The reluctance of Mitterrand and of the mainstream news media to go public with the information may be understandable and, in the eyes of some, even defensible: Mitterrand wished to protect his daughter and mistress from intrusive media publicity. Such a concern would have weighed particularly heavily when Mazarine remained a minor, during which time her protection from unwarranted media attention would have depended on a deal being struck between the Elysée, media owners and journalists. What is clear is that the case in support of the public concealment of Mazarine's identity cannot be based on the grounds that her existence was simply part of Mitterrand's private life.

Second, to ensure the secrecy surrounding Mazarine, the Elysée indulged in practices which represented a misuse, indeed abuse, of presidential authority. For example, the writer Jean-Edern Hallier was the victim of telephone tappings and financial threats against his publishing ventures (Palou, 2007). Hallier's private life and professional career were grossly interfered in so as to protect Mitterrand's secret. Overall the Mazarine case can be seen as a prime example of journalists failing to bring information of public interest into the mediated public sphere. In the light of this culture of journalistic deference to top politicians and especially the President, it is perhaps not suprising that Sarkozy was so taken aback by a question from an American correspondent about the state of his marriage to Cécilia in the early weeks of his own presidency, with an angry President bringing the television interview to a premature halt.

Health – more accurately, bad health – is another area that politicians generally wish to keep in the private domain. However, in this case the motivation is not the threat of public scandal, but rather the fear of lasting damage to the desired image of good health – fitness for purpose – that politicians wish to project. Thus, for a long time President Pompidou was keen to keep the gravity of his illness out of the media spotlight, with the result that his death in 1974 came as a shock to the nation. In 2002, President Chirac initially tried to deny that he used a hearing aid, while after his minor stroke in 2005 Elysée sources repeated that the President was 'in fine fettle' ('*en pleine forme*') and that he was continuing to work while in hospital. His daughter and communication adviser Claude sought to manage news coverage of his entry to and, more importantly, exit from hospital in an attempt to play down any possible negative media attention (Revel, 2007: 8–9).

Mediatized images of illness or physical frailty are to be avoided at all costs. Not only are intimations of mortality an electoral liability, but they are virtually guaranteed to attract political rivals in a 'feeding frenzy' around the ailing body. Moreover, good health can no longer simply be equated with the absence of illness. Instead politicians increasingly wish to exploit more positive images. For instance, in the summer of 2005 Prime Minister de Villepin clearly intended that pictures of himself emerging from the sea after a vigorous swim should be given widespread public dissemination – indeed the swim may well have been staged as a photo-opportunity for the cameras. It certainly received widespread media coverage, both in the press and on television. Similarly, authorized media pictures of Sarkozy cycling or jogging are intended to send out the message that he is physically in good shape, full of vigour and therefore up to the exacting demands of a top job. They also support a key aspect of Sarkozy's political image as a dynamic 'man of action'. When Sarkozy collapsed when out jogging in 2009, the Elysée was at first thrown into confusion over what had happened and then rushed to brief journalists so as to limit any potential damage to the President's image (Bouilhaguet, 2010: 123–6).

The most infamous health story of the Fifth Republic concerned President Mitterrand, who was diagnosed as suffering from prostate cancer towards the start of his first seven-year term in office. Mitterrand not only hid the news from the media and the public until almost the end of his second term, but also encouraged a falsely positive picture of his state of health to be disseminated. The Mitterrand case is especially interesting for two reasons. First, there is the substantive question of whether the President was in a fit state to perform the duties of the office, especially in the final months of his second term. The response appears to be 'yes, but on occasions only just'. A full-blown political crisis requiring active and prolonged presidential intervention may have exposed Mitterrand's physical incapacity, called the Elysée's public handling of the illness into greater question and led to demands for more transparency in the publication of information. Second, there is the question of how private a governing politician's health can be deemed to be. In Mitterrand's case the President's doctor, Claude Gubler, wrote a controversial book about the medical cover-up (Gubler and Gonod, 2005). Its original publication in France just after Mitterrand's death in 1996 was quickly halted by the national judicial authorities on the grounds that the work constituted 'a particularly serious intrusion into the intimacy of [Mitterrand's] private and family life' (Le Monde, 19 February 2005). However, the book was re-released for publication in 2005 after a decision by the European Court of Human Rights which argued that while the original court decision was justified, a perpetual ban on publication could not be legitimately defended: almost ten years after the President's demise the private secret had already so much entered the public domain that the status of the information had been irreversibly altered.

Alongside this media tradition of deference and collusion, there has also emerged a practice of what Ramonet calls 'revelatory journalism' (*'journalisme de révélation'*) (not to be confused with investigative journalism) that focuses on 'the private lives of public personalities and scandals linked to corruption and political racketeering' (Ramonet, 2007: 25). In the 1980s and 90s, for instance, links between the judiciary and the media ensured that cases of corruption against leading politicians featured prominently in the news media. Such coverage was not confined to the 'usual suspect' of *Le Canard enchaîné*, which has always indulged in revelatory journalism and whose irreverence towards elite politicians is legendary. Taking pride in exposing the secrets of politicians in what it would claim to be the public interest, *Le Canard enchaîné* has also frequently set the agenda for mainstream news outlets in the area of political scandal (Martin, 2005b). From the mid-1980s to the early 2000s *Le Monde* championed the cause of a French version of investigative journalism that was particularly targeted on a variety of scandals and alleged abuse of state power associated with the Mitterrand presidency (Collard, 2008).

One notable area of revelatory journalism concerns money. This is often a subject that politicians wish to keep secret, well away from the media spotlight and public eye. It is also an area where they are vulnerable to media exposure and to opponents, from both within and outside their political party, 'dishing the dirt'. During the Fifth Republic the news media have given extensive coverage to the financial affairs of several leading politicians of right and left, calling their probity into question and demanding greater transparency on behalf of the electorate. A by no means exhaustive list would include the revelations about the tax returns of Prime Minister Chaban-Delmas in the early 1970s that contributed to his destabilization within the ranks of the Gaullist Party, the alleged receipt by President Giscard d'Estaing of a gift of diamonds from the Emperor Bokassa, the property deals of Prime Ministers Pierre Bérégovoy and Alain Juppé in the 1990s, and the airline tickets for personal use purchased in cash by President Chirac during his first term at the Elysée as well as allegations of financial malpractice concerning his tenure as Mayor of Paris (1977–95). *Le Monde*, for instance, was severely critical of Chirac's alleged involvement in financial corruption before and during his presidency (Péan and Cohen, 2003), while negative reporting during Chirac's first presidential term included revelations in *Paris Match* and *L'Express* about possible irregularities in the funding of his holidays.

The alleged (and in some cases proven) involvement of executive politicians from President Chirac downwards in a series of financial scandals has not just tarnished the reputation of the whole political class in the eyes of many voters, but also allowed the news media to forge a new relationship with a more active judiciary to expose political corruption and malpractice. Occasionally the results have been quite devastating for individual politicians. In 1993, for instance, a recent Socialist Prime

Minister, Pierre Bérégovoy, committed suicide in the wake of media allegations concerning the funding of his purchase of a flat in Paris. In his oration at the funeral, President Mitterrand criticized the media coverage in strongly condemnatory terms (Favier and Martin-Roland, 1999: 485–91).

The Gaymard affair is a good illustration of a financial secret being made public as a result of media exposure and thereby fatally undermining the politician concerned. In February 2005 it was revealed by *Le Canard enchaîné* that the Minister of Finance, Hervé Gaymard, was renting at considerable public expense a huge flat in a highly desirable part of Paris. Other media picked up the story, putting the minister on the defensive (Communod, 2005). Although technically Gaymard had committed no offence in law, the revelation was embarrassing because as part of his ministerial brief he had previously called on the need for financial restraint in public expenditure. Moreover, as the affair unravelled the minister was shown to have lied to the media about the extent of his property holdings. Thus, not only did Gaymard make a serious error of political judgement, but he compounded the offence by his maladroit handling of his communications response to the initial media allegations. Indeed the failure of his reactive communication strategy was itself the subject of critical commentary in some sections of the media and became an integral part of the evolving news story. In the absence of support from within the government or from the Elysée, Gaymard quickly became a political casualty of the media onslaught and was forced to resign from his ministerial post.

Royal and Sarkozy

The two main candidates in the 2007 presidential election experienced no reluctance in using aspects of their private lives for the purpose of constructing their images as serious presidential candidates. One of the axes of Royal's campaign was to present herself as a maternal figure, compassionate and understanding (clearly seeking to contrast herself with Sarkozy). For example, during a prime-time television debate with 'ordinary citizens' – *J'ai une question à vous poser* (*I have a question to ask you*) on TF1 – she left the podium and walked across to comfort a disabled person in what was to become one of the most talked about aspects of the programme in the next day's newspapers. During the 2007 campaign the news media frequently called Royal 'the Madonna' because of the 'look' of the candidate, the way she interacted with voters and her positioning on certain key issues (Gaffney, 2010: 179–91). An attractive, photogenic woman, Royal frequently dressed all in white during the campaign, perhaps symbolically indicating to party militants and potential voters that she was untouched by the whiff of scandal and corruption that had so affected political elites in France in recent years.

Prior to the campaign Royal had overtly related her sex, and in particular her role as a mother, to the stance she adopted on certain political issues, such as her opposition to pornography on television and violence in schools. In 2007 she presented herself as someone who not only understood but also empathized with the insecurities and anxieties of the French electorate, responding to them with policies that emphasized the importance of 'tough love'. She was also willing to use her family in the pre-campaign period, posing for photos in *Paris Match* with her daughter. During her time as a government minister in the early 1990s Royal had famously publicized her role as a 'working mother' by allowing the press and the main private national television network, TF1, to photograph her in hospital shortly after the birth of her fourth child as she continued to work on ministerial correspondence. Royal, in short, had a long track record of being willing to mediatize her status as a woman and her role as a mother as an integral part of her constructed public image.

Sarkozy's concern with image projection also long predated the 2007 campaign. Between 2002 and 2007 Sarkozy actively fostered a positive relationship with the news media, particularly television. His 'coronation' in 2004 as leader of the UMP was stage-managed for the benefit of the television audience, with the party providing its own video images for use by the news media. Sarkozy's appearances on political debate pro- grammes, such as *Cent minutes pour convaincre* (*One hundred minutes to convince*) on France 2, provided him with a mass audience platform to transmit his political ideas and to demonstrate his style of straight talking, devoid of the vague circumlocutions that so frequently characterized television interviews with other leading politicians. He was popular with television news management because his appearances on this genre of political programming were guaranteed to attract a significant audience share in a highly competitive broadcasting market. The relationship between Sarkozy and television during this period was, therefore, based on mutual dependence: Sarkozy needed the medium to put across his message, while the editors of television's political output needed Sarkozy to boost their viewing figures.

As a testimony to his media management skills, Sarkozy, although still 'only' Minister of the Interior, was in 2006 the political figure credited with the largest quantitative media impact, coming ahead of his two nominal superiors in the executive branch, President Chirac and Prime Minister de Villepin (Girard, 2007). In the 2007 presidential campaign, Sarkozy outperformed Royal, less due to any partisan or sexist conspiracy on the part of the media against the Socialist candidate (Murray, 2010), but rather because of stark differences in the capacity of the two leading candidates to impose both themselves and their favoured issues on the media agenda (Gerstlé and Piar, 2008: 40–6). Sarkozy proved himself to be more in tune with the demands of mediatized campaigning in terms of the coherence of his message, the timing of key announcements, the organization of his support team and the relationship between the candidate and the 'embedded' journalists assigned by news media outlets to cover his campaign (Guibert, 2007).

For all of his political career Sarkozy has projected a political image as a man of strong views and authority. Some of his statements as Minister of the Interior, for example at the time of the 2005 riots on the outskirts of Paris, were highly inflammatory in their articulation of his desire to root out the troublemakers, whom he called 'scum' ('*racaille*'), and restore order by using a 'pressure hose to clean out the municipal housing projects' ('*nettoyer la cité au Kärcher*'). As part of the preparation for his presidential candidacy, Sarkozy sought to balance this authoritarian image with that of himself as an ordinary family man, loving husband and father. Promotion of a spouse and family – especially in the case of male politicians – can help provide a more rounded, human image to the public, and especially to women voters, who in 2007 constituted more than half of the total French electorate. This image softening may be particularly useful for a politician such as Sarkozy who needed to counterbalance those aspects of his public image based on a projection of 'firmness' and 'order'.

Sarkozy experienced no reluctance in constantly using aspects of his private life for the purpose of image construction. Until their marital problems became the big news story of the summer of 2005, the close relationship between Sarkozy and his wife Cécilia had been mediatized at length by the government minister. In his best-selling book *Témoignage* (*Testimony*), Sarkozy speaks about his overwhelming love for 'C' and says how emotional it is for him even to write her full name (Sarkozy, 2006). Their young son, Louis, was mobilized in the effort to help his father's presidential ambitions through an appearance on video footage at the UMP rally in 2004, which marked Sarkozy's takeover of the party leadership: '*Bonne chance mon papa*' ('Good luck, dad') (Artufel and Duroux, 2006: 43–50).

Indeed, the extent to which Sarkozy exploited his spouse and family for political self-promotion through controlled media exposure was ground-breaking in the French context, especially in its focus on the intimate aspects of the private sphere. It was not surprising, therefore, that when the official transfer of presidential power from Chirac to Sarkozy took place at the Elysée in May 2007, the mediatization of the event on television included a mix of public and private as the formal aspects of the official ceremony meshed with the ongoing story of Sarkozy's tempestuous marital relationship. Indeed, much of the media interest in the event focused on Sarkozy's spouse and family – from the Prada dress worn by the new 'first lady' to the non-existent tear ostentatiously wiped from her face by her husband.

The high point of this marketing of the personal by Sarkozy came after his election victory and involved the early months of his new relationship with Carla Bruni. In the wake of his divorce from Cécilia only a few months after arriving at the Elysée, Sarkozy entered into a whirlwind romance with the singer and former model that he was only too keen to publicize via the news media. Staged photo opportunities were arranged at Euro Disneyland, in Egypt and in Jordan, while at his first presidential press conference in January 2008 Sarkozy was at pains to remark that his new relationship was not a light-hearted fling: '*C'est du sérieux*' ('It's serious'). In short, for a few months in late 2007 and early 2008 the French President unashamedly played up his new romantic relationship, keen to propagate the fairy-tale of a French version of John F. Kennedy's 'Camelot' years in the US White House at the start of the 1960s. For many French media outlets this phase of the Nicolas/Carla romance had all the elements of a soap opera, with the President not just a principal character in the drama but the author and narrator of its unfolding romantic plot.

Mediatization of the private sphere, especially its more intimate aspects, as part of a politician's public communication strategy can, however, be dangerous territory with considerable rebound potential from both the media and public opinion. By using his spouse and family for the purposes of electoral self-promotion, Sarkozy had in the eyes of many journalists, given up his right to protection from media intrusion. Sarkozy had previously discovered the downside of marketing the personal when Cécilia left him – temporarily – in 2005 and she was then seen in a new relationship which was itself covered in depth by certain media outlets (Aubry and Pleynet, 2006: 201–51), while Sarkozy went on television to acknowledge that his marriage was in difficulty 'like that of millions of French people'. Sarkozy stopped the publication of a biography of his wife by exerting pressure on the publisher, and while the book was later published by a different company, it took the form of a thinly veiled fictional romance that had little media or public impact (Domain, 2006).

Sarkozy also complained to the owner of *Paris Match*, Arnaud Lagardère, about the magazine's coverage of Cécilia's liaison with her new male companion, Richard Attias (Gadault, 2006: 189–206). The editor of the magazine, Alain Genestar, who had approved a cover picture featuring Cécilia and Attias, was later removed from his post in a move widely interpreted as Sarkozy exacting his revenge (Genestar, 2008; Maurice, 2009: 254–64). When the marriage finally disintegrated, the President had to engage in a reactive, damage limitation communication strategy. The French media had a field day in covering first the insider gossip and then the public revelation of the couple's divorce – the first time that a President has divorced in office. In this context it might be noted that while an overwhelming majority of French voters considered that the Sarkozy divorce had no political significance, there was still huge public interest in the story, stimulating the appetite of the media for more insider information.

Moreover, even when there is cooperation between politicians and the media in the construction of a story – as in the early coverage of Sarkozy's romance with Carla Bruni – there is always the risk of a critical public response. The mediated image of a contemporary French President is necessarily complex and multi-faceted. It is particularly important, for example, for the incumbent to project an image consonant with the function of head of state. For instance, the President is required to provide a symbolic presence on various mediated public occasions such as the national holiday on 14 July and Armistice Day on 11 November. Even if the sacerdotal presidency of the Gaullian era is no longer in vogue, there is still an expectation among French voters that the President should behave in a manner appropriate to the supreme office and maintain certain high standards of protocol.

In his public appearances President Sarkozy has frequently deviated from this ideal, most memorably when in early 2008 in response to a member of the public who refused to shake hands with him he lost his cool: *'Casse-toi, pauvre con!'* ('Get lost, asshole!'). Footage of this incident was quickly made available on the web, exemplifying the way in which public and semi-public utterances of the President that in the past would not have been distributed by the mainstream media are now standard fare on online video sites such as Dailymotion and YouTube. In response, Sarkozy appointed an internet adviser at the Elysée with responsibility for monitoring web content about the President.

Sarkozy's opinion poll ratings plummeted at the start of 2008, humiliatingly overtaken by those of his Prime Minister who had largely abstained from mediated self-promotion. One of the principal reasons for the decline in Sarkozy's popularity, especially among traditional conservatives and older voters, was the perception that their 'bling-bling' President had become too focused on his private life at the expense of his public responsibilities. In the light of the poll findings and the negative municipal election results in the spring, Sarkozy's advisers urged him to readjust the thrust of his public utterances away from his personal life and towards more conventional political issues. In terms of refocusing his political communication, although not necessarily boosting public confidence in his capacity to resolve France's problems, Sarkozy was helped by the French presidency of the EU in the second half of 2008 and above all by the dominance of the financial/economic crisis as the major national and international news story throughout much of 2008 and 2009. However, his personal opinion poll ratings never recovered from the misdirected mediatized focus on his private life, with the crossover from a majority of positive to negative taking place at the start of 2008 and continuing up until the disastrous regional election results of the spring of 2010.

Conclusion

While some might bemoan the recent emphasis on the private sphere in the image projection of elite politicians as a 'dumbing down' of French political communication and/or regard this as further evidence of the Americanization of another facet of French political culture, it is not our purpose to make normative judgements. Instead this conclusion will confine itself to some brief analytic observations.

First, it is now clear that the previously well-delineated boundary between public and private spheres no longer exists in France, whether in politicians' controlled communication or in political journalism. It is not just that as a result of changing political practices, media behaviour and social mores, the boundary between the private and public spheres has shifted over the years, although it is self-evident that this has been the case. Nor is it just that there is now no political, journalistic or popular consensus as to where the dividing line is or where it should be drawn. It is rather that a simple bipolar antithesis of public versus private fails to convey the complexity of contemporary political communication and journalism with its open secrets, private revelations, non-attributable leaks, on- and off-the-record briefings, gossip, hearsay, rumour and spin. As Seymour-Ure reminds us with reference to the behaviour of the British Prime Minister, 'everything private is potentially public' (2003: 50). The example of Cécilia is interesting in this context, because it is clear that she did play a political role alongside her husband, promoting the career development of some advisers and politicians (such as Rachida Dati) and blocking that of others. When their marriage broke down irretrievably in 2007, some of Sarkozy's closest advisers who had been frozen out of the inner circle by Cécilia returned to positions of influence. The state of the relationship between Sarkozy and Cécilia was therefore a legitimate matter of public interest in that it had political ramifications, even if this was not the aspect highlighted in media coverage of their marital breakdown.

Second, the phenomenon of the mediatization of the private lives of French politicians both under controlled conditions and through journalistic commentary is not as novel as one might imagine. It certainly did not begin with Sarkozy. In 1954, for instance, René Coty's wife was photographed by *Paris Match* performing a variety of domestic tasks at the Elysée following her husband's accession to the presidency, while among the featured photos from the new President's 'family album' was one showing him posing in a swimming costume alongside his similarly attired daughter (Delporte, 2007: 54–5). Nonetheless, there undoubtedly has been a qualitative shift in the extent to which, in terms of image projection, the personal has become political, and much of the responsibility for this can be attributed to Sarkozy. In seeking to mediatize his personal life for electoral gain, first as presidential candidate and then as President, he has gone further than any previous political figure in France in changing the rules of behaviour that govern the mediatization of elite politicians.

While the phenomenon may not be new in itself, what is striking is the reduction in the degree of control that a political figure can now exert over what becomes public when compared to only a few years ago, notwithstanding the tough privacy legislation. The younger generation of French politicians is learning to embrace these developments, aware that there is little chance of the clock being turned back. In contrast, by no means all contemporary politicians have been happy or even willing to mediatize aspects of their private lives for electoral purposes. Some, especially among the older generation, have been reticent and uncomfortable in the face of the altered rules of the political communication game. For example, Prime Minister Fillon has kept his wife and children largely out of the public spotlight (Bouilhaguet, 2010: 55–7). Moroever, it should be emphasized that ideas, values and policy pronouncements continue to inform candidates' political communication, while issue-oriented forms of political journalism still exist. Electoral politics in France has certainly not been reduced to a simple personality contest, nor is 'policy lite' by any means the only form of political journalism available.

Finally, from a cross-national perspective it is apparent that France is emulating aspects of political communication, electoral marketing and celebrity politics that are considered commonplace in other western democracies (Corner and Pels, 2003; Seaton, 2003; Stanyer and Wring, 2004; Street, 2004). As a result, even if one makes allowance for the strong privacy laws, the apparently well-entrenched notion of French exceptionalism in this area of politics now has to be subject to significant qualification. While it is certainly not the case that France now has a political communication culture exactly similar to that of the USA or UK, it is true that it is now more difficult than previously to understand the French experience without taking into account the transfer of practices across national boundaries. As with executive news management, so with image projection – it is now less appropriate to talk of a specific French model and more useful to think in terms of a French variant of a transnational template. It is clear that in the mediatization of the private lives of politicians, the public/private interface will continue to be a territory of ill-defined and fluid frontiers, where the imperatives of voter outreach, the impact of technological developments, the pressures of media markets, new forms of journalism and the desire of the public for revelation will combine to make it ever more difficult for politicians and the media not to indulge in the exposure of at least some aspects of the personal.

7 THE FRENCH MEDIA ON THE WORLD STAGE

- The export of media content and formats
- Agence France-Presse
- French media ownership stakes in foreign markets
- External broadcasting
- The case of France 24
- Conclusion

The main stakeholders in France's media policy community are actively involved in promoting and implementing different initiatives by the country's domestic media in European and global markets. These externally directed media activities need to be situated within the broad context of France's cultural, diplomatic and economic presence on the world stage (Maclean and Szarka, 2008). Thus, any analysis of the transnational role of the French media needs to acknowledge France's long-standing commitment to the international dissemination of its values and cultural artefacts as well as the country's self-perception and recognized status as an important 'second tier' power in world politics. In addition, it must be remembered that in various non-media business sectors such as pharmaceuticals and telecommunications, French companies have in recent years successfully exploited the liberalization of markets at supranational and global levels to become European or even world leaders in their fields (Gordon and Meunier, 2001: 13–40). In short, culturally, politically and economically France regards itself – with some justification – as a significant global player.

There is also a particular media context that heavily influences – some might say determines – French media activity outside of its national borders. This is the growth of an increasingly interdependent global media system (Thussu, 2006), the development of which has been driven by technological shift, the changing economics of media industries worldwide and public policy decisions taken by a mix of national governments and international bodies. Both the precise extent of media globalization and the novelty of the phenomenon may well be a matter of academic debate (Hafez, 2007; Tunstall, 2007). However, there is no doubt that the concept has become an integral part of the discourse of various political and media actors over the past couple of decades. The belief in the notion of global media now exerts an important influence on government policy and the corporate strategies of media companies in France, as in other major western democracies (Held and McGrew, 2000: 5).

This chapter focuses on selected activities of the French media on the world stage. These activities, often heavily supported in financial terms by the French government, can be divided into four main analytic categories: the export of media content and formats; the work of the French news agency, Agence France-Presse; ownership shares of French companies in foreign media markets; and the role of external broadcasting via transnational radio and television provision. This chapter briefly considers each of these four areas of activity in turn. It then focuses on an in-depth analysis and evaluation of a specific recent initiative – the launch of the international rolling news channel, France 24 – as a case study of the strengths and weaknesses of France's current media activities on the world stage.

The export of media content and formats

The first external activity undertaken by the French media consists of the export to markets around the world of content and formats produced in France primarily for domestic consumption. TV France International is the association of French television programme exporters that includes producers, distributors and the distribution arm of broadcasting companies among its ranks. Its mission is to promote the sales of French television programmes in global markets and to facilitate international coproduction. Part funded by the film industry and by government, the association is made up of around 140 French exporters who together realize 90 per cent of all international sales in this area of economic activity.

According to the association's official figures, in 2008 sales and pre-sales of French television programmes abroad totalled over €150 million, a figure in line with that of previous recent years. The three main programme sectors of sales activity were fiction (€26.8 million), documentaries (€28.7 million) and cartoon animation (€30.7 million). Cartoon animation thus retained its position as the single most valuable French television export genre, albeit with a marked decline compared to the three previous years, in each of which export sales of cartoon animation exceeded €40 million. Sales of programme formats for local adaptation totalled €13 million. Across all genres as a whole, Western Europe (notably, Italy, Germany, Spain and Belgium) was France's main export market, with about two-thirds of total programme sales in 2008 (€72 million). North America was only France's third most important export market, behind Central and Eastern Europe. The USA, therefore, is not a major importer of French programme content or formats, with the result that France has a huge trade imbalance with America in this domain. To help give an indication of the level of performance of French media in this area of activity, in comparison, export sales of British television programmes in the same year amounted to £980 million (over €1100 million), i.e. more than seven times the French total. Moreover, with sales of £350 million, the USA was the single biggest export market for British programmes.

Agence France-Presse

News agencies have been classically defined as:

> *wholesale* media, gathering and packaging 'news' (much of it about currently developing events in the political, economic and sporting arenas) for the purpose of distributing it to other – *retail* – media, mainly newspapers and broadcasters, who then packaged this material for their own distinctive readers and audiences.
>
> (Boyd-Barrett and Rantanen, 2010: 233, original emphasis)

While in the digital age this definition has to some extent broken down in the face of technological change and new modes of news content distribution, it remains the case that for a media entity to qualify as a news agency, 'the business-to-business provision of news content and allied services for other media should be a salient feature of its operations' (Boyd-Barrett and Rantanen, 2010: 233). The French news agency, Agence France-Presse (AFP) undoubtedly meets this criterion.

The AFP can trace its history back to the creation of the privately run Havas agency in 1835 as the world's first international news agency. Along with other news agencies such as Associated Press (USA), Wolff (Germany) and Reuters (Great Britain), Havas was already an integral part of the globalization of mediated communication during the latter half of the nineteenth century. In response to the takeover of Havas during the Second World War and its conversion into a propaganda tool for the Vichy government as the *Office français d'information* (French information bureau), the French news agency was reconstituted at the Liberation in 1944, given a new name and established as a state enterprise – an integral part of the wide-sweeping state-managed reform of the French media system undertaken at this time (see Chapter 1).

A statute passed in 1957 defines the fundamental principles that are intended to guarantee the independence of the agency and the freedom of its journalists. The AFP was given a very particular juridical status (*un organisme autonome doté de la personnalité civile et dont le fonctionnement est assuré suivant les règles commerciales*) that makes it neither a state-owned nor a commercial entity. Its governing council consists of three main groups: representatives of the French news media, the agency's own journalists and the state, with the latter being in a small minority. The single biggest client of the AFP is the national government and different state bodies, which purchase subscriptions for the agency's various services. In practice, these official subscriptions represent a large indirect financial subvention to the agency, somewhere around

40–50 per cent of its total revenues (the exact level is difficult to calculate with any precision), down from over 60 per cent in the late 1970s (Boyd-Barrett, 2000: 9). While the state plays an important role in outlining the strategic objectives of the AFP, the news agency is independent of the government in its daily operations. It has certainly not functioned as a state news agency or a propaganda arm of the political executive; rather it has been recognized for its professionalism by its commercial and media clients.

The AFP is currently one of the largest news agencies in the world. Every day it files 5,000 text stories in six languages (English, French, Spanish, German, Portuguese and Arabic), with other languages such as Chinese and Japanese offered through partner agencies. It also files 20 television news reports, up to 3,000 photographs and 80 still and interactive graphics on a daily basis. The agency has journalists drawn from more than 80 nationalities reporting for a worldwide audience. It has global regional centres in Washington, Hong Kong, Nicosia and Montevideo and bureaux in a wide range of countries.

Among its media clients, the domestic market is the most important: local and national newspapers, radio stations, television channels and the internet (where the recycling of agency news constitutes a high proportion of news content on many websites). In this respect the AFP is not particularly distinct from most other national and international news agencies (Boyd-Barrett, 2008: 70), although unlike Reuters it does not specialize in financial news. At the domestic level the existence of the AFP means that French 'retail' media outlets and commercial clients can use the services of their own national, Paris-based news agency rather than those of foreign competitors.

Internationally, the agency has notably strong links with France's former colonial territories and has recently built up a notable presence in South East Asia. Yet it is also a competitive actor across international media markets, where the AFP offsets what would otherwise be a significant degree of Anglo-American domination of the field. The news agency plays an important substantive and symbolic role as a French media presence in the world of national and international news agencies, with a status higher than the country's economic or political importance would now justify. It has benefited and built upon its 'first mover' advantages in the field: a combination of expertise, networks, brand and authority. Both domestically and internationally, therefore, the existence of the AFP demonstrates the determination of the relevant organizational stakeholders, most notably the national government, to ensure a major French representative in this sphere of news media activity – to display to both the nation and the world that France continues to regard itself as a major global player in transnational news gathering and distribution.

In recent years, however, the news agency has been going through turbulent economic times. The financial crisis affecting the French press led to the cancellation of their subscriptions by several regional newspaper titles, including *La Provence* and *Nice Matin*. Moreover, in addition to the traditional rivalry with other major international news agencies, such as Associated Press, the AFP now faces competition from all the new information sources, news websites and social media that have been spawned by the 'Web 2.0' developmental phase of the internet. The future reputation of the agency will continue to depend on a clear distinction being maintained between state funding and operational independence (the political issue), while in terms of the AFP's strategic development a more comprehensive adaptation to the world of online information provision and distribution is now seen as essential for the future economic well-being of the agency (the commercial issue) (Pigeat *et al.*, 2010).

French media ownership stakes in foreign markets

Several French media companies have a direct presence in foreign markets. This is often done through minority shareholdings or joint ventures with local partnerships: for instance, in the 1990s Vivendi had an ownership stake in the British satellite broadcaster, BSkyB. In the final years of the twentieth century, Canal+ expanded its operations across different continental countries, acquiring a stake in pay-TV in Spain, Italy and Poland among others. It quickly became one of Europe's most successful subscription-based broadcasters, with the result that 'at its peak Canal Plus was Europe's largest pay-TV operator with 15 million subscribers across Europe' (Chalaby, 2009: 157). However, Canal+ had to pull out of these markets as a result of the group's financial problems in the early 2000s. This included its enforced withdrawal from the Italian pay-TV market, in which it was compelled to sell its holdings to Murdoch's News Corporation. Through its subsidiary, Canal Overseas, the Canal+ group was in 2010 involved in television production, programming and distribution in Poland, various African countries and Vietnam.

Other French companies with a market presence outside France include the NRJ Group, which owns commercial radio stations in various continental European countries. The Lagardère group is a huge international player in magazine publishing and as a result is France's biggest corporate success story in global media markets. Other French companies, such as Bayard and Marie-Claire, have also been successful in the magazine sector internationally. Conversely, no French newspaper group is a major player at the European or global levels. In the television sector the TF1 group, which owns the largest private television company in France, is largely focused on the domestic market, with the notable exception of its ownership of Europe's leading sports entertainment group, Eurosport, which operates five television sports channels, including Eurosport Asia-Pacific.

In the public sector, France Télévisions is involved in the Arte cultural channel in partnership with German public television. Arte is available in several European countries including Austria, Belgium and Switzerland, as well as in the two host countries. Audiences for Arte's highbrow programme output, that includes opera, art house films, serious documentaries, quality drama and intellectual debate programmes, are undoubtedly small. Yet as well as serving the symbolic function of embodying Franco-German cooperation in the media field, the channel provides a distinctive public service presence in a European broadcasting environment where commercial companies, fixated on audience ratings and the financial bottom line, dominate the field.

The expansion of Vivendi is a good example of a French company reaching out into external markets. Indeed, the merger of Vivendi with the American film giant Universal in 2000 represented an audacious attempt by a French company to become a major global multimedia player. Across the world there are fewer than ten major media conglomerates that between them dominate global entertainment and communications markets. These include TimeWarner, Viacom, Disney, Bertelsmann and News Corporation, all of which are either in American ownership or have a major base in the USA (Herman and McChesney, 1997; Tunstall and Machin, 1999). These companies do not just have a worldwide media presence across different global regions; they also tend to be vertically integrated, with a stake in each stage of the value chain of production, programming and distribution.

Rupert Murdoch's News Corporation, for example, has media interests in Australia, Asia, the UK, continental Europe and the USA. The company owns satellite distribution systems; it runs several television channels including the rolling news network, Fox News, and various sports, film and general entertainment channels; it controls the Twentieth Century Fox film business which gives it a stake in programme production; it owns the social networking website MySpace; it has been a leading player in the acquisition of sports rights for television coverage; and it is involved in the businesses of encryption technology and subscriber management systems, two key areas of activity in digital television. Murdoch's interests have always been media-focused.

In contrast, the French company Vivendi was originally a water utility company, the Compagnie Générale des Eaux, which became involved in the distribution of cable services in the 1980s and, after its takeover of the advertising company Havas in 1997, entered the French media market as a major player by gaining control of the pay-TV company Canal+. This move guaranteed Vivendi a role not just in the media sector in France but also in the media markets of those other countries where Canal+ was involved in the supply of pay-TV. Under the leadership of its dynamic chief executive, Jean-Marie Messier (Briançon, 2002), Vivendi expanded its media portfolio in an attempt to take advantage of the technological convergence in media industries across telephony, television and the internet, becoming involved in mobile phone services and setting up its own internet portal, Vizzavi. Control of sports and film rights are generally considered to be major economic drivers in the pay-TV industry. Consequently, a deal with a major US movie company such as Universal was an attractive proposition to Vivendi management, as it seemed to offer Vivendi the opportunity to move their corporate game to a higher level and to compete with the major players of the global media economy. At its height, Vivendi Universal was one of the leading media companies on the world stage.

Messier's convergence strategy may have appeared perfectly sound in theory. The growth of digital broadcasting and the expansion in internet services appeared to underline the importance to media companies of combining ownership of programme rights with control of the means of distribution to audiences: the holy grail of a combined stake in both content and conduits. The US mega-merger in 1999 between the media giant TimeWarner and the internet company America OnLine (AOL) seemed to demonstrate the mutual compatibility between traditional media organizations and new internet companies. Yet even this particular conjunction of US interests failed to live up to stock market expectations following the end of the speculative dot.com boom only a few months after the merger.

Messier's strategy also quickly encountered major problems. His investment decisions proved to be overly ambitious, with either the technology failing to deliver or customers unwilling to sign up to the promised new services. Vivendi Universal quickly ran into financial difficulties and the stock markets lost confidence in Messier's capacity to steer the company through troubled waters. As the share price plummeted, Messier continued to defend his decisions, making statements increasingly at odds with the reality of the company's market position. In 2002, Pierre Lescure, head of Canal+, was sacked in a diversionary attempt to shift responsibility for Vivendi's economic woes. A few weeks later, Messier himself resigned, leaving behind a media conglomerate which was a pale shadow of the company of only a few years previously. Vivendi Universal had been severely damaged by a mix of Messier's personal hubris, corporate overreach and poor investment decisions (Orange and Johnson, 2003). It was little consolation that around the same time other European media companies, such as Kirch in Germany and ITVDigital in the UK, made similar costly errors in their attempts to benefit from the media's digital expansion.

Vivendi was the principal flagbearer of French hopes in global media markets. The failure of Vivendi Universal under Messier deprived France – at least temporarily – of a media company with truly global ambitions. The complicated ownership structure of Vivendi Universal also revealed the complexities of being a successful player in the highly competitive, interdependent global media economy of the early twenty-first century. The Vivendi débâcle can certainly be viewed as an example of failed French outreach into world markets. From a different perspective the saga could also be framed as the unsuccessful Americanization of a previously wholly French company – a view apparently taken by many in the French cinema industry at the time (Hayward, 2005: 70).

External broadcasting

The final French media activity on the world stage is evident in the development of transnational radio and television provision. The three main components are the external services radio company, Radio France Internationale (RFI), the global Francophone generalist channel, TV5MONDE, and the rolling television news channel, France 24. During the Sarkozy presidency all three components were brought under the umbrella of a new holding company entitled French External Broadcasting (*Audiovisuel Extérieur de la France* – AEF) in an attempt to provide coherence to French initiatives in this field.

In terms of its mission, RFI is the French equivalent of the BBC World Service. Following the break-up of the ORTF, France's overseas radio services were originally organized as part of the public radio company, Radio France. In 1986, however, RFI was constituted as a separate self-standing public service company and it retained this status prior to Sarkozy's reform. With a large network of correspondents, including ten permanent foreign bureaux, RFI is the leading French radio station for international news. It broadcasts in French and various foreign languages and also runs an Arabic language station, Monte Carlo Doualiya, which produces programmes for transmission to audiences across the Middle East and North Africa.

TV5MONDE was established in 1984 when it was knows as TV5. It is the leading French language global television channel. In addition to news, it transmits a programme schedule consisting of films, drama, sport and documentaries. The role of TV5MONDE is to supply French language content across the globe to French-speaking audiences and those interested in French and Francophone content. More than 200 million households across the globe can receive TV5MONDE, with different editions depending on the global region, and its viewing figures make it one of the leading global networks alongside MTV and CNN. Its ownership structure includes France Télévisions and Arte, as well as Belgian, Swiss, Canadian and Québécois broadcasting organizations (Brochand, 2006: 435–68). While TV5MONDE is formally a Francophone rather than a simply French channel, most of its funding comes from the French government.

Launched at the end of 2006, the transnational news channel, France 24, represents a belated attempt by stakeholders in the French media policy community to join the competitive world of global television news providers. France 24 entered an international marketplace in which several other suppliers of news, including most notably the US-based CNNI, BBC World News (UK), Deutsche Welle (Germany) and Al Jazeera (Qatar), had already established themselves as significant players over several years. CNN, for example, established its reputation through its coverage of the first Gulf War in 1990–1, while Al Jazeera has been particularly successful in providing an Arab perspective on events in the Middle East, including the war in Iraq. During this period of growing international competition, France was a surprisingly notable absentee from this sector of media production and distribution. An initial lack of political will, the weakness of the national public service broadcasting institutions, the start-up and operational costs of the enterprise and the fragmented nature of France's external broadcasting supply all contributed to what in retrospect seems an astonishingly prolonged absence of a French contribution in this important sector of global media provision.

The case of France 24

The establishment of France 24 as a transnational news provider was made possible by two main developments in communications technology that originated during the latter part of the twentieth century. The first was satellite broadcasting, which allowed for transfrontier transmission of television programming (Negrine, 1988). Without the capacity for cross-border distribution, French television signals would have remained territorially constrained by national boundaries – as was effectively the case up until the 1980s – due to broadcasters' dependence on terrestrial transmission methods (see Chapter 1). The impact of satellite technology in opening up what had previously been largely self-contained national media systems across Western Europe and elsewhere was itself part of a broader process of transnationalization (see Chapter 2). The second technological development was the internet, which allows users across the world to access text, audio and video content irrespective of the original geographic location of the transmission source (Castells, 1996).

Yet while technological change and other facets of media globalization provided the opportunity and context for the launch of France 24, the establishment of the service was in no way simply determined by the independent influence of technological or communication variables. Nor did France 24 come into being in response to market demand or as a result of the simple application of technocratic planning or professional expertise. Instead the new service was the product of an explicitly political initiative taken at the very heart of the French state. The origins of France 24 are, therefore, interesting in that the impetus came primarily from the political sphere rather than from media companies. No private broadcaster saw any commercial gain to be secured from entering the market of global news provision, while public service broadcasters in France lacked the financial means, the political autonomy and the entrepreneurial ambition to undertake the task on their own initiative. Without the active implication of the state as the main actor driving the new venture, the project would quite simply never have come to fruition. In particular, the wholehearted support demonstrated by President Chirac, one of the early backers of the project after his re-election in 2002, was crucial (Blet, 2008: 77). In short, the French decision to go ahead with a transnational news channel was a top-down state initiative that illustrated the primacy of political considerations and, in particular, the power of the President to kick-start the policy-making process.

The immediate stimulus to the decision to go ahead with the project was official concern that the French government's position in the run-up to the 2003 invasion of Iraq by the US-led coalition had not been given sufficient space on existing English-language news channels, especially those based in the USA. French political elites across the party spectrum argued that France's voice in international matters, notably its opposition to the invasion, had at best been marginalized and at worst vilified in the news reporting of channels such as CNN and Fox News. More generally, in the new international climate of post-9/11, there was a strong sense that the battle 'for hearts and minds' required a transnational rolling news channel to provide a French perspective on world events.

This in turn was based on a judgement that such a media presence had become an indispensable part of the toolkit for the exercise of national political influence on the world stage. Permanent membership of the UN Security Council, the possession of an independent nuclear deterrent and extensive use of the standard array of diplomatic initiatives could no longer be regarded in themselves as sufficient guarantors of global status, power and influence. While the reality of a 'CNN effect' on the political handling of foreign and diplomatic issues by governments may be open to question (Robinson, 2002), there is no doubt that French political elites considered that the absence of a French-based news provider in the transnational public sphere had become a significant impediment to the exercise of influence in international fora, on world opinion-leaders and on global public opinion. In respect of the impact on French policy-makers in shaping attitudes towards the creation of a transnational news provider, a 'CNN effect' was, therefore, clearly evident. Indeed, the debate in France in the early part of the millennium was often framed in terms of the need for 'a French-style CNN' ('*CNN à la française*').

Key planning issues

Despite official backing from the very top of the political system, French policy-makers had to overcome a series of difficulties in the run-up to the launch of the new service. The first issue to be resolved was who would run the channel. The government wanted the TF1 group, owner of France's most popular television network and flagship channel, to be involved in the ownership of France 24, while France Télévisions wanted to be in total operational control. As we saw in Chapter 4, France has no organizational equivalent of the BBC, whose size and output of Anglo-phone content make it a natural UK player in global media markets. In the television sector, for instance, France Télévisions does not have a reputation among international audiences on a par with that enjoyed by the BBC. Moreover, since the break-up of the ORTF in the 1970s there has been no single public broadcasting company which could maximize its influence internationally or benefit from synergies in the employment of resources across radio and television – at least not until Sarkozy's reform of external broadcasting. In the absence of a 'French BBC', ownership of

France 24 was initially shared on a 50:50 basis between TF1 and France Télévisions. However, the joint partnership represented a fragile, and in the end short-lived, compromise with TF1 keen to renege on the deal. In 2009, the publicly funded holding company AEF took over full ownership of France 24.

Second, TF1 did not want the France 24 channel to be available within France for fear that it would provide unwanted competition for its own rolling news service, La Chaîne Info (LCI), which was available to domestic audiences on a subscription basis via different distribution platforms. Audiences within France currently have a choice between three rolling news channels, two of which (i-Télé and BFM TV) are available without payment on the digital terrestrial platform. In contrast, the France 24 channel can be accessed by French audiences on satellite (free) and cable (subscription) systems, but crucially not on the digital terrestrial platform. As a result, the impact of the France 24 channel on the domestic television audience remains small (Blet, 2008: 119).

Third, a prolonged debate took place – and, given the sensitivities involved, probably needed to take place – regarding the language(s) in which France 24 would broadcast. In particular, the question of whether the news channel should broadcast only in French was an important aspect of the pre-launch debate. In the end it was decided that the channel would in the first instance provide content in three languages – French, English and Arabic – so as to maximize audiences and extend its potential for influence among elite opinion-formers who were regarded as the channel's main target audience. The Arabic service has a particular mission to serve elite audiences in the Middle East, a global region that France considers vital for its own national interests and that has become a highly contested media market for the rolling news channels of different states: 'many Western governments are expanding their international broadcasting operations in pursuit of "soft power" in the Middle East' (Painter, 2008: 15). Transmitting in other languages, notably Spanish, was considered an option to be explored in the future, although there are no immediate plans in this respect. Broadcasting solely in French was not considered to be a point of principle.

This was an interesting result in the light of long-standing French sensitivities about the status of their language. French political elites have taken various steps to protect the language internally – for example, explicitly including it in the Constitution in 1992 as the official language of the Republic and enforcing a variety of measures to minimize the use of English in the French media, official documents and commercial communication, most obviously through the application of the 1994 Toubon law 'concerning the use of the French language'. In addition, France has a long-standing commitment to the spread of French across the globe – notably through its involvement in the Francophonie organization – and to the international dissemination of French culture, evidenced in significant financial support from the government to domestic film production and overseas cultural institutes among other things. The decision not to fetishize the monopoly use of French for France 24 was a pragmatic recognition that French is no longer in the lead group of global languages, that English is the lingua franca of political, economic and cultural elites across the world and that to broadcast only in French would severely reduce France 24's potential impact.

It came as a shock, therefore, that at the start of 2008 President Sarkozy announced that France 24 would henceforth broadcast only in French (with the use of appropriate subtitles) on the grounds that French taxpayers' money should support broadcasts only in the national language. If implemented, this measure would have placed France 24 in a hugely disadvantageous market position and out of step with other global news providers, such as Deutsche Welle, which alternates between German and English, and Al Jazeera, which launched an English language service in 2006 to complement its Arabic network. Fortunately, this ill-considered presidential proposal, which would have effectively killed off any realistic hopes of France 24 establishing itself as a major news provider in the transnational public sphere, was quietly dropped in the subsequent governmental reorganization of France's external broadcasting services.

Mission, structure and funding

According to its website, the mission of France 24 is 'to cover international current events from a French perspective and to convey French values throughout the world' (www.france24.com/en/about-france-24). At a formal level, this mission statement significantly differentiates France 24 from both CNNI and BBC World News. Although it is frequently regarded by its critics as a vehicle for the transmission of US hegemonic values, CNNI does not see itself as explicitly promoting the viewpoint of the USA, while BBC World News places itself within the public service tradition of the Corporation in its attachment to due impartiality in its news coverage and does not seek to frame events from a particularly British perspective. In short, neither CNNI, nor BBC World News situates itself primarily with reference to its country of origin, with both preferring to regard themselves as global news providers. By contrast, the mission statement of France 24 has strong overtones of the 'voice of France' role controversially attributed to the national state broadcasting organization by President Pompidou at the start of the 1970s. Is this mission statement compatible with professional norms of balance and due impartiality? Does it mean that France 24 is in effect an adjunct of the French state? A response to these two related questions requires a disentangling of different elements related to France 24's structures and functioning, including its organizational framework, funding, editorial content, framing and style of presentation among other things.

In terms of both organization and funding, the French transnational news provider certainly enjoys close ties to the state. The establishment of France 24 initially contributed to a fragmentation of France's external broadcasting supply that the government quickly found to be unsatisfactory. Prior to the launch of the news channel, France's external broadcasting consisted of two components, one in radio (RFI) and the other in television (TV5MONDE). The arrival of the French transnational news channel was destabilizing for both RFI and TV5MONDE in two important respects. First, it introduced a new competitor for public funding into the external broadcasting mix. Second, it complicated the overall configuration of France's external broadcasting supply and contributed to a picture of organizational fragmentation that was exacerbated by a division of political responsibility for external broadcasting across different government ministries (including Foreign Affairs, Culture and the Prime Minister's office).

President Sarkozy quickly moved to secure a 'joined-up' policy in this important area of French media provision by bringing the separate external broadcasting services under the umbrella of a new holding company. AEF was established in 2008 and has a 100 per cent ownership stake in RFI and France 24, as well as 49 per cent in TV5MONDE. France's foreign partners in TV5MONDE were strongly opposed to the company being seen by the French government simply as another part of France's external broadcasting and successfully fought to ensure the channel's survival as a broader Francophone entity. At RFI the transition to the new model was accompanied by a reduction in the station's activities, the suppression of broadcasts in certain languages, the lay-off of staff and the longest strike in French public broadcasting since the 'events' of 1968. RFI is now in danger of being marginalized by France 24 in the government's strategy for France's external broadcasting (or, more accurately, external multimedia) activities, with critics wondering, for example, how long the French taxpayer will continue to fund two competing international news websites.

Appointed by the President, the chief executive of both AEF and France 24 is Alain de Pouzilhac, who has spent his career in the worlds of advertising and communication. The managing director of both companies is Christine Ockrent, who has had a distinguished career in journalism in France and the USA and, purely coincidentally, is also the long-standing partner of Sarkozy's Minister for Foreign Affairs, Bernard Kouchner. In the light of this relationship between the worlds of politics and journalism, the suitability of Ockrent's appointment was not surprisingly the subject of considerable debate, much of it critical, among France 24 journalists and more generally in the French media.

France 24 claims to have over 1,000 correspondents throughout the world. Very few of these – perhaps around 50 (Blet, 2008: 151) – are directly employed, with the overwhelming majority from a network of partners with whom the channel has signed cooperation agreements (including France Télévisions, TF1, RFI and Global Radio News). France 24's global network of correspondents is considerably smaller than that on which BBC World News can depend, with some global regions such as Latin America having no correspondent based there who is specifically employed by France 24. Finally, the funding for France 24 comes overwhelmingly from government grant, approved each year by parliament. The initial operating budget of around €80 million per year was comparatively small by the standards of international news channels. In 2009, the state funded France 24 to the tune of €92 million, plus an additional €25 million to help the television channel secure a fuller global distribution and increase its Arabic output to a 24-hour daily schedule.

Content and presentation

There is no evidence, however, that the organizational and funding links with the French state have an adverse impact on France 24's editorial content in terms of structuring the news agenda: just as the AFP cannot be considered a government news agency, so France 24 is certainly not a government news outlet. To retain credibility with its worldwide audiences, France 24 cannot afford to be seen as a propaganda adjunct of the French state. In addition, several of the 250+ journalists of over 30 different nationalities employed by the company have previously worked in non-French news organizations such as CNNI and BBC World News and bring to their work for France 24 their professional experience gained outside of a French employment context. Despite this, France 24 has closer ties to government than, say, BBC World News in Britain, because of the stronger tradition of state interference in the broadcasting media in France and a concomitantly weaker tradition of political independence.

The impact of France 24's mission statement on its editorial operations is evident in several respects. First, and most obviously, events in France are given higher priority by France 24 than by other transnational news providers. On the home page of the France 24 website, for instance, France is the only nation state mentioned in the geopolitical division of news rubrics. All other countries, including superpowers such as the USA and China, are covered within the geopolitical rubrics devoted to five global regions: Europe, Africa, Middle East, Americas and Asia & the Pacific. There is, therefore, a certain ethnocentric bias towards France in the selection of items for the news agenda, clearly apparent for example in France 24's extensive coverage of the French presidential election campaign in 2007 (Blet, 2008: 104–6). Even on the website's weather pages, the report for Paris is the opening item.

Second, events in Africa, especially in Francophone sub-Saharan African states such as the Ivory Coast, Mali and Senegal and in the Maghreb countries of Algeria, Tunisia and Morocco, receive more coverage than on other transnational news services. This is not just because a local variation of French is spoken by an estimated 115 million African people spread across 31 African countries. More importantly, France's long colonial history on the African continent and its political, economic, cultural and defence links with several African states ensure that Francophone Africa is regarded by French political elites as part of France's private preserve (*pré carré*) for the exercise of French influence (Chafer, 2008).

Third, a French perspective influences the framing of coverage of European and global events. The role of French actors is highlighted, as in coverage of Sarkozy's contribution to the resolution of the global financial and economic crisis in 2008–9 or Bernard Kouchner's peace efforts in the Middle East, even if this is less pronounced than in television news coverage by the French national channels.

Fourth, France 24 gives a substantial space to the arts, literature and culture – notably French and Francophone culture – in its schedules. This is regarded by France 24 management as a particularly distinctive feature of its content provision in comparison with transnational competitors.

Finally, French-style debate and discussion programmes are an integral part of the schedules, giving the service (along with Al Jazeera English) a 'more discursive' character than several of its competitors (Chalaby, 2009: 185). In the autumn of 2009, for example, France 24 ran a series of ten weekly debates on the so-called 'French model'. The series was chaired by different presenters on each of the language channels, with a separate expert as an invited guest. Discussion focused on various topics, including education, health, the economy, secularism and social/racial integration. This series of programmes took place at the same time as the French government was holding a nationwide debate via public meetings and the web on the controversial question of French national identity, and so a clear link could be established between the national political agenda and the France 24 debate series.

In short, French values influence several aspects of content and framing, most notably when French national interests abroad or an aspect of contemporary France (politics, society, economy) are perceived to be at stake. The France 24 website is particularly reliant on the wire services of news agencies such as Agence France-Presse. In contrast, the dependency on footage from other international news agencies, including Reuters and Associated Press Television News, and from the European Broadcasting Union's EuroVision News picture library for much of its video content frequently prevents France 24 from fully differentiating itself from its rivals and from projecting a uniquely French perspective on world events.

The television schedules (and web pages) of the three language versions of the service are for the most part identical. The television schedules consist of ten-minute news programmes at the top of the hour and on the half hour. Magazine and debate programmes occupy the slots between the news bulletins, with an item of current affairs or an issue for debate treated in some depth. France 24 does not confine itself to a repetitive rolling news approach; indeed, it accords a relatively low priority to breaking news when it comes to modifying its scheduling. The pictures and text for the news bulletins are the same for the French-, English- and Arabic-language versions; the running order of news items, however, may differ slightly, with a French story more likely to feature more prominently on the French-language version. In contrast to several of its global news competitors, France 24 uses the same terminology in its coverage of a story across all three language versions. Moreover, it does not gear its content to suit particular global regional markets, thereby eschewing a 'glocalization' approach. Compared to most rolling news channels, the visual presentation is kept simple, with just one band of alternative changing news text at the bottom of the screen. There is some streaming of programmes throughout the weekly schedule: for instance *The Week in Africa/Asia/Europe/France/the Americas/the Maghreb/the Middle East* at the same time on successive days of the week.

Distribution and audiences

France 24 can be accessed via television, internet and mobile phone. The television channel is available in its different language versions on the main satellite positions and commercial feeds (satellite, cable, DSL) in Europe, the Middle East, Africa and the east coast of the USA. It is not part of mainstream cable packages in most parts of North America because of the heavy carriage costs imposed by cable operators, nor is it available via satellite in South America. The Middle East is seen by France 24 management as a particularly crucial global region and in April 2009 the number of hours broadcast on the Arabic service increased from four to ten (the French- and English-language versions transmit round the clock). The French- and English-language versions are available in around 80 million households worldwide and the Arabic version in about 50 million households. Since the same household can receive different language versions, this gives France 24 a cumulative reach of around 100 million households across 160 different countries. A live television feed in each language is also available on the relevant version of the France 24 website.

On the internet, the homepage of France 24 is devoted to the top news stories of the day. In addition to the geopolitical sections on France and the five global regions, there are rubrics devoted to business and technology, sport, culture, health, earth, science, recent programmes on the France 24 television channel and weather reports. A section entitled 'Observers' uses eyewitness accounts of international events sent in by 'observers' – i.e. ordinary citizens – who are signed-up contacts for France 24 either based in a certain part of the world or specialized in a certain subject. The 'observers' submit video, photographic or textual material, which, although not produced in-house, is selected, checked, if necessary translated, and explained by France 24's professional journalists. The 'Observers' pages also include discussion forums. Finally, there is a section entitled '*Reportages*' that contains video reports on selected current affairs stories. Video podcasts are available for download to an MP3 player or computer. There is some discreetly placed advertising material on the website, but there are no obtrusive advertising pop-ups. The site is professionally produced and easily navigable for the user. The service's RSS feeds allow users to receive the latest headlines directly on their computer. Finally, the three language services of France 24, including live television feed and video-on-demand, are also available via mobile telephony irrespective of the local network operator. In January 2009, AEF and France Telecom-Orange signed a strategic global partnership for news over the web, mobile phones and television with the objective of extending the international reach of both France 24 and RFI.

According to its chairman, France 24 primarily targets opinion-leaders rather than a mass audience. These include established opinion-leaders in politics, business, international organizations, the media and the universities, and the 'new opinion-leaders' who are heavy users of communications technology, avid news consumers and interested in international events and issues. In other words, in sociological terms France 24 aims to attract the traditional upper level socioeconomic groups and key decision-makers in different countries, as well as a new demographic of younger, media-savvy, educated professionals. In linguistic terms it is important for the service to reach out beyond Francophone audiences, even if its success in reaching French-speaking elites in North African countries such as Tunisia and Morocco is noteworthy. Geopolitically it is crucial that the service attracts users in the Middle East so that a French perspective on the Israeli-Palestinian conflict becomes an accepted part of the news media mix in this global region. This will be a particularly difficult market for France 24 as it is already crowded with competition from several other international news suppliers, with CNNI and BBC World News benefiting from the advantages of their embedded position with local audiences. For instance, a survey covering the period June to September 2008 that measured audience reach for English-language news channels in elite Middle East households ranked CNNI number one (21 per cent), followed by BBC World News (15.6 per cent), Al Jazeera English (9 per cent), CNBC (4.8 per cent) and Euronews (3.6 per cent), with the English-language version of France 24 not mentioned.

Accurate audience figures for France 24 are difficult to obtain because of the methodological difficulties involved in measuring an elite tranche of a worldwide transnational audience. According to a European Opinion Leaders Survey[1] conducted in 2007 (the first year of France 24's existence), France 24 secured an 8.8 per cent weekly reach, trailing well behind CNNI (31.3 per cent), BBC World News (26.9 per cent) and Euronews (19.4 per cent), but ahead of Al Jazeera English (3.5 per cent) (survey results quoted in Chalaby, 2009: 188). More recent surveys show France 24 doing well in Francophone states in sub-Saharan Africa and in the Maghreb countries of North Africa, but comparatively poorly in Europe where the service attracted less than 5 per cent market share during its first three years of operations. Traffic on France 24's website has increased steadily, with management trumpeting the success of the site in attracting users from outside France, including the USA.

---

1 The European Opinion Leaders Survey 2007 was conducted across 17 European countries among an elite universe of 32,000 individuals drawn from the worlds of business, government, law, media and academia. Fieldwork ran from April to August 2007 and 2,021 responses were received. Those surveyed are experts in their field, whether key decision-makers in the EU, members of think-tanks, news editors, senior business people or members of the *International Who's Who* (BBC press office release, 8 October 2007) (see www.bbc.co.uk/pressoffice/bbcworld/worldstories/pressreleases/2007/10_october/eols.shtml).

Influence and evaluating success

Apart from the fact that it exists after long and difficult birth pains, how does one evaluate the impact of France 24 and assess its potential for future success? One promising sign is that it clearly presents itself as a multimedia operation. The management and staff have been aware from the very beginning that their range of services cannot be reduced to old-fashioned television broadcasting. The internet not only allows France 24 to reach users in those parts of the globe where its television service is not fully available, but allows them to interact with France 24 staff. Its journalists are young (average age in the early thirties) and are accustomed to working in a multifunctional fashion across both television and the internet.

Only time will tell whether the objective of reaching out to the key target audience of opinion-formers in the transnational public sphere – the transnational power elite – has been a success. In terms of global audience reach it is clear that in relative terms France 24 lags well behind CNNI and BBC World News, even if it is performing reasonably well in some global regions. In his analysis of international television news channels, Chalaby puts forward a typology that distinguishes between those channels 'that tell stories *beyond* their borders' (e.g. CNNI, BBC World News and Al Jazeera English); those that 'tell stories *within* their borders' (such as Euronews and Sky News); and, finally, those 'that tell stories *about* their borders' (including Deutsche Welle, Russia Today and France 24) (Chalaby, 2009: 173, original emphasis).

Chalaby allocates channels to each section of his typological framework based on what he calls 'their degree of transnationality'. This concept embraces three key features: 'the extent of operational integration at global level, geographical spread of newsgathering facilities and character of the news agenda' (Chalaby, 2009: 186). It is the combination of these organizational, production and content variables that gives a news service a transnational impact in terms of audience reach and political influence, although, somewhat curiously, Chalaby does not regard the geographic spread of the audience as in itself an independent feature of such a service's transnationality. For Chalaby, France 24 fails to be placed in the premier league of international news providers because of its deficiencies in terms of operational integration, newsgathering and content. In most global regions it is not perceived to be as relevant and authoritative as the big hitters. In particular, crucially he regards the news agenda of France 24 as nation-centric in scope. In this sense, France 24, unlike CNNI, BBC Word News and Al Jazeera, does not 'report the world to the world' (Chalaby, 2009: 187).

It is easy to understand Chalaby's downbeat evaluation of France 24's contribution to global news provision. It is certainly unlikely that in the foreseeable future France 24 will pose a viable challenge to the dominant position of the three majors on the world stage, while in Europe Euronews has achieved levels of popularity well ahead of the French transnational service. If success is measured by the gold standard of the extent to which other news providers use content produced by France 24 on their own services, as frequently happens for example with content produced by Al Jazeera, then France 24 has a vertiginous mountain to climb. We are certainly a long way from any possible discussion of a 'France 24 effect'. If, however, a more modest criterion of success is employed, such as the capacity of French elites to enjoy a media platform to put forward different, alternative and even oppositional views on issues of global importance such as climate change, then France 24 may be said to perform a useful, and even necessary, counterpoint function. This is itself important, when too frequently it seems that an Anglo-American world view predominates in both global news coverage and the international community of decision-makers – and as the Iraq war demonstrated, not always with beneficial results.

Conclusion

How successful have the French media been on the world stage in recent years? The answer is at best mixed. France has certainly not been as successful as it would have wished. French independent production companies are often weak and under-capitalized by international standards, while programme exports have been hindered by language constraints and the cultural specificity of much of the content. In terms of producing a Gaullist-style 'national champion' in global media markets, the results are also poor. Vivendi Universal represents a 'heroic failure', TF1 has been largely content to be a big player in the domestic market and France Télévisions cannot rival the BBC in terms of its external commercial activities and is in any case operating under severe financial constraints.

In the realm of external broadcasting, France 24 is a welcome initiative, but is probably unlikely ever to reach the status of the major global news providers. TV5MONDE is a Francophone success story, while RFI increasingly looks to be the poor relation of the external broadcasting triumvirate. In this regard for a long time one aspect of the failure of France's 'reaching out' strategy was political confusion. Turf wars between the Ministry of Foreign Affairs on the one hand and the Ministry of Culture on the other militated against the formulation and implementation of a 'joined-up' policy in external broadcasting. The result was a fragmentation of effort across the main media players: RFI, TV5MONDE and France 24 (Brochand, 2006, 435–68). The new holding company set up by Sarkozy should help in this regard, yet it is also the case that fragmentation is to some extent inevitable: the mission of TV5MONDE is to supply French language content to those with a knowledge of French, while that of France 24 is to put across a French perspective on global events in different languages. These are two quite separate objectives, catering for different audiences and requiring different skills on the part of the content providers.

With particular regard to television, Chalaby is scathing about the failures of French ventures in transnational markets, referring to what he calls the 'French crash' over the past decade (Chalaby, 2009: 155–60). He puts forward four sets of reasons for France's decline in transfrontier television. The first is linguistic and in particular the dominance of English (to which could be added Spanish) in global markets. The second is cultural, with exposure to French cultural artefacts less evident than in the past, with the result that these now have less resonance with non-Francophone audiences (Morrison, 2008). The third reason is political: the tradition of state intervention and dirigisme that has resulted in so many poor policy decisions in the media field, including the high power satellite TDF1 and French backing for the European MAC transmission standard in the 1980s. The final reason given by Chalaby is what he calls 'an overzealous regulatory agency' (2009: 160) in the form of the CSA, that along with the government helps protect the domestic media market from competition. Chalaby concludes (2009: 160):

> The damage is now irreversible. France has lost too many industrial and cultural battles not to have lost the war, and spending taxpayers' money on channels like TV5MONDE and France 24 will make no difference. It is an edifying tale for those who like to dabble with interventionism and protectionism.

Is this critique fully justified? In the linguistic and cultural fields the national government has been active in protecting and promoting French interests internationally. There are clear limits to what any French government can do in these areas, as it is forced to follow a strategy that focuses on what might be called the 'orderly management of decline'. French language content on the internet, for instance, is hugely exceeded by that in other languages, notably English. There is no reason, however, why a government of a country like France should simply give up a proactive defence of the national language and culture. Indeed, it could even be argued that these activities are related to a government's primary function of defending the territorial integrity of the state.

With regard to the other two parts of Chalaby's critique – poor quality state intervention and over-regulation – four points can be made in response. First, Chalaby focuses on examples of state intervention in major projects (*grands projets*) in the technological field that date from over two decades ago. That particular form of entrepreneurial state interventionism, described by one commentator as 'high tech Colbertism' (Colbert was King Louis XIV's powerful finance minister), has been out of vogue for many years (Cohen, 1992). One might note in passing that it had its successes, such as modernization of the national telephone network and the development of a high-speed train network, as well as its failures.

Second, not all intervention by the French government and regulatory agency in media operations can be said to have had negative consequences or to have been a waste of taxpayers' money. Active government intervention has been particularly important, for example, in helping to sustain the French film industry as the leader in Europe.

Third, state investment in some international media ventures seems a perfectly reasonable public policy choice. For example, the withdrawal of a French presence from an area such as international television news channels would seem perverse at a time when every other major country regards such activity as an important part of its diplomatic efforts (Painter, 2008: 5). Several external radio services and news channels, such as the BBC World Service and Deutsche Welle, depend on public money for some or all of their income. This is an area of media activity where financial investment by the French state is perfectly defensible.

Finally, it is important to remember that some of the more recent spectacular failures in French media ventures on the world stage, notably that of Vivendi Universal, were the result not of wrong-headed government intervention but of corporate hubris and miscalculation by the chief executive of a private company. If the state may not have always made sensible decisions in terms of promoting French media interests internationally, the private sector has also had its fair share of policy failure in recent years.

CONCLUSION

Of the many important developments that have affected the structures and functioning of the French media in recent years, four in particular are worth highlighting in this short concluding chapter. The first is the widespread impact of technological innovation on media provision. The combination of digital switchover and the spread of the internet has brought about the most wide-sweeping changes on the supply side of the French media landscape since the launch of the national roll-out of television more than 50 years ago. As a result, a wide range of media content is now accessible both online and offline via different media outlets, technological platforms and communication devices. This so-called 'digital revolution' has radically transformed the production, packaging and distribution of media content.

Technological change has impacted on mainstream media in different ways and to differing degrees. For instance, the internet poses a huge challenge to the economics of newspaper publishing, pushing the industry into a structural crisis the outcome of which it is still impossible to predict with any sense of certainty. As circulations decline and advertisers migrate to online platforms, French newspapers are in crisis. While newspaper groups struggle to monetize their content on the web, it is at least possible that we are witnessing the terminal decline of newspapers in their familiar newsprint format. The traditional business model of newspaper publishing has collapsed, while a new economic model of online publishing has not yet proved its viability.

In the television sector the provision of new thematic and generalist digital channels has led to a decline in the audience shares of the long-standing channels from the analogue era and jeopardized their attractiveness for advertisers. It has also allowed new entrants to come into the market both as network distributors and content providers, has extended viewer choice in the constructed schedules of linear television and has facilitated access to a range of new broadcasting and narrowcasting services. Finally, while the internet is an additional means of distribution for established mainstream media outlets, it is also a new medium in its own right, allowing a wide diversity of providers of information to bypass the traditional media and establish a direct link with users. In addition, the global reach of the internet has permitted the entry of foreign players, such as Google, into previously largely protected French media markets.

The second development, itself linked to technological advances and a corollary of changes on the supply side, can be found in new forms of demand and practices of media usage by audiences. The biggest changes in this respect are evident in the ways in which young people interact with the media. Newspaper reading, listening to the radio and watching television have all declined among this generational cohort over the past decade. In contrast, the internet is increasingly the medium of choice for the 18–34 age group and internet use by this section of the population has grown enormously over the past few years. In addition, for all audiences, especially the young, media usage has become more mobile than in the past. The ubiquity of handheld devices has resulted in an increase in the amount of media content – including news – that is accessed by users on the move. Rituals of news consumption at fixed times of the day via the discrete media of press, radio and television are still well-entrenched among several sections of French society. Alongside these, however, are relatively new practices of rolling news consumption by media users operating in an ambient news culture: news on demand irrespective of time and place. Mobile phones with sophisticated applications, for example, have become the first source of breaking news for many French citizens.

New communications technology has also empowered citizens to become more active participants in the process of news production through the uploading of text, graphics, photos and video on to the internet, some of which content may well find itself being used by the mainstream media. The relationship between professional news producer on the one hand and a citizen confined to the role of news receiver on the other is no longer valid. Of course, media audiences were never simply passive decoders of news texts; however, their influence on the process of news production was mostly indirect and collective. Now it can be direct and individualized. While the impact of this phenomenon of user-generated content should not be exaggerated – professional journalists overwhelmingly dominate the process of news-gathering and production – it is clear that new modes of interdependence between journalists and their audiences have been fostered by the possibilities offered by new technology – including participatory social media such as Facebook and Twitter – that have allowed 'ordinary citizens' to contribute to the process of news gathering in hitherto unimaginable ways.

The third development lies in the policy arena, where one of the striking features is the continued tradition of state intervention. While the media have long been the focus of public policy in France, it might have been anticipated that the expansion of media in recent years would have been accompanied by their commercialization and deregulation, with a concomitant reduction in the policy-making and regulatory role of the state. A huge degree of commercialization has certainly taken place, both in ownership and content, especially in the broadcasting sector when compared to the restrictive era of the state monopoly. Wherever one looks in the contemporary media landscape, market pressures are inescapable, even in public service media organizations such as Radio France and France Télévisions. However, the state tradition established at the Liberation of seeking to manage, regulate and promote the domestic media is still much in evidence. Providing financial aid to newspapers, protecting national media sectors from foreign ownership, setting quotas in different genres of broadcast content and defending the interests of the French film industry are just some of the practices that continue to be undertaken by the state, often with the support of indigenous media companies. To this list can be added the more recent initiative of managing the roll-out of digital television services nationwide.

Indeed, during the Sarkozy presidency, the political executive has been instrumental in formulating and implementing two major media policy initiatives. The first has been to help the newspaper industry survive a combined structural and cyclical economic crisis and adapt to the era of online publishing. The second has been to reform the structures and alter the mode of funding of public service television with the avowed objective of enhancing its specific contribution in the competitive environment of digital media. There has certainly been a considerable and extensive marketization of the French media landscape since the Liberation, but it has not resulted in the state's simply abandoning its policy-making and regulatory functions, as is evident in these two initiatives undertaken by President Sarkozy and more routinely in the daily work of state officials at the Ministry of Culture and Communication and at the CSA.

The final development is linked to the use of the media by Sarkozy both before and since his election to the presidency in 2007. Sarkozy's impact on the contemporary French media is by no means confined to his high profile policy initiatives. He has been particularly active in occupying media space, structuring the news agenda and engaging in practices of executive news management. He has also focused on the construction and projection of his image, with an emphasis – as a presidential candidate and then in the early months of his presidency – on intimate aspects of his private life. In both news management and image projection, Sarkozy has built on the legacy of his predecessors, but he has gone further than any of them in the attention he has paid to the routinized mediatization of presidential activity and the constructed image of himself in a leadership role.

In looking at the contemporary media landscape in France one is struck by aspects of radical change intertwined with elements of historical continuity. In all four of the aspects alluded to in this concluding chapter – technology, social usage, public policy and executive communication – it is possible to see new outlets and/or practices sometimes replacing, sometimes working alongside, sometimes being superimposed on, occa- sionally being successfully resisted by, established structures and modes of behaviour. One can also see several instances of the French experience being strongly influenced by the communication practices and media policy initiatives of other western democracies (with reference, for instance, to practices of executive news management and the project to develop an international news channel).

Indeed, the impact of transnational variables on the French media landscape might well be considered a fifth important development in its own right. It is certainly undeniable that in many respects media structures and behaviour in contemporary France are neither unique nor exceptional. It may even be the case that, as Hallin and Mancini argue, 'the differences among national media systems ... are clearly diminishing. A global media culture is emerging ...' (2004: 294). Yet as this book has shown, the French media landscape still retains elements of national distinctiveness, particularly in its political and policy dimensions. These continue to make a single country case study relevant not just to those interested in contemporary French media and politics, but also to those who wish to cite the French experience as part of a broader, cross-national, comparative endeavour.

BIBLIOGRAPHY

Achilli, J.-F. (2006) *Sarkozy, Carnets de campagne*. Paris: Robert Laffont.

Achilli, J.-F. (2007) *'Jusqu'ici tout va bien … Nicolas Sarkozy, une partie de campagne'*. Paris: Ramsay.

Albert, P. (1998) *La presse française*. Paris: La documentation française.

Albert, P. (2008) *La presse française*. Paris: La documentation française.

Albertazzi, D. and P. Cobley (eds) (2010) *The Media: An Introduction*. Harlow: Longman.

Amaury, P. (1969) *Les deux premières expériences d'un ministère de l'information en France*. Paris: Pichon et Durand-Auzias.

Ambiel, D. (2005) *Fort Matignon*. Paris: Plon.

Artufel, C. and M. Duroux (2006) *Nicolas Sarkozy et la communication*. Paris: Éditions Pepper.

Aubry, É. and M. Pleynet (2006) *Pas de deux à l'Élysée*. Paris: Éditions Héloïse d'Ormesson.

Bachmann, S. (1997) *L'éclatement de l'ORTF*. Paris: L'Harmattan.

Barjon, C. and S. des Déserts (2007) 'L'énigme Cécilia', *Le Nouvel Observateur*, 2230: 6–16.

Bazin, F. (2009) *Le Sorcier de l'Élysée*. Paris: Plon.

Bédeï, J.-P. (2008) *L'info-pouvoir*. Paris: Actes Sud.

Berretta, E. (2010) *Le Hold-Up de Sarkozy*. Paris: Fayard.

Blet, C. (2008) *Une voix mondiale pour un État: France 24*. Paris: L'Harmattan.

Bongrand, M. (2006) *Le marketing politicien*. Paris: Bourin Éditeur.

Bouilhaguet, A. (2010) *La carpe et le lapin*. Paris: Éditions du Moment.

Bourdon, J. (1990) *Histoire de la télévision sous de Gaulle*. Paris: Anthropos/INA.

Bourdon, J. (1999) *Haute Fidélité*. Paris: Seuil.

Boyd-Barrett, O. (2000) 'National and international news agencies: issues of crisis and realignment', *Gazette*, 62/1: 5–18.

Boyd-Barrett, O. (2008) 'News agency majors: ownership, control and influence reevaluated', *Journal of Global Mass Communication*, 1/1–2: 57–71.

Boyd-Barrett, O. and T. Rantanen (2010) 'News agencies', in D. Albertazzi and P. Cobley (eds) *The Media: an Introduction*. Harlow: Longman.

Briançon, P. (2002) *Messier Story*. Paris: Grasset.

Brochand, C. (2006) *Histoire générale de la radio et de la télévision en France, Tome III 1974–2000*. Paris: La documentation française.

Carton, D. (2003) *'Bien entendu … c'est off': Ce que les journalistes politiques ne racontent jamais*. Paris: Albin Michel.

Castells, M. (1996) *The Rise of the Network Society*. Oxford: Blackwell.

Castells, M. (2009) *Communication Power*. Oxford: Oxford University Press.

Cavelier, P. and O. Morel-Maroger (2008, 2nd edn) *La radio*. Paris: Presses Universitaires de France.

Chafer, T. (2008) 'From confidence to confusion: Franco-African relations in the era of globalisation', in M. Maclean and J. Szarka (eds) *France on the World Stage*. Basingstoke: Palgrave Macmillan.

Chalaby, J.K. (2002) *The de Gaulle Presidency and the Media*. Basingstoke: Palgrave Macmillan.

Chalaby, J.K. (ed.) (2004) *Transnational Television Worldwide: Towards a New Media Order*. London: I.B. Taurus.

Chalaby, J.K. (2009) *Transnational Television in Europe: Reconfiguring Global Communications Networks*. London: I.B. Taurus.

Charon, J.-M. (1991) *La presse en France de 1945 à nos jours*. Paris: Seuil.

Charon, J.-M. (2005, 2nd edn) *La presse quotidienne*. Paris: La Découverte.

Charon, J.-M. (2008, 2nd edn) *La presse magazine*. Paris: La Découverte.

Chauvau, A. (1997) *L'Audiovisuel en liberté?* Paris: Presses de Sciences Po.

Chemin, A. and G. Catalano (2005) *Une famille au secret*. Paris: Stock.

Cheval, J.-J. (1997) *Les Radios en France*. Rennes: Éditions Apogée.

Chirac, B. (2001) *Conversation: Entretiens avec Patrick de Carolis*. Paris: Plon.

Chupin, I., N. Hubé and N. Kaciaf (2009) *Histoire politique et économique des médias en France*. Paris: La Découverte.

Clift, B. (2003) *French Socialism in a Global Era*. London: Continuum.

Cohen, E. (1992) *Le Colbertisme 'high tech'*. Paris: Hachette.

Cole, A. (1994) *François Mitterrand: A Study in Political Leadership*. London: Routledge.

Collard, S. (2008) '*Le Monde* and Mitterrand: challenging the "yellow line" ', *The Web Journal of French Media Studies*, 7: 1–18.

Collins, R. and C. Murroni (1996) *New Media, New Policies*. Cambridge: Polity Press.

Communod, N. (2005) *L'affaire Gaymard*. La Chatelle: Editions MIRNO Graphie.

Corner, J. and D. Pels (eds) (2003) *Media and the Restyling of Politics*. London: Sage.

Cotta, M. (1986) *Les miroirs de Jupiter*. Paris: Fayard.

Cotta, M. (2008) *Cahiers secrets de la Ve République, tome II 1977–1986*. Paris: Fayard.

Cour des comptes (2009) *France Télévisions et la nouvelle télévision publique*. Paris: La documentation française.

CSA (2009a) 'Délibération du 21 juillet 2009 relative au principe de pluralisme politique dans les services de radio et de télévision', www.csa.fr/infos/textes/textes_detail.php?id=128952 (accessed 17 September 2009).

CSA (2009b) 'Le baromètre de la diversité à la télévision', www.csa.fr/infos/diversite/barometre.php?rub=2 (accessed 14 February 2010).

Dagnaud, M. (2000) *L'État et les médias*. Paris: Éditions Odile Jacob.

Dagnaud, M. (2006) *Les artisans de l'imaginaire*. Paris: Armand Colin.

Dakhlia, J. (2008) *Politique people*. Paris: Bréal.

D'Almeida, F. and C. Delporte (2010) *Histoire des médias en France*. Paris: Flammarion.

DDM (Direction du Développement des Médias) (2002) *Tableaux statistiques de la Presse, Édition 2002*. Paris: La documentation française.

DDM (Direction du Développement des Médias) (2009) *Chiffres clés de la presse: Résultats détaillés de 1985 à 2007*. Paris: La documentation française.

Delporte, C. (2007) *La France dans les yeux*. Paris: Flammarion.

Domain, V. (2006) *Entre le coeur et la raison*. Paris: Fayard.

Donnat, O. (2009) *Les pratiques culturelles des Français à l'ère numérique: Éléments de synthèse 1997–2008*. Paris: Ministry of Culture and Communication, www.pratiquesculturelles.culture.gouv.fr/doc/08synthese.pdf (accessed 20 November 2009).

Doyle, G. (1999) 'Convergence: "A unique opportunity to evolve in previously unthought-of-ways" or a hoax?', in C. Marsden and S. Verhulst (eds) *Convergence in European Digital TV Regulation*. London: Blackstone.

Doyle, G. (2002) *Media Ownership*. London: Sage.

Duhamel, A. (2009) *La marche consulaire*. Paris: Plon.

Duhamel, O. and M. Field (2008) *Le Starkozysme*. Paris: Seuil.

Duplan, C. and B. Pellegrin (2008) *Claude Guéant*. Paris: éditions du Rocher.

Eck, H. (ed.) (1985) *La Guerre des Ondes*. Paris: Armand Colin.

Eck, H. (1991) 'Radio, culture and democracy in France in the immediate postwar period 1944–50', in B. Rigby and N. Hewitt (eds) *France and the Mass Media*. Basingstoke: Macmillan.

Elgie, R. (2003) *Political Institutions in Contemporary France*. Oxford: Oxford University Press.

États généraux de la presse écrite (2009) *Livre vert*. Paris: La documentation française.

Eveno, P. (2008) *La presse quotidienne nationale: fin de partie ou renouveau?* Paris: Vuibert.

Favier, P. and M. Martin-Roland (1999) *La Décennie Mitterrand: 4. Les Déchirements (1992–1995)*. Paris: Seuil.

Feintuck, M. (1999) *Media Regulation, Public Interest and the Law*. Edinburgh: Edinburgh University Press.

Ferenczi, T. (2000–1) 'The media and democracy', *CSD Bulletin*, 8/1: 1–2.

Fillioud, G. (2008) *Mémoires des deux rives*. Paris: Éditions du Moment.

Foley, M. (2000) *The British Presidency*. Manchester: Manchester University Press.

Franceschini, L. (1995) *La régulation audiovisuelle en France*. Paris: Presses Universitaires de France.

Frèches, J. (1989) *Voyage au centre du pouvoir*. Paris: Éditions Odile Jacob.

Gadault, T. (2006) *Arnaud Lagardère: L'insolent*. Paris: Maren Sell Éditeurs.

Gaffney, J. (ed.) (2004) *The French Presidential and Legislative Elections of 2002*. Aldershot: Ashgate.

Gaffney, J. (2010) *Political Leadership in France: From Charles de Gaulle to Nicolas Sarkozy*. Basingstoke: Palgrave Macmillan.

Genestar, A. (2008) *Expulsion*. Paris: Bernard Grasset.

Gerstlé, J. and C. Piar (2008) 'Les campagnes dans l'information télévisée', in P. Perrineau (ed.) *Le vote de rupture*. Paris: Presses de Sciences Po.

Giazzi, D. (2008) *Les médias et le numérique*, http://danielegiazzi.typepad.fr/ump/2008/09/rapport-les-mdi.html (accessed 23 September 2009).

Girard, L. (2007) 'Nicolas Sarkozy en tête de la médiatisation en 2006', *Le Monde*, 30 January.

Giscard d'Estaing, V. (2006) *Le Pouvoir et la Vie: Choisir*. Paris: Compagnie 12.

Gordon, P.H. and S. Meunier (2001) *The French Challenge*. Washington, DC: Brookings Institution Press.

Green, D. (1995) 'Preserving plurality in a digital world', in T. Congdon, A. Graham, D. Green and B. Robinson, *The Cross Media Revolution: Ownership and Control*. London: John Libbey.

Gubler, C. and M. Gonod (2005) *Le Grand Secret*, Paris: Éditions du Rocher (originally published in 1996, Paris: Plon).

Guibert, P. (2007) *La téléprésidente*. Paris: Plon.

Guillauma, Y. (1988) *La presse en France*. Paris: La Découverte.

Hafez, K. (2007) *The Myth of Media Globalization*. Cambridge: Polity.

Halimi, S. (2005, 2nd edn) *Les nouveaux chiens de garde*. Paris: Raisons d'Agir.

Hall, S., C. Critcher, T. Jefferson, J. Clarke and B. Roberts (1978) *Policing the Crisis*. London: Macmillan.

Hallin, D.C. and P. Mancini (2004) *Comparing Media Systems*. Cambridge: Cambridge University Press.

Harcourt, A. (2005) *The European Union and the Regulation of Media Markets*. Manchester: Manchester University Press.

Hayward, J. and V. Wright (2002) *Governing from the Centre*. Oxford: Oxford University Press.

Hayward, S. (2005, 2nd edn) *French National Cinema*. London: Routledge.

Heffernan, R. (2006) 'The prime minister and the news media: political communication as a leadership resource', *Parliamentary Affairs*, 59/4: 582–98.

Held, D. and A. McGrew (eds) (2000) *The Global Transformations Reader*. Cambridge: Polity.

Helms, L. (2008) 'Governing in the mediaage: the impact of the mass media on executive leadership in contemporary democracies', *Government and Opposition*, 43/1: 26–54.

Herman, E.S. and R.W. McChesney (1997) *The Global Media*. London: Cassell.

Hewitt, N. (1991) 'The birth of the glossy magazines: the case of *Paris-Match*', in B. Rigby and N. Hewitt (eds) *France and the Mass Media*. Basingstoke: Macmillan.

Huchon, J.-P. (1993) *Jours tranquilles à Matignon*. Paris: Grasset.

Humphreys, P. and M. Lang (1998) 'Digital television between the economy and pluralism', in J. Steemers (ed.) *Changing Channels: The Prospects for Television in a Digital World*. Luton: University of Luton Press.

INA (Institut national de l'audiovisuel) (2009) 'Le baromètre thématique des journaux télévisés', www.ina-entreprise.com/observatoire-medias/ina-stat/index.html (accessed 21 September 2009).

Institut Charles de Gaulle (1994) *De Gaulle et les médias*. Paris: Plon.

Institut Montaigne (2006) *Comment sauver la presse quotidienne d'information*. Paris: Institut Montaigne.

Iosifidis, P., J. Steemers and M. Wheeler (2005) *European Television Industries*. London: British Film Institute.

Jäckel, A. (2010) 'Cinema', in D. Albertazzi and P. Cobley (eds) *The Media: An Introduction*. Harlow: Longman.

Jackson, J. (2001) *France The Dark Years 1940–1944*. Oxford: Oxford University Press.

Joffrin, L. (2008) *Le roi est nu*. Paris: Robert Laffont.

Jost, F. (2009) *Télé-réalité*. Paris: Le Cavalier Bleu.

Jost, F. and D. Muzet (2008) *Le Téléprésident*. Paris: éditions de l'aube.

Kedward, H.R. (1978) *Resistance in Vichy France*. Oxford: Oxford University Press.

Kedward, H.R. (1985) *Occupied France*. Oxford: Blackwell.

Kernell, S. (2006, 4th edn), *Going Public: New Strategies of Presidential Leadership*. Washington, DC: CQ Press.

Kleinsteuber, H. (2010) 'The media in Europe', in D. Albertazzi and P. Cobley (eds) *The Media: An Introduction*. Harlow: Longman.

Kuhn, R. (1995) *The Media in France*. London: Routledge.

Kuhn, R. (2004) 'The media and the elections', in J. Gaffney (ed.) *The French Presidential and Legislative Elections of 2002*. Aldershot: Ashgate.

Kuhn, R. (2005a) 'The myth of exceptionalism? French television in a West European context', in E. Godin and T. Chafer (eds) *The French Exception*. Oxford: Berghahn.

Kuhn, R. (2005b) ' "Be very afraid." Television and *l'Insécurité* in the 2002 French presidential election', *European Journal of Communication*, 20/2: 181–98.

Kuhn, R. (2007) 'Media management', in A. Seldon (ed.) *Blair's Britain, 1997–2007*. Cambridge: Cambridge University Press.

Kurtz, H. (1998) *Spin Cycle: How the White House and the Media Manipulate the News*. New York: Touchstone Books.

La Croix (2010) *Baromètre de confiance dans les média*, www.la-croix.com/illustrations/Multimedia/Actu/2010/1/20/barometre-medias.pdf. (accessed 5 March 2010)

Lancelot, A. (2005) *Rapport au Premier Ministre sur Les Problèmes de Concentration dans le Domaine des Médias*. Paris: Diréction du développement des médias, www.ddm.gouv.fr/IMG/pdf/rapport_lancelot.pdf. (accessed 14 September 2009)

Le Galès, P. (2008) 'The ongoing march of decentralisation within the post-Jacobin state', in P.D. Culpepper, P.A. Hall and B. Palier (eds) *Changing France: The Politics that Markets Make*. Basingstoke: Palgrave Macmillan.

Le Lay, P. (2004) in Les associés d'EIM (eds) *Les dirigeants français face au changement*. Paris: Huitième Jour.

Léger, L. (2007) *Claude Chirac*. Paris: Flammarion.

Levy, D. (1999) *Europe's Digital Revolution*. London: Routledge.

Lutaud, L. and T. Dromard (2006) *Les Dessous de la presse people*. Paris: Éditions de la Martinière.

Maclean, M. and J. Szarka (eds) (2008) *France on the World Stage.* Basingstoke: Palgrave Macmillan.

Magoudi, A. (2009) *J'vais vous dire un truc ... Les plus belles déclarations de Nicolas Sarkozy.* Paris: La Découverte.

Maigret, É. (2008) *L'Hyperprésident.* Paris: Armand Colin.

Maler, H. and A. Schwartz (pour Acrimed) (2006) *Médias en campagne.* Paris: Éditions Syllepse.

Mamère, N. and P. Farbiaz (2009) *Petits arrangements entre amis.* Paris: Jean-Claude Gawsewitch.

Marlière, P. (2009) 'Sarkozysm as an ideological theme park: Nicolas Sarkozy and right-wing political thought', *Modern & Contemporary France*, 17/4: 375–90.

Martin, L. (2005a) *La Presse écrite en France au xxᵉ siècle.* Paris: Librairie Générale Française.

Martin, L. (2005b) *Le Canard enchaîné.* Paris: Nouveau Monde.

Martin, M. (2002) *La presse régionale.* Paris: Fayard.

Masure, B. (2009) *Journalistes à la niche?* Paris: Hugo&Cⁱᵉ.

Maurice, J.-C. (2009) *Si vous le répétez, je démentirai ....* Paris: Plon.

Médiamétrie (2010) www.mediametrie.fr/.

Mehl, D. (1996) *La télévision de l'intimité.* Paris: Éditions du Seuil.

Meier, W.A. and J. Trappel (1998) 'Media concentration and the public interest', in D. McQuail and K. Siune (eds) *Media Policy: Convergence, Concentration and Commerce.* London: Sage.

Ministry of Culture (2009) *Pratiques culturelles.* Paris: Ministry of Culture, www2.culture.gouv.fr/deps/mini_chiff_00/fr/pratiq.htm (accessed 20 November 2009).

Missika, J.-L. (2006) *La fin de la télévision.* Paris: Éditions du Seuil.

Moores, P. and C. Texier (1997) 'The campaign and the media', in J. Gaffney and L. Milne (eds) *French Presidentialism and the Election of 1995.* Aldershot: Ashgate.

Morrison, D. (2008) *Que reste-t-il de la culture française?* Paris: Éditions Denoël.

Muller, M. (2005) *Garantir le pluralisme et l'indépendance de la presse quotidienne pour assurer son avenir.* Paris: Conseil économique et social.

Murdock, G. (2000) 'Digital futures: European television in the age of convergence', in J. Wieten, G. Murdock and P. Dahlgren (eds) *Television Across Europe*. London: Sage.

Murray, R. (2010) 'Madonna and Four Children: Ségolène Royal', in R. Murray (ed.) *Cracking the Highest Glass Ceiling*. Santa Barbara, CA: Praeger.

Musso, P. (2008) *Le SarkoBerlusconisme*. Paris: éditions de l'aube.

Musso, P. (2009a) 'Sarkozysme, néo-télévision et néo-management', *Modern & Contemporary France*, 17/4: 391–406.

Musso, P. (2009b) *Télé-politique: Le sarkoberlusconisme à l'écran*. Paris: éditions de l'aube.

Muzet, D. (2006) *La Mal Info*. Paris: éditions de l'aube.

Negrine, R. (ed.) (1988) *Satellite Broadcasting: The Politics and Implications of the New Media*. London: Routledge.

Negrine, R. (2008) *The Transformation of Political Communication*. Basingstoke: Palgrave Macmillan.

Negrine, R. and S. Papathanassopoulos (1990) *The Internationalisation of Television*. London: Pinter.

Negrine, R., P. Mancini, C. Holtz-Bacha and S. Papathanassopoulos (2007) *The Professionalisation of Political Communication*. Bristol: Intellect.

Neveu, E. (2001) *Sociologie du journalisme*. Paris: La Découverte.

Neveu, E. (2005) 'Politicians without politics, a polity without citizens: the politics of the chat show in contemporary France', *Modern & Contemporary France*, 13/3: 323–35.

Norris, P., J. Curtice, D. Sanders, M. Scammell and H. Semetko (1999) *On Message: Communicating the Campaign*. London: Sage.

Orange, M. and J. Johnson (2003) *Une faillite française*. Paris: Albin Michel.

Organisme de Justification de la Diffusion (2010) 'Bureau presse payante grand public', www.ojd.com/chiffres/section/PPGP. (accessed 18 March 2010)

Painter, J. (2008) *Counter-Hegemonic News*. Oxford: Reuters Institute for the Study of Journalism.

Palou, A. (2007) *Allô, c'est Jean-Edern*. Paris: Michel Lafon.

Péan, P. and P. Cohen (2003) *La face cachée du 'Monde'*. Paris: Millet et une nuits.

Pedley, A. (1993) 'The media', in M. Cook (ed.) *French Culture since 1945*. London: Longman.

Perrineau, P. (ed.) (2008) *Le vote de rupture: Les elections présidentielle et legislatives d'avril-juin 2007*. Paris: Presses de Sciences Po.

Perrineau, P. and C. Ysmal (eds) (2003) *Le vote de tous les refus: Les elections présidentielle et législatives de 2002*. Paris: Presses de Sciences Po.

Pfetsch, B. (2008, 2nd edn) 'Government news management: institutional approaches and strategies in three western democracies reconsidered', in D.A. Graber, D. McQuail and P. Norris (eds) *The Politics of News, The News of Politics*. Washington, DC: CQ Press.

Pigeat, H., M. Cotta, F. Boé, J.-M. Colombani and F. Teitgen (2010) *Comité de réflexion sur l'avenir de l'AFP*. Paris: La documentation française, www.ladocumentationfrancaise.fr/rapports-publics/104000197/ (accessed 29 April 2010).

Pingaud, D. (2002) *L'Impossible défaite*. Paris: Seuil.

Pingeot, M. (2005) *Bouche cousue*. Paris: Julliard.

Plenel, E. (2010) 'Le journalisme pris au piège', in E. Plenel (ed.) *N'oubliez pas! Faits et gestes de la présidence Sarkozy*. Paris: Don Quichotte.

Portelli, S. (2009) *Le Sarkozysme sans Sarkozy*. Paris: Grasset.

Powrie, P. (ed.) (2006) *The Cinema in France*. London: Wallflower Press.

Quivy, V. (2009) *Profession: Elkabbach*. Paris: Éditions du Moment.

Ramonet, I. (2007) *La tyrannie de la communication*. Paris: Gallimard.

Revel, R. (2007) *L'Égérie*. Paris: JC Lattès.

Reymond, M. and G. Rzepski (pour Acrimed) (2008) *Tous les médias sont-ils de droite?* Paris: Éditions Syllepse.

Ridet, P. (2008) *Le président et moi*. Paris: Albin Michel.

Rieffel, R. (2010) *Mythologie de la presse gratuite*. Paris: Le Cavalier Bleu.

Risser, H. (2004) *L'Audimat à mort*. Paris: Seuil.

Robinson, P. (2002) *The CNN Effect: The Myth of News, Foreign Policy and Intervention*. London: Routledge.

Rocco, A.-M. (2006) *Serge Dassault*. Paris: Flammarion.

Rouger, A. (2008) 'What future for local news? The crisis of the French regional daily press', *Journalism Studies*, 9/5: 822–31.

Sabato, L.J. (2000) *Feeding Frenzy: Attack Journalism and American Politics*. Baltimore, MD: Lanahan.

Saint-Cricq, R. and F. Gerschel (2009) *Canal Sarkozy*. Paris: Flammarion.

Salmon, C. (2007) *Storytelling*. Paris: La Découverte.

Sarkozy, N. (2006) *Témoignage*. Paris: XO.

Sassoon, D. (2006) *The Culture of the Europeans*. London: Harper Press.

Schlesinger, P. (1990) 'Rethinking the sociology of journalism: source strategies and the limits of media-centrism', in M. Ferguson (ed.) *Public Communication: The New Imperatives*. London: Sage.

Schrameck, O. (2001) *Matignon Rive Gauche*. Paris: Seuil.

Schudson, M. (2000, 3rd edn) 'The sociology of new production revisited (again)', in J. Curran and M. Gurevitch (eds) *Mass Media and Society*. London: Edward Arnold.

Seaton, J. (2003) 'Public, private and the media', *The Political Quarterly*, 74/2: 174–83.

Séry, M. (2003) 'Télévision et insécurité', *Le Monde Télévision*, 1 March.

Seymour-Ure, C. (2003) *Prime Ministers and the Media*. Oxford: Blackwell Publishing.

Smith, A. (1973) *The Shadow in the Cave*. London: Allen & Unwin.

Smith, A. (1979) *The Newspaper: An International History*. London: Thames & Hudson.

Stanyer, J. and D. Wring (2004) 'Public images, private lives: the mediation of politicians around the globe', *Parliamentary Affairs*, 57/1: 1–235.

Steemers, J. (2004) *Selling Television*. London: British Film Institute.

Street, J. (2003) 'The celebrity politician: political style and popular culture', in J. Corner and D. Pels (eds) *Media and the Restyling of Politics*. London: Sage.

Street, J. (2004) 'Celebrity politicians: popular culture and political representation', *The British Journal of Politics and International Relations*, 6/4: 435–52.

Talbott, J. (1981) *The War Without a Name*. London: Faber & Faber.

Tessier, M. and M. Baffert (2007) *La Presse au défi du numérique*. Paris: Ministère de la Culture et de la Communication, www.culture.gouv.fr/culture/actualites/rapports/tessier/rapport-fev2007.pdf (accessed 20 September 2009).

Thomas, R. (1976) *Broadcasting and Democracy in France*. London: Crosby Lockwood Staples.

Thussu, D.K. (2006, 2nd edn) *International Communication*. London: Hodder Arnold.

Tunstall, J. (2007) *The Media Were American: U.S. Mass Media in Decline*. New York: Oxford University Press.

Tunstall, J. and D. Machin (1999) *The Anglo-American Media Connection*. Oxford: Oxford University Press.

Vedel, T. (2008) 'Internet', in P. Perrineau (ed.) *Le vote de rupture: Les elections présidentielle et legislatives d'avril-juin 2007*. Paris: Presses de Sciences Po.

Vedel, T. (2009) 'Pluralism in the French broadcasting system: between the legacy of history and the challenges of new technologies', in A. Czepak, M. Hellwig and E. Nowak (eds) *Press Freedom and Pluralism in Europe*. Bristol: Intellect.

Vedel, T. (2010) Oral presentation on the French case at the workshop on 'The Changing Business of Journalism & Its Impact on Democracy'. Oxford: Reuters Institute for the Study of Journalism, 5 February.

Veillet, P. (2009) 'Sarko et les medias', *Médias*, 22: 30–9.

Victor, B. (1999) *Le Matignon de Jospin*. Paris: Flammarion.

Ward, D. (2004) *A Mapping Study of Media Concentration and Ownership in Ten European Countries*. Hilversum: Commissariaat voor de Media.

Willerton, J.P. and M. Carrier (2005) 'Coalition management in the face of ideological and institutional constraint: the case of France's Gauche Plurielle', *French Politics*, 3/1: 4–27.

Zeldin, T. (1977) *France 1848–1945, Volume Two: Intellect, Taste and Anxiety*. Oxford: Oxford University Press.

INDEX

The Media in Russia

Anna Arutunyan

9780335228898 (Paperback)
2009

eBook also available

This book introduces readers to the Russian media, its current landscape, and its history by outlining the chief challenges faced by Russian journalists on their quest for media freedom.

Key features:

- Provides vivid examples and case studies of the power play between television and the State during the tumultuous 1990s
- Details a comprehensive historical overview supported with examples from relevant publications
- Demonstrates a clear outline of various different forms of media

www.openup.co.uk

OPEN UNIVERSITY PRESS
McGraw - Hill Education

Media and Society
Second Edition

Graeme Burton

9780335227235 (Paperback)
2010

eBook also available

This popular introductory book provides a clear introduction to the key ideas within media studies. The friendly writing style and everyday examples, which made the first edition a favourite with students and lecturers alike, has been retained and updated in this new edition.

Key features:

- Uses examples and case studies from the real world
- Shows how key concepts can help to understand the relationship between the Media and society
- Provides a clear explanation of how critical perspectives on the Media construct thinking about media businesses, texts and audiences

www.openup.co.uk

Media Convergence

Tim Dwyer

9780335228737 (Paperback)
2010

eBook also available

The process of 'media convergence', in which new technologies are accommodated by existing media industries, has broader implications for ownership, media practices and regulation. Dwyer critically analyses the political, economic, cultural, social, and technological factors that are shaping these changing media practices.

Key features:

- Uses case studies to show the impact of major traditional media players moving into the online arena
- Provides a road map of current and future trends for policy makers and media activists
- Discusses how people may access digital media content in the future

www.openup.co.uk

 OPEN UNIVERSITY PRESS
McGraw - Hill Education

The Media in Italy

Matthew Hibberd

9780335222858 (Paperback)
2007

eBook also available

Featuring a timeline of key Italian events, the book begins with the Unification - or Risorgimento - of Italy in 1861, and charts the rise of Italy from a fragmented and rural-based society through to a leading industrialised and urbanised world power. It details Fascism's reliance on the exploitation of the mass media, analyses Italy's remarkable post-war recovery, the development of democratic institutions and the contribution that a pluralistic media has made to this. Finally, it examines Silvio Berlusconi's rise to high political office and questions whether the involvement of Italy's leading media mogul in politics has harmed Italy's international reputation.

Key features:

- Shows how governing parties and individuals have been able to assert influence over media intuitions
- Emphasises the importance of the Catholic Church in the development of the Italian media
- Demonstrates how a unique Italian media system has been shaped by issues of citizenship, democracy and nation-state

www.openup.co.uk

OPEN UNIVERSITY PRESS
McGraw - Hill Education

The Media in Latin America

Jairo Lugo-Ocando

9780335222018 (Paperback)
2008

eBook also available

This book provides a comprehensive and critical overview of some of the most important media systems in Latin America. Drawing on original and critical essays from some of the most prominent authors in the field, the author approaches the subject with a country-by-country analysis, exploring the most relevant aspects of the media in each society.

Key features:

- Looks at the effect of media history
- Analyses the interrelationship of the media and the state
- Discusses media regulation and policy and ownership

www.openup.co.uk